THE GREAT CHARLIE

Robert Payne

The Great Charlie

Foreword by G. W. Stonier

Brick Tower Press
Habent Sua Fata Libelli

Brick Tower Press
1230 Park Avenue
New York, New York 10128
Tel: 212-427-7139
bricktower@aol.com • www.BrickTowerPress.com

Library of Congress Cataloging-in-Publication Data
Payne, Robert
The Great Charlie, A Biography of the Tramp
Includes biographical references, index, and photos.
ISBN 978-1-883283-95-7

1. Payne, Robert— 2. Biography—Charlie Chaplin 3. Performing Arts 4. Silent Film 5. Robert Payne Library, Volume 2.

First Trade Paper Printing, September 2012
The Great Charlie
—*A Biography of the Tramp*

CHARLIE

OF COURSE we all know him. There he goes, with his brisk morning waddle, or quiet on a corner where the world passes, in movement, in silence, in black and white. From our weekly shadow-show no other image so transcends. Babylon may fall, Garbo smile, revolution rage, crime not pay, wars come and go: he remains. Eternity, in a flicker, has been his. Only one Charlie.

Yet when we come to talk or think about him – and the gap between one film and the next makes critics of us all – there pops up a bewildering array of Charlies. Clown, mime, sentimentalist, libertarian, last of the dandies, champion of the underdog, tumbler, mask dancer – which is it to be? He has given the Pygmalion touch to caricature, and regards us with the big sad eyes of humanity. He's the alivest poppet that ever walked. He has slid down a sunbeam. Don Quickshuffle, says one; Goat-foot, exclaims another. Monkey tragedian! Troll! Son of a dustbin! . . . So it goes on. A few, having considered, inquire whether his boots aren't too big for him, or he for them.

And back to the screen, with an added divinity (whatever we may say or feel), comes the old Charlie. Boots and cane, moustache, bowler, prim coat, ebullience of bags. That's all. With anyone else they wouldn't fetch elevenpence three-farthings.

Charlie, you might say, was a job lot. He had been picked up by Chaplin – let me refer to the book you are about to start on and I have just laid down. Yes, the boots belonged to one Fred Sterling, and the walk (which Chaplin elaborated remembering 'the strangely menacing way men walk when they are wearing their shoes on the wrong feet') to an old cabbie in the Kennington Road. Mack Swain's moustache was clipped down to a nose-smudge of the kind affected by British officers in the Boer War. The hold-all trousers and the perched hat were Fatty Arbuckle's; it, the hat, neither too large nor too small, being 'balanced gravely like a yacht on the water, on Charlie's

curly hair'. In the pages that follow, many such appreciative
touches will fill in the picture. Cane and cutaway were added.
The waistcoat arrived later. So, in an early film-studio, Charlie
was vamped out of props handy and out of a poor boy's memory;
even Charlie's behaviour – or at least the first raw manifesta-
tions of it – had its origin in a fat town councillor of Jersey who,
a summer or two before, had disorganised a fête by smiling at
women, kissing children, saluting soldiers and everywhere
getting in the way of the camera. Charlie also set out to get in
the way of the camera.

The point well made is that this rare, great figure – and,
damn detraction, great he is, with the stature of Falstaff, Don
Quixote, Hamlet (for Hamlet, too, may be part comedian) – so
extemporised, came living and took everyone by surprise,
including Chaplin, who has been inquiring into him and wondering about him till this day. Antics flowed from him naturally,
adventure was soon his, he encountered romance and suffering,
and (while the world flooded with laughter) he was engaged in
the most scrupulous self-discovery.

Do you recollect that story of Hans Andersen called *The
Shadow*? One night to a southern town comes a traveller; hearing music and laughter across the way, he leans out of the
window, and the light at his back flings a shadow. The shadow
detaches itself, saunters into the house opposite, and does not
return till all hours. For several nights this happens, and the
traveller is powerless to prevent its happening. His shadow has
become realler than himself. In the end it is he who must tread
the Other's heels.

Some such paradox haunts, elates, and perhaps terrifies every
great artist. Balzac on his death-bed called for Bianchon, the doctor
from one of his novels, as the only man who could save him; of
Shakespeare nothing remains when the plays have sucked his
life-blood, and Dickens' silhouettes danced over him while he
still breathed. Even more striking may be the emergence, the
assertive independence, not of a crowd, but of oneself: Andersen's
Shadow. This is the clown's experience and the poet's. Grimaldi
(see page 71), dying miserably and unrecognised, was told that
he should go and see Grimaldi. Among the great clowns,
naturally, we look for Chaplin's co-equals: all that survives of

them is tributes, tears, an anecdote or a pencil sketch. But what
of those poets, single-voiced, who were no less slaves of a shadow?
Think of Byron, of Baudelaire. The latter – who, by the way,
had a deep if melancholy affection for clowns – provides a very
exact comparison. He also 'discovered' himself, sometimes in
the odds and ends of inferior writers; his poetry of the damned
was a dictation to which painfully and unceasingly he must
attend; and for two hours a day he would devote himself to
that *toilette de guillotine*, without which he – or the Other – would
not descend the stairs to take his place in drawing-room or café.
One sees Chaplin submitting to the ruthlessness of Charlie,
putting the final touches to dilapidation, brushing the threadbare cloth, pulling the shirt tail to just its right emergence from
the trouser seat, springing the cane, further whitening the
mask, revolving the eyes, pausing over the blown button-hole
– no, *that* a few moments later shall be plucked from a dustbin
– before he takes the garishly lit floor. That metamorphosis or
act of creation differs in no way from the poet's except in its
means. One walks, the other talks. Charlie is wildly, dramatically,
ideally comic; and he would not be so if he did not embody the
sort of convergence brought about by great art. His knockabout
attains the spell-bound grace of a Nijinsky, and only by continually warding off tragedy can he keep a balance of fun. In the
precariousness lies the perfection.

Let me quote two passages touching this equivocation, this
tragic haunting which is the essence of clowning.

Charlie [writes Robert Payne], is never a character easy to
define and circumscribe. It is not only that he is continually
eluding us, but he is always suggesting he is something else,
always mimicking, always chameleon-like, taking on the
character of his surroundings. When he mimics the cop, the
cop can hardly arrest him, for that would be like arresting
himself. When he mimics the children, they are first stunned,
then they laugh uproariously, because it never occurred to
them that a man could be instantly transformed into a child.
But it is when he mimics himself that the complexities really
begin, for since he is obviously the great god Pan, and even
wears, thinly disguised, the goat-mask – for what else is

the moustache but a sketchy replica of the goat's black muzzle, and why the baggy trousers unless it is to hide the cloven hoofs and legs thickly covered with curly hair? – we enter a world where a god mimics himself in the pure enjoyment of himself, and there seems neither rhyme nor reason for the doing of it. 'Since I am a god or a fallen angel,' he seems to be saying, 'I can do what I damned well please. . . .'

So he sticks two forks into two rolls and conjures up twinkling feet, footlights, the theatre; he roller-skates to his lady or, like a child, to himself alone; as Hitler he scampers up a curtain and visibly, airily makes our globe his plaything. He can't quite be brought back. Robert Payne tries to nail him as Pan: you will have noticed the reference. Now that is a manner of speaking. Of course, Charlie never could be the great god Pan, if only because he is that great indefinable, Charlie; but it may be useful and even necessary (since one thing can only be defined and understood in the terms of another) to assume identification for the time being. Divine comedy, divine farce, have their roots wherever man dreads death and seeks the violence of laughter and action. The origins and pre-history of Charlie, no less than his personal legend, will be found here inscribed with a wealth of allusion. The fact that another book – but that might be even more difficult to write – could trace out a more saintly or tragic predisposition does not at all rob this one of its value.

The wonderfully haunting mask is what has grown on Charlie with the years. Its eloquence depends not at all upon words, which, introduced by circumstance, issue from some quite minor if agreeable source. Horseplay and illusion are over; the moment comes; loneliness would, but must not, will not, shriek.

Is it possible that the mask of Charlie, which suggests Pan, also suggests a skull, and we laugh because of the very effrontery of this walking skeleton who has appeared from nowhere with no authority at all, except the authority which comes from the dead? It may be that the strange mask which Chaplin invented does represent something which exists at the very edge of life. 'I am always aware that Charlie is playing with death,' Chaplin told me once. 'He plays with it, mocks

it, thumbs his nose at it, but it is always there. He is aware
of death at every moment of his existence, and he is terribly
aware of being alive.'

I said something about the messenger in Æschylus who
announces: 'I see the dead are killing one who lives,' and
suggested that Charlie is a kind of *revenant*, a pale ghost of
the past, but instead of trying to kill the living, he attempts
to give them more abundant life.

'Yes, yes,' Chaplin said. 'There is death in him, and he is
bringing life – more life. That is his only excuse, his only
purpose. That is why people recognised him everywhere.
They wanted the ghosts to come and bring them life.'

Well, that is Chaplin talking, or, on an occasion, being induced
to talk. Charlie, like Brer Rabbit, goes on saying nuffin'; and it
is, quite rightly, his book. Half its entertainment comes from the
tumbling, articulate prose notations of antics which exist
properly only in themselves. I have enjoyed in this way a whole
week's gala of Chaplin films, including several I have never seen:
the bawdiness of *Work*, the moment of horror in *The Face on the
Bar-Room Floor*, and *Sunnyside* exist for me now in the most
agreeable of limbos. The photographs, in fact, are almost not
needed.

G. W. STONIER

CONTENTS

ILLUSTRATIONS

INTRODUCTION

THIS is a study of Charlie the Clown, who first appeared on this earth on a winter's day in 1914. I have been interested in studying his ancestry, his moods, his expressions, his adventurous career and the sources from which he derives his strength, and Mr Charles Chaplin has been allowed to enter the discussion only by implication, or on those rare occasions when he has broken silence and had illuminating things to say about his distant relative. I have begun with the premise that Charlie exists in his own right like Don Quixote and all the great heroic archetypes, and I have assumed that Charlie has never for a moment scorned reality, but has waged perpetual war with it to his own infinite jest and amusement. I cannot see Charlie as the epitome of the common man pitting his feeble strength against the organised forces of his age; if this were all, there would be no reason to applaud him, for then he would be doing no more than anyone else. This study is concerned with the Clown, the generator of laughter and the divine creator of merriment, that whirling gust of joy which drives through the universe like a Milky Way.

In a recent article Mr Al Capp, creator of the comic strip character Li'l Abner, has observed that we laugh at Charlie because he is more unfortunate than ourselves. He wrote: 'No matter how badly off any of us was, we were all in better shape than that bum. The fact that we had enough spare cash to buy a ticket to that movie made us superior to him. That was the first thing that made us feel good. Next, we saw him starving. That wasn't going to happen to us – another reason for feeling superior, better off at least than one person.' This is drivel.

We laugh, because laughter to most of us is the closest we ever get to divinity. 'Men,' wrote St Thomas Aquinas, speaking with all the authority of the Church, 'must live together merrily – this is the law.' It follows that to laugh at misfortune is a crime against the Holy Ghost, a *skandalon* for which no penance is known, a sin so terrible that there is no name for it except

15

whatever is the opposite of charity. One of the saddest commentaries on our age is therefore provided by the comic strips,
where the misfortunes of the poor, the orientals and the insane
are held up for our contemptuous approval, and Superman, an
archetype who lies at the opposite pole to Charlie, is shown as
the inheritor of all earthly blessings. It may be so. But it is odd
that the Sunday morning rocking chairs should be filled with
people revelling in the feats of Nietzsche's *alter ego*, and odder
still if the divine providence which guides the universe should
have brought about a world where Superman in his eternal void
becomes the arbiter of destinies. Against the wickedness of Superman and all unconsecrated authority we shall see Charlie waging
war, but this is not to say that he wages war against reality.

So this is a book about Charlie, half god, half man, and always
vagabond, brother to St Francis and the moon, the loveliest
thing that ever graced the screen. Look how he crosses the
stage, the only real thing there, the rest being toys he plays
with. His moustache is but a little shadow for his nose, his eyes
are crafty as the eyes of Hercules, his battered hat is a sign of
authority greater than Superman's magic interstellar boat. What
is certain is that he is a better guide than those faceless men in
rubber cloaks who have no gift for laughter. 'What is humour?'
asked Chaplin once, and answered, speaking with all the authority
of his knowledge of Charlie, 'It is a kind of gentle and benevolent
custodian of the mind which prevents us from being overwhelmed by the apparent seriousness of life.' Chaplin's critics
are accustomed to point out to him that he knows very little
about humour. It seems a pity, for the answer he gave is one
which St Thomas Aquinas would have approved of, and so would
the friars of the Middle Ages, and so would children, who have
a keener sense of humour than their elders.

Where does the clown come from? Where does he go?
What purpose lies beyond the pale mask of the clown? By what
stages did he travel into the world? Who invited him? What
mysterious tasks does he fulfil? These are questions which were
once important, and may be important again, and so I make no
apology for the rather long introduction. It was necessary to
trace the sources where they could be found, and to treat the
clown with the utmost gravity.

'It is a desperate business being a clown,' Chaplin said once. It is perhaps even more desperate than he knew, for as the world grows more authoritarian, comedy vanishes through the back-window and wisecracks (which are not wise and very rarely crack anything open) take the place of the great explosions of comedy which were once our birthright, and which possessed the magic power of reducing us to our human proportions at the same time that they uplifted us to the highest heavens. It was not for nothing that Dante spoke of Beatrice smiling in the place of blessedness. What else was she smiling at if not at the beautiful madness of the divine comedy? As for Chaplin, it should be enough to say that he is one of the greatest jesters of the age, and like all great jesters he raises serious questions, and it would be an impertinence to treat his work less than seriously. He is a man who knew exactly what he wanted to say, and how to say it, and exceptionally determined upon repeating it in every key until he should be heard. The pity is that we have so rarely listened, and a whole generation has arisen which knows almost nothing of his work.

We can hardly blame them: it is not their fault that the early comedies are often difficult to procure. Mostly we see them by chance. I saw *The Circus* and *Tillie's Punctured Romance* recently in a warehouse in Greenwich Village, and would not have known they were being shown unless a Czech barber had told me about them. I found *Carmen* in an obscure underground theatre on Hollywood Boulevard, which closed after the showing of a few films. *One A.M.* and *The Kid* were mercifully revived recently by the Museum of Modern Art in New York. I saw a torn and silver-splashed copy of *The Pilgrim* in Kunming, *A Dog's Life* in New Delhi, and a whole series of fading one-reelers in Paris, where copies printed in World War I were being shown nearly thirty years later. *City Lights* I have seen four times in the past year, but I saw *Modern Times* for the last time fifteen years ago, and what is written here is based on a fallible memory and the lengthy report of a recent private showing from a friend. In the last months I have obtained nearly all the Keystone, Essanay and Mutual comedies from various Hollywood and New York agencies. Nearly all these films are falling to pieces. They have been cut abominably, sound has been added, many are faded

and spotted, and in a few years nothing will be left of them.
Someone must get to work. I have read that film more than forty
years old gradually decomposes. There is need for the art-
restorers of film. Meanwhile there is every reason why those
early films should be carefully looked after, preferably in the
colleges and universities – not that they should be regarded
academically, but simply that they should be preserved.

For help in the writing of this book it is pleasant to thank
Mr Chaplin who very kindly discussed Charlie with me on a
number of occasions, and allowed me to see the scenario of
Footlights. I have not discussed *Footlights* in the book, because a
scenario is not a film. I am indebted to Dr Ruth Bunzel for
delightful illuminations on the delight-makers. It is also pleasant
to thank Dr Lawrence Clark Powell of the University of
California in Los Angeles, Miss Abi Russell of Alabama College,
and the director of the Widener Library at Harvard University
who gave me permission to reproduce Grimaldi's last letter; I am
grateful to the Film Library of the Museum of Modern Art, the
theatre collection of the New York Public Library, the Bettmann
Archive, Mr Raymond R. Stuart of Hollywood and Mr Irving
Klaw of New York who have given me permission to reproduce
the photographs.

November 1951   ROBERT PAYNE

CHAPTER I

THE GREAT GOD PAN

PAN was the son of Hermes, the divine prince of knaves and liars and the herald of the dead. No one knew who his mother was, and no one seemed to care. As a child, wrapped in the skins of mountain goats or in the skins of hares, he was brought to the banquet of the gods, and because he delighted in everything he was called 'everything', for Pan means 'everything' in Greek. Such was one story; there were many others, including the story that all the gods fathered him and therefore he was 'everyone'. But it is more likely that the true origin of his name comes from the word *paon*, meaning a grazier. He was the god of the woodlands in Arcadia, and from the very beginning he seems to have had his goat's feet. Silius Italicus talks lovingly of the god Pan who left no imprint in the dust when he walked and could be seen turning round to laugh at the antics of his shaggy tail. The Homeric Hymn describes him as 'the goat-footed, two-horned lover of the dance' who haunts the snowy mountains and the inaccessible crags, but sometimes he comes running down to the foothills where he slays the wild beasts and then, having won his victory, he plays a tune on his pipe in the evening. Sometimes he approaches the dark fountains, the springs in the mountain caves, and there he is seen singing to the nymphs as they dance, and his song re-echoes from the tops of the mountains. Sometimes, for no reason at all, he gives a shriek, and everyone runs in panic.

Today we know far more about the rustic god than we knew forty years ago, but he still escapes us. We know, for example, that ancient Greek tragedy developed from the worship of Dionysos, but Dionysos himself was often confused with Pan, and Pan lies somewhere at the beginnings of the theatre. The

19

origin of the stage was the goat-cart from which jests were flung. The art of tragedy itself derived from a fertility cult centred around a goat, beginning, as Aristotle says, in trivial and ludicrous things, with much satire and dancing, until at a later stage it developed a dignity of its own. At this late date it is impossible to trace the origins, which were unknown even to Aristotle, but it is a reasonable assumption that a fertility cult in a time of drought is a serious thing.

There may have been tragedy, real tragedy as we know it, in the days when the god Pan was first worshipped, and if he was partly goat the reason was simple: he was the only beast the Arcadians could tame, and there was something altogether frightening in the way he could elude the hunters by roaming on the topmost crags. He looked crafty and evil. He was credited with fabulous sexual powers. He represented the terror of the woodlands, the menacing dark presences which lurked behind the trees. He was nimble-footed, ludicrous, powerful, so powerful indeed that he could create those solemn silences which suddenly descend on woodlands, and he could also create thunder. He was the voice laughing quietly which the hunter heard as he went through the forest. *Run quicker. This is no place for you. What are you doing here?* In a sense he was the whole earthly world laughing at man's puny endeavours. Dionysos came from abroad, from Thrace, and he was a late adherent to the circle of the Greek gods, having wandered all the way from India. He was not essentially Greek. It is possible that the first of the Greek gods, the one most intimately discerned by the woodland-dwellers, the one who was most powerful, most terrifying, most difficult to placate was the great god Pan. In the end his power faded away, for there was no place in the solemn ceremonies of urban Greece for a mountain goat. In the first century of our era Plutarch speaks of a voice crying over the midnight sea: 'Great Pan is dead'; but everyone knew the oracle was false. The mocking spirit of the woodland remained, and is still heard today.

It is possible to reconstruct the ceremonies of the great god Pan. It is evening in Arcadia, the time of twilight and the task, of the goat's face seen through the trees and the sudden stirring of the leaves. On the blue crags, high in the sun, the goats are leaping, but the meadows lie deep in shadow. As the light fades the young men and women of the village dressed in goatskins come from their huts, walking softly at first, then leaping to the beat of drums, with great flying leaps imitating the goats on the highest crags, and behind them comes the empty cart, and behind the cart come the flute-players and the old people and young children, while at the head of the procession walks the priest with the goat-mask. As they come near the sacred place on the edge of the forest, singing the *tragoi*, the shouting grows louder, for they are now in sight of the ram itself, the animal caught in the thicket, the sacrificial beast, and they are about to follow a ritual more ancient than Babylon. The shouting ceases, drums beat, fires are lit, and on a crude altar the throat of the bleating ram is cut by the priest in the goat-mask, for only the goat-priest may kill the ram. Once killed, the flesh is torn apart and those who are not quick enough in snatching it are beaten with leeks or onions, for the *phallos* is the emblem of Pan and the vegetables supply the substitute. Then dancing and singing by torchlight, and with many jests from the cart, with rustic plays performed by players whose faces are smeared with blood, they journey back to their huts, and in some way the journey has now become the journey from birth to death, and also the pity of the journey seen in itself; and so in all these sacred processions there is war between the pity and the journey.

Such then is the ceremony as we can imagine it. The goat becomes the symbol of fertility and daring, of insolence and the wide-ranging mind, of mental as well as sexual powers. We remember that the glitter of his horns on the high crags is the last living thing seen by the villagers before the sun sets. He comes before the horse and the bull, and something of the ancientness of the woodlands clings to him. His beard, his cloven hooves, the characteristic strong odour he gives off in the rutting season, the richness of his wool, all these have marked him out, so that almost inevitably he became the god of the woods and fields, of flocks and shepherds, a terrifying and fearful god who lived in the highest caves. The syrinx, the shepherd's pipe, was invented by him, and he makes people dance to his tune.

We have spoken of him as a sacred character, the totem of the obscure Arcadian tribes, but this is not the whole story, though

it is the most important part of the story. In some such way both
tragedy and comedy had their origins, but the victory of Pan was
short-lived, and though he was finally conquered by Dionysos
coming from Thrace, he was also bested by Apollo coming from
Asia Minor long before Dionysos assumed his splendours. We
shall never know exactly how Apollo won his victory, but some
hint of it is given in the ancient story of King Midas, who wandered
at the beckoning of Bacchus to the shores of the river Pactolus.
Bathing in the river, he lost his prodigious power of turning
everything to gold and became a peasant, worshipping Pan,
who was so encouraged by the presence of the great king that
he challenged Apollo, saying that he could blow more sweetly
on his pipe than Apollo could ever play on his lyre. The error
was fatal. Apollo rose, wearing his laurel crown and his immense
robe of Tyrian purple, and after Pan had played a few weak notes
on his pipe, the sun-god struck the lyre and the mountain-god,
Tmolus, awarded the prize to him. Pan returned to his woods.
He still had a hold on the peasants of Arcadia: stories are told
about him in Greece even to this day; but the new god of the
East, a new conquering civilisation, was sweeping over the
primitive rustic cults of Arcadia, and Pan lost his pre-eminence.
For a while Pan disappeared under the skirts of Dionysos who
decorated sensual licence with all the panoply he derived from
the East, and held his own festivals, and tore the goat apart as
though it had always belonged to him; but the goat-god with
the leering face, the reed flute and the goatherd's staff was
indestructible. More than all the other Greek gods except
Zeus and Apollo he confronts us still with the terms of an ever-
lasting and vital predicament.

Who is he? Where does he come from? Where will he go?
We shall never know the complete answers because they are
inextricably woven into the human comedy. The great god
Pan, the high and presiding genius of sensuality who is also the
mocker of sensuality, the laughter among the leaves, the solemn
rogue who sits at the pit of every man's stomach, the eternal
wanderer on the high cliffs of the mind – take everything away,
and he remains. There is no reason to mock him or be afraid of
him, though he is terrible enough, and he is older than any of us.
If we call him the spirit of licence in a trammelled world, then

we should remember that liberty derives from the ancient Roman god Liber, whose emblem was also a *phallos* and whose worship was performed by naked youths. Pan *is* the spirit of licence, and to those who disapprove of licence it should be enough to say that by licence we entered the world and by licence we enjoy it and by the licence of the mind we have made the prodigious discoveries which enable us to destroy ourselves; and all this was implicit in Pan from the very beginning.

Frowned upon, pushed out of the way, thrown from Olympus to wander in the Arcadian forests where the wolves howled, the great god Pan survived. That face of terror and joy, those vast powers, ruled over the mediæval carnivals. The old English mummers brought him on to their stagecarts and crowned him with leaves, and beyond the Atlantic the Indians of America performed his rites, not that he had ever been to America, but they found it necessary to invent him for themselves. He was *l'homme moyen sensuel*, the creature of ribald human instinct, the gypsy of the world, loathed (as the gypsies are) by Communists and Fascists alike, because he fits into no preordained pattern and holds all patterns in contempt, and in our own increasingly mechanical and authoritarian age he is the perpetual outcast.

In his purest form he appeared on the screen for the first time in February 1914. There were some who ascribed a peculiar blessing to the arrival of such a portentous personage in such an unhallowed year. But he came jauntily, swinging his cane, wearing a seedy cutaway, a dilapidated derby hat, enormous outturned boots, baggy pants and an absurd toothbrush moustache. As for the cane, it was all that was left to him of the goatherd's flowering staff. Head erect, pale from exhaustion, with livid black rings round his eyes, his mouth twitching, he came down a street in Venice, California, as though he owned the place, and if he was hungry and down-at-heel, it was observed that there was something of the prince about him. Sometimes he gave a little skip like a goat or like a child, and there was an expression of extraordinary contentment on his pale ghost-like face. He was glad to be back again.

CHAPTER II

KID AUTO RACES AT VENICE

THE film was called *Kid Auto Races at Venice*. In this film Charlie appeared for the first time wearing his strange, subtle and faintly terrifying mask. It was the second film he ever appeared in; the first, called *Making a Living*, belonged purely to the Keystone tradition, with Chaplin appearing as a dude with a Chinese moustache: it had nothing to recommend it. *Kid Auto Races* came like a bolt of lightning.

The story of how Chaplin came to wear the mask has been often told. It has been suggested that the bits and pieces which went to form the uniform of Charlie were accidental and contrived on the spur of the moment. It is not quite true. The complete picture of Charlie had been in Chaplin's mind for a long time: it had come out of his studies of London street-types. He took Mack Swain's moustache, and cut it down until it resembled the moustaches worn by British officers during the Boer War. He wore Fatty Arbuckle's immense trousers – this was admittedly an afterthought, but the out-turned boots were part of the general pattern he had thought out, and so was the small delicately poised bowler hat, and this too belonged to Arbuckle. On Charlie the hat was only a little too small. It balanced gravely, like a yacht on the water, on Charlie's curly hair. The bamboo cane was another afterthought, and for Chaplin's purpose the most precious of all, for it offered immense possibilities of 'business'. As for the boots, which belonged to Ford Sterling, Chaplin was puzzled about how to imitate the walk he wanted until he remembered the strangely menacing way men walk when they are wearing their shoes on the wrong feet. That splayed walk derived from an old cabman in London's Kennington Road, who suffered from bad feet and wore boots of abnormal size and slithered along the road in a painful and ludicrous manner. The surprising and beautiful thing was that all these odds and ends fitted together. They formed a new character whose possibilities Chaplin only half understood, though he was to explore them at length. The character had emerged suddenly, fully formed. All Chaplin ever added to the costume was a checkered waistcoat, and even this was sometimes abandoned without any harm to the portrait of the clown, who was not a tramp or a vagabond when he first appeared, but someone who came from nowhere, mocked everyone in sight, continually got in the way of the prop camera, brawled with the cops, pretended that the auto races were being run for his benefit alone, ordered everyone about and danced his silly dances for no purpose at all. Without slapstick, without custard pies or bathing beauties, a new kind of comedy had arisen, and there was no name for it.

But the comic character which Chaplin had suddenly invented did have a history, and its history can be traced – to a fat town councillor in the island of Jersey, who amused and alarmed Chaplin in the summer of 1912 by the way in which he pompously directed the parades during a fête and continually got in front of the camera. By some magical means this absurd man succeeded with infinite aplomb in nudging everyone else out of camera range, until the Pathé cameraman became explosive. There he was, eternally smiling at the women, saluting the soldiers, kissing the children, and Chaplin promised himself that one day he would play such a part. When Chaplin asked Mack Sennett what part he should play at the auto races, he was told: 'Don't worry. Just get in the way of the camera.' Chaplin saw his chance. So the clown was born, but the clown had none of the pomposity of the town councillor, and if he ogled at the women, it was not because he wanted to be seen ogling them on film. What the clown derived from the town councillor was a delicacy of movement, a certain insistence on his own importance, a power to nudge people out of the way; and if the clown was also absorbed in his own self-importance, it was for reasons which had nothing to do with the town councillor. But occasionally, no more than once every few years, it would be possible to detect on Charlie's face something of that amazing town councillor, who finally succeeded in clearing everyone out of camera range until at last he stood there alone, beaming incomprehensibly and stupidly at a lens. But where the town councillor was enormously fat and resembled in his utterances the Monsieur Homais of *Madame Bovary*, Charlie was atrociously thin and if he resembled anyone else other than the great god Pan, it was one of those sharp-witted street urchins who crowd through the pages of *Oliver Twist*, only now the street urchin had grown old and wise in the ways of the world.

No one has troubled to enquire the name of the town councillor who held office during a fête on the island of Jersey in the Channel Islands in August 1912. It seems a pity, for without him there might have been no Charlie. As we might have expected, Charlie came to birth as the result of an odd encounter of fortuitous things. One man's moustache, another's hat and trousers, someone else's boots, an old cabman in Kennington Road, a town councillor in the Channel Islands. To these Chaplin added his natural grace and dignity, a recollection of Max Linder's suavity, and an almost terrifying mask.

As he remembers the day, Chaplin says he was aware that everything he was doing assumed profound significance in his mind, but he was not quite certain where the significance lay. His horror of the first film was burning in his mind. He was terror-stricken at the thought of failure. By assuming the new disguise, he was abandoning everything he had learned, and he would have to make his way through unknown territory. He had played many parts, but never a part like this. Usually he played a drunken toff who railed at the actors on the stage, threw things at them, coughed at awkward moments, burst out into absurd trilling songs at the moments when they were most absorbed in their own affairs, tripped them up with his walking stick as he leaned out of a box conveniently located on the stage – he had played such a part times without number on tours through England, France and America. Nearly always he had been the toff, with his monocle, his morning-coat, his high collar, his polished shoes and his sense of outraged dignity. Now he was something else altogether, a mysterious and many-sided figure passionately absorbed in amusing himself in an oddly capricious way, twirling his cane, laughing at everybody, a man who refused under any circumstances to take anything seriously and yet was wildly, ferociously determined to have things his own way against all the obstacles the universe set in front of him (for the character was split down the centre from the very beginning) and at the same time there was a casual tenderness in his gestures, and if he mocked everybody, he was also mocking himself.

There were fantastic complications in this pale godlike figure he had invented on the spur of a few horror-stricken moments. 'Even then,' Chaplin said later, 'I realised I would have to spend the rest of my life finding more about the creature. For me he was fixed, complete, the moment I looked in the mirror and saw him for the first time, yet even now I don't know all the things there are to be known about him.' Chaplin talks about Charlie without familiarity and with enormous respect, and he is not in the least convinced that Charlie's arrival on earth was an accident. Somehow, by some means unknown, Chaplin had tapped powerful forces. Explosive comic forces were let loose, but from the very beginning, Chaplin was aware of the tragic overtones.

How explain the extraordinary creature who was now about to live his own independent life? What did he represent? Where had he come from? It was simple enough to see where the parts were derived, but the whole was not the sum of the parts.

Chaplin examined his creation and attempted to discover what Charlie was about. He saw that the big feet were naturally funny, that the bowler hat with its claim to a lost respectability was exactly the right size to rest nimbly on his head and could be made to assume an infinity of amusing positions, and that the baggy trousers had the effect, whenever he turned his back, of making him resemble the rear end of an elephant. There was something absurdly comic in this waddling elephant who could be instantly transformed into a dancer. The heavy trousers and heavy boots chained him to earth, but they only just held him down. An airy spirit was contained in the baggy clothes. Charlie's essential lightness does not appear on the posed photographs, but it does appear on the screen, and E. E. Cummings has caught it admirably in a sketch which shows Charlie twirling in the air, a rose in one hand, the cane in the other, but the cane has been transformed into a conductor's baton as Charlie beats time to his own perpetual dance. It was this airy spirit which led Charlie into comedy; the tragedy lay mostly in the boots and trousers.

Cummings wrote once in another connection that the expression of a clown is chiefly to be seen in his knees, and this, too, was true of Charlie, who was a compound of opposites, light and heavy, innocent and evil, invincibly noble and miserably wretched, bird and elephant. So, birdlike and elephantine, Charlie blunders and dances through the world, and like Pan he is wholly human, resembling nothing so much as the whole human comedy wrapped in a single frail envelope of flesh.

The shape of the animal was unique; so was the shape of the mockery. He was enraged with the children who got in his way, and when he saw them looking surprised by his rage, he immediately assumed a look of hurt surprise, as though to say: 'What! I am in a rage, and you are frightened! What nonsense this is!' Thereupon they burst out laughing happily. Then Charlie laughs. The children are delighted, but there comes a moment when he finds their laughter unendurable, so once more he bursts out in another roar of rage, and the children laugh all the louder until they realise he is in dead earnest: then their laughter freezes at the moment his laughter begins. He has calculated the precise moment, he knows exactly when the knife descends, but when this extraordinary process of mockery has come to an end, there is no punishment: Charlie skips out into the centre of the road-way and having mocked the children, he now mocks the cops and the cameraman. The mockery is lighthearted, but there are undertones of tragedy. The mockery, of course, comes from long practice. He mocked the actors on the stage when he performed in Fred Karno's Circus, but he also mocked the audience. Now for the first time he mocks himself and enters those heady regions where the mocker mocks himself mocking himself and then goes on to mock himself mocking himself mocking himself and so *ad infinitum*, as though mockery was something that could be held up between parallel mirrors and reflected interminably in a long gallery of gradually diminishing brightness.

For an understanding of Chaplin's use of mockery *Kid Auto Races at Venice* is of quite extraordinary significance, for in that short film which took only forty-five minutes to make and lasted a bare ten minutes on the screen – it was spliced with another film called *Olives and Their Oil* to form a full reel – he was reaching out into all the potentialities which Charlie was later to reveal. The jaunty walk, the pathos, the innumerable tricks played with the cane, the fantastic power of mimicry which could not be used in *Making a Living* because a man in a top-hat and wearing a villainous moustache is in no position to mimic any-one, the way he would tip his hat or shrug his shoulders, and the way all these could be used to mock and embarrass, were clearly demonstrated in this extraordinary film, where he sketched out the first rough portrait which was to develop depth and dimension later.

In that first film so many complex and contrary things were happening at once that it is worth while to pause and examine one or two of them. The most noticeable thing about the new clown was that he was a stranger and had no place there, was only there on sufferance and could not be removed only because he was far more cunning than those who attempted to remove him. His chief desire is to interfere with everyone and attract attention to himself, as though there was some mysterious message which he wanted to deliver. What is the message? It is never disclosed, or rather it is disclosed by implication only too obviously. The street has been roped off on both sides to allow the kids' auto race to take place down the middle. All the on-lookers are jam-packed behind the ropes with policemen pressing them into line, while Charlie insists on wandering freely in the middle of the road. What he is saying clearly enough is: 'What is all this nonsense of ropes? Why allow yourselves to be hemmed in by these ridiculous cops? If you want to walk across the road, why don't you?'

It is not, of course, as simple as that, for when the mood takes him he will assist the cops and herd the people in line and gaze at them with a tender benevolence, without sorrow, noting the fact that they are placid and obedient and even applauding their obedience. He is without malice, and yet he suffers from sudden fits of merciless rage directed against the first object he sets eyes on. Wonderfully urbane and passive, he will yield to incredible fits of aggressiveness, and some of these fits are real, while others are disguised, produced simply to amuse himself or to amuse someone else or because he is bored with his own urbanity. What is masterly is the endless complexity of the character who is never a tramp, never a fool, but resembles most of all a god

Jean-Gaspard Deburau

Joseph Grimaldi

*Tillie's
Punctured
Romance,*
1914

who has unaccountably found himself on this earth, and having concealed his godlike nakedness with the first clothes he was able to find and wandered unheedingly into the world's traffic, discovers that the world is completely inexplicable and obeys laws he will not even attempt to understand. Behind the dead-white mask and the sad eyes there is the memory of a state of former magnificence, an earthly paradise in which no one was ever roped off and no little boys pedalled furiously in wooden automobiles to the imminent danger of innocent wayfarers.

Charlie is never a character easy to define and circumscribe. It is not only that he is continually eluding us, but he is always suggesting he is something else, always mimicking, always chameleon-like taking on the character of his surroundings. When he mimics the cop, the cop can hardly arrest him, for that would be like arresting himself. When he mimics the children, they are first stunned, then they laugh uproariously, because it never occurred to them that a man could be instantly transformed into a child. But it is when he mimics himself that the complexities really begin, for since he is evidently the great god Pan, and even wears, thinly disguised, the goat-mask – for what else is the moustache but a sketchy replica of the goat's black muzzle, and why the baggy trousers unless it is to hide the cloven hooves and legs thickly covered with curly hair? – we enter a world where a god mimics himself in the pure enjoyment of himself, and there seems neither rhyme nor reason for the doing of it. 'Since I am a god or a fallen angel,' he seems to be saying, 'I can do what I damned well please. I can even mimic myself if I feel like it.'

Yes; but what language does he speak? He is a mime, and he speaks the language of mimicry, but the mouth opens and closes – in a great number of the films that followed the mouth was set rigidly – and presumably he is talking in communicable terms to the crowds of children he addresses. Evidently he is talking some kind of divine gibberish. Everyone understands him perfectly, but he speaks in a language without grammar, without a known vocabulary, without any recognisable prosody. Mr T. S. Eliot has complained bitterly in some of his recent poems: 'I've got to use words when I talk to you.' Charlie successfully overcomes the difficulty. He uses words, but they are not words as we know them; it becomes increasingly clear that he is employing magic spells, strange abracadabras, and this is enough. The abracadabras are immediately understood by the children, even though the policemen are outraged, and never understand a word he says.

That first film, that first epiphany of Charlie on the streets of Venice, is rewarding because it reveals the full measure of Charlie without the complications of plot or story. Having fallen from heaven or wherever the ancient rustic gods dwell, he has jumped up, dusted his pants and discovered to his intense surprise that it is a warm day in December,[1] the kids are having an auto race and there is a cameraman in attendance. What could be better? He proceeds to announce his arrival to the world. He knows he will be regarded as a nuisance. He knows that the rulers of the world, represented by the cops, are immersed in the task of creating order out of the natural disorder of human beings, but he imagines they will have the good sense to pay attention to him, forgetting that they are as little interested in the coming of Pan as they would be in the descent of Christ in a thunder-cloud. Magic has gone from the world. His task – a task which the children instantly recognise – is to bring it back again.

From the very beginning then, Charlie announces that his enemies are the cops and the cameramen and that he is on the side of natural man. He has no patience with law and order. Whenever he flares up in one of those outrageous bursts of temper, it is because he sees the futility of the law, the idiocy of those heavy men with batons who interfere in a child's auto race as though the race, the crowd, everyone taking part, were there simply so that the policemen could enforce the law, when every-one knows that a child's auto race only becomes splendid when everyone is allowed to do what he pleases, when all the autos jam together and the drivers spill out. A child's auto race should be fun. It isn't, because the police are always interfering. As for the cameraman, who insists on filming the race and does every-thing he can to forget Charlie, he is beneath contempt. He must be outraged into fulfilling his proper task, which is to film Charlie while the children take care of themselves. In order to

[1] Careful enquiry has failed to reveal the exact day the film was made, but it appears to have been one day during the last week of December 1913. The film was released on 7 February 1914.

outrage the cameraman, Charlie does openly all the things which
people wish they could do in public, though they never have the
courage to do it. He thwacks a cop on his backside, sticks out his
tongue, struts down the street, pulls a cop's moustache, in-
solently mimics the flat-footed magisterial stride of the cop. He
does all the absurd and wonderful things which people do when
they think they are alone and not being seen. He is the exhibi-
tionist in all of us. And the children, who are exhibitionists by
divine right, applaud him, torn between their desire to see the
auto race and the more urgent desire to see Charlie for the pure
pleasure of watching him at his antic play. Whatever he does
commends itself to them. If he trips up a cop – excellent. If a
cop trips him up – excellent. Captivated by the deft beauty of
his clowning, by the clown's sense of bodily grace and rhythm,
they are instantly removed from the world of right and wrong,
and enter a world where everything is permissible.

At this moment dangers appear. Since Charlie possesses a
godlike immunity, since he can dart away from punishment,
there is nothing to prevent him from doing anything he pleases.
He is the possessor of prodigious powers. In his capacious
pockets lurk thunderbolts, and when he prods a cop neatly in the
seat of the pants with his only too flexible cane, he is not demonstrating his insolence so much as demonstrating the threat of the
vast powers he secretly possesses, a secret he shares with the
children, for it is unthinkable that he should ever harm them.
But as we know too well merely to possess vast powers is
dangerous, and if it should happen that Charlie runs a cop
through with his cane and transfixes him to the ground, as one
transfixes a butterfly with a pin, the death of the cop would be
amusing; and in the same way, if Charlie's head were broken by
a cop's baton, that too would be amusing. It would seem that in
the world of comedy killing has a meaning which is totally
distinct from its meaning in real life. In comedy it is inconceivable that people should really die. They may assume the
postures of death, and then we howl with laughter, and the
nearer they approach to the postures of death the louder is the
laughter.

These conclusions should give us pause. At its best comedy is
a desperate thing. Comedy is never so comic as when the comedian

B

teeters on the edge of death. We remember the hilarious
moments when the comedian is caught up on the hour-hand of a
clock high up on a skyscraper. He looks down, and there is Fifth
Avenue below him, the people invisible and the automobiles
streaming along like ants. How marvellous! How comic! The
minute-hand creeps round and hooks on to the comedian's coat,
and ever so slowly rips through the cloth. Then the comedian
lets go his hold on the hour-hand. He falls two feet, but some
miraculous threads of the coat caught on the minute-hand hold
him up. He sighs with relief, adjusts his spectacles and gives a
weak little smile. At that moment the clock bell rings the hour
and the heavy black hour-hand, jerking sharply, hits him over
the head. He is knocked out. When he wakes up from his stupor
he gazes at the automobiles in Fifth Avenue streaming below
and smiles indulgently, happy to be in a place where there is
such an excellent view of New York. Seeing a balloon high up
over Washington Bridge, he makes gestures with his hands
as though he were swimming, still smiling, but the smile freezes
when the last threads of his coat-tail snap. Now he is dangling
on the hour-hand. His spectacles fall off, and he watches them
until they become no more than a speck in the grey air above
Fifth Avenue.

We find this kind of thing irresistibly comic. Why? Andrè
Malraux in *La Condition Humaine* tells the story of a small
Chinese woman who slaps the face of her dead husband in bed,
and while the old man's face wobbles grotesquely from side to
side, the children are overcome with ringing laughter. What has
happened? What is there about extreme danger or death which
sometimes makes us laugh? There is very little difference
between Harold Lloyd dangling on an hour-hand and a man
dangling on a rope. He is as close to death as a man can be without dying. Is it possible that the mask of Charlie, which suggests
Pan, also suggests a skull, and we laugh because of the very
effrontery of this walking skeleton who has appeared from
nowhere with no authority at all, except the authority which
comes from the dead? It may be that the strange mask which
Chaplin invented does represent something which exists at the
very edge of life. 'I am always aware that Charlie is playing
with death,' Chaplin told me once. 'He plays with it, mocks it,

thumbs his nose at it, but it is always there. He is aware of death at every moment of his existence, and he is terribly aware of being alive.'

I said something about the messenger in Æschylus who announces: 'I see the dead are killing one who lives,' and suggested that Charlie is a kind of *revenant*, a pale ghost of the past, but instead of trying to kill the living, he attempts to give them more abundant life.

'Yes, yes,' Chaplin said. 'There is death in him, and he is bringing life – more life. That is his only excuse, his only purpose. That is why people recognised him everywhere. They wanted the ghosts to come and bring them life. It's very strange, isn't it?' And saying that, he shook his head, pretending to be bewildered, sitting there at one o'clock in the morning on the steps of the house in Beverly Hills, the darkness thick on the hills. 'You see,' he went on, 'the clown is so close to death that only a knife-edge separates him from it, and sometimes he goes over the border, but he always returns again. So in a way he is spirit – not real. And because he is always returning, that gives us comfort. We know he cannot die, and that's the best thing about him. I created him, but I am not him, and yet sometimes our paths cross. You know, it is a very enviable thing to be a clown.'

Chaplin has asked himself many times what the devil Charlie is up to. Who is this pale ghost-like creature, who has come from nowhere and will go nowhere because he is always present in the air, the vagabond with a suicide's rope round his neck and the look of perplexity and power on his mask-like face? Chaplin has not solved the conundrums presented by the presence of Charlie. In a sense all the films are an attempt to solve the single problem: *Who is he?* At different times and different places he has talked superbly about the clown. He said once: 'I walk on to the stage, serious, dignified, solemn, pause before an easy chair, spread my coat-tails with an elegant gesture and sit – on the cat.' But in fact he never did sit on the cat, which was always to be found in his coat-pocket, smiling its Cheshire cat smile. There was a great deal of the conjuror in him. At another time he said that Charlie is like the ordinary man, baffled by the world:

He does not cut a dashing figure as he blunders through a drab and commonplace existence. Heroism with him, except on great occasions, never soars to greater heights than his interviews with his landlord. His fortunes always drag a little behind his expectations, and fulfilment lies always just out of reach. And as he shambles along with dwindling hopes he is smitten more than ever with a sense of his own unfitness and inadequacy. When he sees on the stage or screen the romantic hero who sweeps through life like a whirlwind, he feels a sense of inferiority and is depressed. Then he sees me shuffling along in my baffled and aimless manner, and a spark of hope rekindles. Here is a man like himself, only more pathetic and miserable, with ludicrously impossible clothes – in every sense a social misfit and failure. The figure on the screen has a protective air of mock dignity – takes the most outrageous liberties with people – and wears adversity as though it was a bouquet. In emergencies he even triumphs over those imposing characters whom the average man has always visualised with so much awe.

This is part of the story, but not the whole of it; and it leaves out the power of the character, his inexplicable rages, the fact that he is at once baffled and completely in command of himself, reverent and irreverent, and gives the impression so often of performing a kind of sacred rite. The mask is many masks, and many-sided. We shall never capture it entirely. But of some things we can be reasonably certain, and among them is the knowledge that something unusually real, terrible and beautiful occurred on the day when Chaplin wore the mask for the first time. We shall find hints towards an understanding of the mask in places where we least expected them.

CHAPTER III

THE DELIGHT MAKERS

UNKNOWN to Chaplin in 1913, there already existed in America clowns who curiously resembled the clown he invented in Venice. They had never appeared on the vaudeville stage or before cameras. They lived in isolated places, and went about their sacred fooling almost unknown to the white inhabitants of America, following traditional patterns handed down through the centuries.

Some four hundred miles away from Venice, in the pueblos of Arizona and in a hundred other places in New Mexico and Nevada, there exist societies known as the *koshare* or 'Delight Makers'. In these societies the men paint their faces black and white, and their bodies with blue and white stripes, they wear their hair parted at the crown and turretted to resemble rams' horns. At certain festivals during the year they are considered sacred. They may commit any improprieties and obscenities they like, and they may burlesque anyone. If any harm comes to them, the whole tribe believes it will suffer misfortune. Their disguise is supposed to make them invisible, though of course everyone sees them and knows they are there. They wear bunches of pine on their arms, and wear long black hanging breechcloths, and they never speak. They come mysteriously, when they are least expected. They may draw a mystic line of cornmeal on the ground: anyone who crosses the line must pay a forfeit. They are believed to have the power to make floods recede and rain fall; they increase fertility in man and plant. They are the spirits of the dead and the ancients, and they are also the ribald spirits of fertility, licensed jesters possessed of sacerdotal powers. With corn-husks in their hair and branches of evergreen in their belts, they frolic through the tribal territory, dancing with shuffling steps. They hold the tribe at their mercy. Yet they are entirely pleasant, and everyone is delighted when they come.

These strange delightful clowns have a long history. The tribes can never remember a time when they did not exist. To call them the 'Delight Makers' is to simplify their purpose. They are there to test the sacredness of the most sacred rituals, which they mimic, pressing close to the priest at the most solemn moments of the ceremonies, imitating him, confusing him, leaping out of nowhere to confound him with their animal presences. They employ all their considerable powers of cunning and insolence to destroy ruthlessly and deliberately, without hurting anyone and generally without touching anyone, the established order. They have another purpose, which is to remind everyone of his common humanity.

During a Roman triumph the victorious general in his chariot led by four pure white horses, accompanied by a long retinue of soldiers, priests and senators, attended by serving-boys and watched by the admiring citizens of Rome, would sometimes hear the words whispered into his ear by the public slave who stood behind him, holding a gold crown over the *triumphator's* head: 'Look behind you, for you are mortal.' The *koshare* fulfil the same function as the public slave and the hosts of young men and girls who danced round the sacred chariot, singing indecent hymns to the victorious general.

The *koshare* mimic ceremonies, but they also mimic individuals. If they see a beautiful girl watching them, they may come up to her, mincing and swinging their hips, extending a condescend-ing hand, mimicking her smile, her dignity, the trembling of her lips, the way she covers her lips with her hands, the way she walks away, the way she stands still, even the way she bursts out crying, until she is wholly at their friendly mercy. Sometimes they amuse themselves with charades. At Taos on St Geronimo's Day a greased pole with sheep and various other spoils is thrown up on the plaza. The 'Delight Makers' come dancing to the pole, then they make sheep tracks in the dust at their feet, and then other 'Delight Makers' appear. They follow the sheep tracks. They pretend they cannot understand why the tracks end at the pole. Then they see the sheep hanging high above them, and they aim little arrows at it, and start to climb the pole, but they all come tumbling to the ground. Afterwards they lower their heads and butt one another, incomprehensibly pretending to be bulls.

So the 'Delight Makers', weaving in and out among the crowds, demonstrate that we are all bound together in a single chain. They are the custodians of the sacred powers, medicine men, doctors, clowns. To show that they are immune from the frailties of the flesh, immortal, they will eat all manner of filth, including live puppies and stones and urine. Occasionally they will utter curses, as when they announce: 'Our daylight fathers, our daylight mothers, after so many days, eight days, on the ninth day you will copulate with rams.' But generally their temper is quiet, and they do no harm unless they are themselves harmed. They have the powers that Pan possessed, and like Pan, the hoary goat-god, they are above all 'deliverers'. Not far from Nazareth, and in the time of Christ, there was a shrine to 'Pan the Deliverer'.

The koshare are not the only sacred clowns among the Indians, but they are the most powerful. There are 'Mud-heads', who wear knobbed soft masks and who seem to derive from the time of the great floods. They, too, grapple with the Plumed Serpent, summon the rain, perform strange indecent dances with bull-roarers in their hands. Then there are the Boogermen among the Cherokees, disease-healers who unexpectedly leap into the sick man's presence to startle him and so drive the evil spirits away. They shuffle their feet to a furious unaccented drumming, going a few paces forward, then stopping abruptly, then scuffling sideways, shaking their knees – the effect is exactly like a gross imitation of Charlie's dancing and limping walk, and like Charlie they wear baggy suits of burlap or old rags, and they are adepts at mimicry. During the dance, the music-master will call upon a Boogerman to answer a question, 'Who are you?' or 'Where do you come from?' The Boogerman must immediately reply with some ludicrous or obscene answer, then he must dance the part, and he does this in the most sprightly manner possible, deliberately breaking the rhythm of the shuffling steps. Finally, having teased and tormented and mimicked everyone in sight, they disappear silently to some remote field where they can remove their disguise, for it would be unthinkable that anyone should see them in their own houses in disguise.

The Boogermen possess little of the charm which is possessed by the 'Mud-heads', nor is their behaviour so complicated. The 'Mud-heads' who may make love realistically on the house-tops and who burlesque everything in sight, are more sacramental. Like the *koshare*, their lunacy seems to spring from a divine source, and it is not to be wondered at that they conceal in their muddy knob-like ears the footprints of people. If they come begging, then food must be given to them; otherwise disaster would befall. If they laugh, you must be silent. They are fearful gods, and their masks have the simplicity of Charlie's: there is no more than the outline of a face, two holes for the eyes, a hole for the mouth.

We come closer to Charlie's mask in the Night Chant of the Navajos, which lasts for nine nights and is attended by complex ceremonies, including the recital of 324 different songs which go to make up a long ritual poem. The cow-mask, the most sacred vestment used in these ceremonies, is formed of a single piece of stretched fabric with black eyes, a black spot for a muzzle or a mouth and two horns. The effect of the juxtaposition of the eyes and muzzle bears a quite extraordinary resemblance to the mask of Charlie. Holiness springs from the mask, which is also reproduced in the sand-paintings. From it come, in a long, soft and unbroken stream, the tender recuperative forces of life, as the medicine men chant:

> *He stirs, he stirs, he stirs.*
> *Among the lands of dawning, he stirs, he stirs,*
> *The pollen of dawning, he stirs, he stirs.*

As for the Navajo clowns who appear in force on the last night of the Night Chant in celebration of the returning flow of life, they are the rowdiest and most boisterous of all. Nothing is sacred to them. Their comic play is as indelicate as the comic play of the ancient Greeks. All the men have a large bladder shaped like a penis under their breechcloths, and with their breechcloths removed, with clumps of grass pulp on their buttocks and a short twig crosswise between their buttocks they jump and hobble to the shouts and laughter of the crowded house-

tops. This may not be amusing to our taste; it is not intended
to amuse the Navajo onlookers. They have created a glorious
drunken indecent shape of a hobbling clown as part of their
ritual, and they are after larger rewards than amusement. The
ceremonies are performed through eight long nights of hushed
and reverent chanting; on the ninth day the dark fermenting
wine is uncorked, and half the wine gushes out in the explosion.
The Balinese have similar revels; so did the Aztecs, from whom
the Pueblos seem to have borrowed many of the forms of revelry.
We forget that orgies of clowning were once considered a part
of life, perhaps the most essential part, and we shall not understand the clowns until we realise they are gods.

In an age when real laughter is rare, we regard the *koshare*
and the Boogermen as strange survivals of some antique creed.
They fulfil sacerdotal functions; we are not accustomed to see
priests mocking the sacraments, and if we did we would call the
priests insane or we would summon the police. Our priests are
modest; they are in love with decorum; they are on the right
side of the law. It was not always so. In the Middle Ages there
were great feasts which the priests attended where the utmost
licence prevailed. They wore masks and monstrous faces at the
hours of office. They danced in the choir dressed as women,
panders and minstrels. They sang bawdy songs from the altar,
and ate black pudding at the horn of the altar while the celebrant
was saying mass. They played dice on the altar steps, and censed
the church with puddings, sausages and old shoes, and thought
little of running and leaping about the church naked or with slit
breeches or following some naked, drunken carouser in procession through the town, and they would make the most indecent gestures and sing the most obscene songs. For five hundred
years they did this. There were complaints from high authorities,
but the Feast of Fools was celebrated at the New Year in a
thousand churches of Christendom, and a mad missal, where all
the accepted canons of taste were solemnly reversed, was employed on this feast-day, which celebrated the New Year, the
Circumcision and the happy folly of men. The Feast of Fools
possessed a respectable ancestry. It can be traced back to the
Roman Saturnalia and far beyond, and it represented a deep and
desperate need: the need to mock the things one loves best only

in order to reverence them the more, the need to see the world in the light of laughter. The Feast provided a release from the conventions of worship; and the celebrant who attended mass on a day after a drinking bout below the high altar was not to be regarded as a man who had sold his soul to the devil. Indeed, his piety was all the greater now that he had seen the Christ through the eyes of laughter.

Forbidden, the *festum follorum* was continually revived, and though the bishops generally took little part in it, the common priests were its chief participants, the most delighted of the delight makers. The end of the seventeenth century saw the end of it as a deliberate part of the annual ritual of Christendom, but it survived in odd places – Mardi Gras in New Orleans is a happy marriage between the ancient Roman processional triumph and the Feast of Fools of the Middle Ages, and if we would imagine the mediaeval feast, it is simple enough: we only have to imagine a wilder, a more roisterous Mardi Gras.

All over the world religions have sanctified folly, but it was always a special kind of folly. There must be mockery in it, but the mockery must do no harm. There must be obscenity, but the obscenity is reserved for a single day or a single occasion: a licensed release from pent-up emotions. Somewhere there must be a clown in command, a *dominus festi*, to ring the sacred bells and call upon the faithful to rejoice. There must be a deliberate reversal of the conventions: the high are laid low, the humble are elevated. There must be free wine flowing, and wreaths of roses on the foreheads of the celebrants, and every man may address every woman, and every child must straddle a father's shoulders. Someone must play music, and everyone must dance in the village squares. The *koshare* and the mediaeval priests at the Feast of Fools were performing the same human function; and in our own day this function has been performed by Chaplin and W. C. Fields and perhaps three others.

Today, the glinting wisecrack has taken the place of the salty humour of the past. In the modern radio auditorium you find the cruellest of recent inventions – the man who raises his arm and tells you when to laugh. 'How are you?' says Groucho Marx. 'So you come from Wichita Falls? Well, well. Fell in the falls, eh!' The bright mechanical laughter follows immediately, and ceases when the hand falls. The manipulated radio audience and the manipulated tape are putting an end to laughter, and encouraging us to become a race of liars, or automatons, or worse. The radio audience laughs for the same reason that the mouth of Pavlov's dog watered. No institutions are mocked; all must be praised; the wisecracks jump on one another's heels; the harsh voice is a machine working with mechanical precision. More terrible than the wars is the end of laughter.

The art of pantomime is dying, and when Chaplin dies it may be altogether dead. There was a time not very long ago when great gusts of earthy laughter smacked against the vaudeville stage; in those days there was froth on the beer, not pretty little bubbles. So it was with the Keystone comedies. There was nothing smart, nervous or jaded in them; no one was trying feverishly to be funny; the fun lay all around them, and they had only to pick it up. In those days the humour was rich and gay and mocking and atrociously impudent, and it was all these things because there was a human need for them, because a man cannot live without the grace of laughter, because he dies in the flesh if his flesh does not laugh with mockery and delight in the world around him. We used to wonder why Field and Chaplin held such power over us. We need not have wondered. They were, and are, a part of our need.

CHAPTER IV

MARIONETTES

But the mystery of Charlie is not solved by an appeal to fooling. The priests of the Middle Ages who performed a sacrament in reverse and censed the churches with puddings, sausages and old shoes were fulfilling an essential function; the function of preserving man's humanity and earthiness; but though there is fooling in Charlie and he does not disdain the puddings, the sausages or the old boots, and he would be an admirable performer at the *festum follorum*, we are conscious that the strange creature whose eyes are almonds and whose mouth resembles the mouth of a tragic mask, is closer to the *koshare* than to the mediæval priestly buffoons. Like the *koshare* he has a special kind of walking, is clothed with a kind of dancing invisibility and in some way derives his strength from the spirits of the dead or of the ancients. There were no white masks at the *festum follorum*, no ceremonies of lighthearted mockery. In mediæval Europe the mockery was cruel and blunt-edged, a deliberate abasement following the exaltations of the church. We remember that the *koshare* were abstemious and when they were obscene, it was with a devilish immediacy, wagging their members as they danced round the priests. Something of that immediacy was lacking in the mediæval carnival, which tended to substitute horseplay with chamber-pots for the naked obscenities which are the most comic of all. These mediæval fêtes were essentially bourgeois; it is unthinkable that the same fêtes were performed in the villages.

To understand Charlie we must follow the clues wherever we can find them. They must lead us inevitably into some of the remote places of the human spirit, among the towers of pride and the valleys of human misery. We cannot isolate the comic spirit and hold it up to the light. We cannot pin it into a museum case. But it is possible that if we could see it steadily for a moment, or thrust through some of the veils where it hides, we might find some of the reasons why it is worth while to be alive, for tragedy offers only the most excellent reasons why it would be better to be dead. There is a sense in which the genuine spirit of comedy is the lightning-flash which alone illuminates our down-at-heels world. 'A joke, sometimes even a bad joke,' said Christopher Fry recently, 'can reflect the astonishing light that we live in. Indeed, laughter itself is a great mystery of the flesh, as though flesh were entertaining something other than itself: something vociferous but inarticulate.'

The philosophers, of course, have set their hearts at contriving a solution to the enigma, and Chaplin has remarked, with some authority, that since philosophers are usually unable to distinguish between a good joke ·and a bad one, they are in no position to pass judgment. 'In laughter,' according to Bergson, 'we always find an avowed intention to humiliate and consequently to correct our neighbour.' Bergson's theory has a respectable ancestry. Hobbes wrote in *Leviathan:* 'The passion of laughter is nothing else but a sudden glory arising from a sudden conception of some eminence in ourselves, by comparison with the infirmity of others, or with our own formerly.' It would have been simpler and more accurate if he had said only: 'The passion of laughter is nothing else but a sudden glory.'

Mr Al Capp, in discussing Chaplin, has recently revived the same dismal theory, which does not explain why we laugh when we are in bed with a girl or when we are just plain happy. Laughter, we are told, is only the extreme of smiling, and smiling is simply the baring of teeth. It may be so; but when Dante saw all the radiance of heaven flooding from Beatrice's smile, we should be under no illusions concerning Beatrice. She is divine; she is not an animal baring her teeth.

But there are some philosophers who have written well and learnedly concerning the spirit of comedy. Among them was Søren Kierkegaard, whose sense of the urgency and anguish of being a Christian did not prevent him from enjoying comedy.

In one of those lyrical fragments of reminiscences which Kierkegaard introduced into his most prophetical works there is

an account of a clown called Beckmann he was accustomed to see
at the Königstadter Theatre at Copenhagen. Beckmann was a
prodigious clown who could play in the most gentle manner
possible and could also give way to the most frightful rages. He
was like Mediterranean weather, now wanton warmth, now the
sickening storm of a sirocco. A fat man with a trailing moustache
and a devil-may-care manner, he usually portrayed a travelling
tinker; and the gaunt hunchbacked philosopher, sitting in his
favourite seat in the royal circle, saw something of himself in
the actor. Beckmann could make you see things which your
reason told you could not possibly exist. He did not walk on to
the boards; he seemed to have been there from the beginning
of time. You would see a travelling tinker, and that was Beckmann; but the surprising, the beautiful, the inexplicable thing
was that there had suddenly appeared on the empty stage a
whole imaginary village, exactly as though Beckmann had tossed
the village out of his cloak when he was dusting it or searching
for fleas. You saw the people emerging from their houses and
greeting the tinker, you saw the dust, the pathways, the river
winding beside the village smithy, the crowds of children
gathered at his heels, and it was all conjured out of a wink, a
gesture, the way he strolled and grimaced and careened across
the stage, a magician who could invent a world with a crook of a
finger, a man without character who could assume the character
of his inventions.

There was something amorphous about Beckmann which put
Kierkegaard in mind of the Greek gods, who could change their
appearance at will. He noted that Beckmann's contours were
masterly, though the shading was weak. It hardly mattered, for
there was no time to watch for shading or depth. Incredible
forces were bottled up in Beckmann, whose rages were superb:

> I call him the Incognito, whose body is the home of the
> crack-brained, insane devil of comedy, a devil who will break
> out of his chains at any moment and destroy everything in
> berserk fury. As for his dancing, it is incomparable. He sings
> a verse, then he dances, dances so furiously that at any moment
> you imagine he will break his neck. The ritual of the dance
> offers him no solace. He is beside himself with rage, yet his

wild laughter has nothing at all to do with the usual comic
foolery. Like Baron Münchhausen, his soul achieves perfection only when he takes himself by the neck and throws himself into a delirious abandon of joy. I have said that anyone can
taste these joys, but it is only a genius, working in the name
and with the authority of genius, who can play with them.
Unless genius is present, the result is disastrous.

There was Beckmann, but there was also Grobecker, whose
voice was harsh and piercing where Beckmann's possessed, even
in its rages, a human warmth. Grobecker was sentimental, but
it was a cold sentimentality. He attracted attention to himself,
not to the world he created, and his *forte* lay in his absurd
postures. Once he took the part of a steward waiting for the
arrival of his masters. Grobecker decided that on their return
from the city nothing would please them so much as a *fête-
champêtre*, a charming introduction to the life of the country.
He could not bring the peasants to life; he could only bring
himself to life as the obedient steward, waiting to serve his
master. But how? He decided to disguise himself as Mercury,
attaching wings to his feet and decorating his head with a helmet;
and then standing on one foot, with one foot outstretched behind
him, leaning forward with an idiotic smile of greeting, he made a
speech of welcome to his masters the moment they came within
earshot. The extraordinary thing about Grobecker was the cold
calculating precision of his mimicry, the clear outlines, the sense
that he was performing according to rigorous laws, and above all
his detachment. 'He was intelligence personified,' Kierkegaard
commented, 'and at the same time he was a sentimentalist
whose sentiments led him into a state of ecstacy. In that mood of
cold detachment he showed his mastery to perfection, though he
lacked Beckmann's fermenting flame. Nevertheless it would be
untrue to say that he was not a genius: he was a genius, and
worthy of his calling.'

Kierkegaard possessed the utmost respect for these clowns.
All his life he was bewitched by the spirit of comedy. He attended
the theatre regularly and continually commented on the performances. It seemed to him that the comic stage with its paradoxes and absurdities, its excesses, its eternal dilemmas, was

quite extraordinarily close to the explosive world of theology where he was at home. It was absurd to be alive, it was absurd to die, and most of all it was absurd to be a Christian. *Credo quia absurdum.* Tertullian's phrase haunted him. He examined 'the category of the absurd' tranquilly, always walking on a tightrope and always in danger of falling, inventing his terminology as he went along because no one had ever explored such a landscape before. Jesus said that salvation is found only by putting everything one has in jeopardy. That, too, was absurd, and yet it was true. Men spent their whole lives on the edge of the abyss 'suspended over 70,000 fathoms', and that was absurd and wonderful beyond belief. He was not the first to note that the universe is essentially comic, but he was the first to give depth and precision to the divine absurdity in the world of faith. He told the story of the Old Testament princess who mysteriously murdered her husbands one by one, and how in the end the one who had greatest faith was not murdered by her, but instead lived tranquilly with her to the end of his days. Then he set the story against a universal background and commented:

> A purely human courage is required to renounce the temporal in order to gain the eternal. . . . . And yet it must be glorious to get the princess . . . and the knight of resignation who does not say it is a deceiver. . . . The only happy one is the heir apparent to the finite, whereas the knight of resignation is a stranger. By my strength I am able to give up the princess, but by my own strength I am not able to get her again, for I am employing all my strength to be resigned. But by faith . . . by faith I shall get her *in virtue of the absurd.*

The sense of paradox which informs so much of Kierkegaard's writings was not so much the result of his natural cleverness as of his humility. Before the paradoxes of life he stands astonished, devout, amazingly childlike. 'Paradox,' he said once, 'is a passion of thought, and the philosopher without a sense of paradox resembles a lover without passion – a foolish fellow. The highest power of every passion is to desire its own destruction, and so it is the highest passion of understanding to desire a stumbling-block. The greatest paradox of the mind is the mind's desire to discover something it cannot think.' In this sense all philosophy becomes a trapeze act, a joyful exploration by the trapeze artist of the heights of the tent. What if he falls? What if he hears the clown's mocking laughter? So irony enters the game, and philosophy itself becomes 'a dance on the rim', played by a dancer with the courage of a highwayman who, when the cart has left him dangling, kicks off his shoes in a final gesture of invincibility.

It is fashionable to decry Kierkegaard and his successors, to lament their irony, the complexities of their paradoxes, the astonishing contours of the landscapes they explored so brilliantly. But though we decry them, we cannot put them away. The world has caught up with them, and the paradoxes which once seemed daring are in danger of becoming commonplaces. Kafka, the most methodical as he was the most daring of Kierkegaard's successors, invented a character K. who is partly Kafka himself desperately trying to escape from his own prophetical visions, but he is also Kierkegaard. He is also Charlie.

Like Kierkegaard, Kafka was haunted by the paradox of faith. The Castle, which lay beyond the mind's reaches, was the source of authority. It sent its messengers to the earth, held its courts of judgment, paraded its beauty over the whole landscape, but the King remained invisible and unapproachable. One could believe in the King, but it stretched the faith to the uttermost to believe in his messengers who sometimes stood in judgment on the people of the earth. They held their courts in abandoned warehouses. If you examined them closely, you saw that they did not know what they were doing. They dressed in a peculiar fashion. Under their immense beards you would sometimes see their badges of authority. Were they policemen, or were they priests? Kafka did not know. He could only report what he had seen. When K. is finally arrested and led out to a deserted quarry where his throat is cut according to the proper ceremonies, he notes that the men arresting him are paunchy, jovial in their uncommunicative way and resemble ham actors. All through the strange divided world in which Kafka moves, we are aware of a resemblance between the world of the Castle and the world of the Keystone cops. Kafka enlarges on the divided world, subtly dissects it, proves its incoherence and patiently draws the portrait of K. as he attempts to make sense of the messengers or the

invitations he occasionally receives from the Castle, those invitations which are always written in enigmatic language or in a
code where the key is unknown. Yet all through the drama K.
behaves with a kind of brooding *insouciance*, always gentle,
always hoping for the best.

The poet Heinrich von Kleist never thought it worth his
while to hope for the best. He saw himself engaged in a fight
doomed from the beginning. But before dying by his own hand,
he wrote the most penetrating of all the short stories which have
been written about the clown. In this story, called *Concerning the
Marionette Theatre*, he simply told a number of anecdotes,
beginning with an encounter with a friend who had long studied
the art of the marionettes. The man was a successful dancer; he
admitted that he learned his art from the puppets, with their little
pellets of lead in feet and hands. The puppets possessed a kind of
reality denied to human dancers. As for the mechanic who held
the strings, he must be himself more than dancer, he must
surrender wholly to the dance of puppets, find his way into their
souls – *yes, into their souls*, he says. Heinrich von Kleist finds himself wondering whether he is talking with a madman, but no, he
looks very calm and he has the air of a man speaking of things he
knows. 'You must understand that the man who holds the
strong strings is very much like a god,' the dancer says. 'And
look what happens. No mortal man can ever reach the grace
achieved by a dancing doll. One becomes a god by holding the
strings, for only a god can deal with nature in these fields of
activity, and when he does this, why, *the two ends of the world's
ring reach out for one another.*'

That holy moment, when artistry achieves its greatest perfection, is discussed at length, and then Kleist goes on to discuss
another story altogether. It is a very strange story, and concerns
an immense tame bear which a Russian nobleman kept in his
house. The nobleman was known as a magnificent swordsman.
Many were puzzled by his accomplishment. One day, it was
learned that he exercised with his sword every day with the
bear, which possessed a wonderful sense of rhythm, and with a
single cuff of its great paws was able to parry all attacks. The
bear's defences were perfect. It possessed the pure grace of art,
the knowledge of the rhythms appropriate for defence. Why is

this? 'It seems to me that the reasons are clear,' the nobleman said. 'The bear behaved instinctively, without using its reason. In the world as it is, as the power of the mind grows dull and weakens, then grace comes forward, more radiant, more dominating. Think, then, of two intersecting lines which cross and then go onward to infinity, and beyond, but suddenly, encountering another plane, they find themselves once more at the point of intersection. Or imagine yourself gazing in a concave mirror, where you image vanishes to infinity and then appears beside you. In exactly the same way, when self-consciousness has passed from you and made its way into the infinite distances, grace is acquired, and this quality of grace, as it appears in the human body, possesses the greatest purity when there is either no self-consciousness or else an infinite self-consciousness: *either the mechanical doll or the god.*'

In effect, Kleist is saying that the greatest dances can take place only when consciousness is at vanishing point or at its height. The doll and the god between them have the mastery of art. There is a perversity in the dance. Sometimes the doll appears, sometimes the god; then they vanish, and all we see is the crass human body attempting to imitate art.

Perhaps the heart of the mystery lies here. We shall never know for certain why we are so deeply moved when we watch a puppet-show or a ballet. There are times when we watch *Les Sylphides* when the dancers seem to acquire their life and movement only from the music, then suddenly the music ceases and they have the appearance of gods. It is the same with Charlie. There are times when he seems to walk down the road as though there was a mechanical engine inside him, a puppet with a clockwork motor. Then the sound of the motor is drowned and you hear the rage of a god.

CHAPTER V

THE WHITE-FACED CLOWN

No ONE knows where the white-faced clowns came from. According to the *Dionysiaca* of the poet Nonnus, the Titans were the first whose faces were painted white, perhaps as a sign of their servitude as gods who had fallen from heaven. There is a ghostliness about the colour white which suggests more than ghosts; some shuddering horror lurks in the colour we call 'dead white', as Melville observed when he came to write the the chapter called 'The Whiteness of the Whale' and spoke of midnight seas of milky whiteness, pale horses, shrouds, frosts and wind-rowed snows as though all of them contained some secret poison, were covered with the devil's spittle. 'Not yet have we solved the incantation of this whiteness,' he wrote, and hinted that the secret of life lay in some white thing shaped like a whale. As for the clowns they seem to have been white from the beginning, perhaps with fear at the world around them, and perhaps after all white is no more than the colour corresponding to 'being haunted'.

There are gaps in our knowledge of the history of the clown. When we first come upon the ancient Greek clown he is already complex, his heart set not on buffoonery but on gentle intimidation. He affects to be a fool in order to outwit the braggarts, but he is not a fool. Instead, he gives the impression of being a remote and fastidious intellectual, but it was not always so. Under that mask, as J. A. K. Thomson observes in his study of the ironical man, there is 'someone far more elemental, simple, grotesque and pitiful'. At any rate clowning in ancient Greece seems to have begun and ripened in the eternal contest between the *alazon* (the impostor) and the *eiron* (the cunning one), with the buffoon standing by as a kind of laughing chorus to their

53

play. The truth is, of course, that we know too little. We do not know how the *eiron* developed, and what origins he had, but we have a right to guess that he was always split across the middle, pitiful and fastidious from the beginning. Socrates was accused of irony, and some clue to the behaviour of the ironical man is given by Alcibiades when he discusses Socrates in the *Symposium*. 'He is the satyr without and the god within,' says Alcibiades. 'Listen to him talk. Why, his language is like the rough skins of the satyrs – nothing but talk of pack-asses and smiths and cobblers and curriers, and he is always repeating the same things. But remember that our statues of the satyrs are hollow, and then you will perceive that Socrates has a rough surface but within him are the divine images.' This was only another way of saying that Socrates looked and often behaved like the great god Pan.

We see the face of Pan again in the chief character of the Atellane farces performed by the citizens of Atella in Campania and transplanted in the third century B.C. to Rome. His name was Maccus, and he was known as the *albus mimus*, the white mime. He had no horns, but he had a goat's beard and a goat's muzzle. He was quick, witty, impertinent, ironical and cruel, the enemy of the boastful shrewish Bucco, and he handed down his shape and disposition to the *Commedia dell' Arte* where he appears under the name of Pulcinella. By this time he had become more complex than ever, so brilliant in his cunning and so animal in his lusts that he had to be divided into two separate characters with the same name. It was explained that the 'upper' Pulcinella was born in the hills of Benevento, the 'lower' Pulcinella in the valleys. One wonders why. Pan had possessed the same attributes, but no one ever suggested that he was born in two separate places at once. In time Pulcinella became Punch, but as we shall see later he was still the great god Pan, living in two worlds even when he descended to being a puppet-show. Finally, one small part of Pulcinella, and that the better part, was torn away to form the image of Pedrolino, whom we know as Pierrot. Here the rough outlines of Pulcinella were softened, and though they wore the same costume as a sign of their identity, Pedrolino never allowed himself to speak, never employed his cunning to the uttermost, and he alone of the *Commedianti dell' Arte* had a face that was completely white. From Pedrolino–Pierrot Chaplin acknowledges the descent of Charlie. He did not, of course, deliberately assume the mask and behaviour of Pierrot. 'In the early days I was interested in getting a job,' he said later. 'I was after fifty dollars a week. It was only later on that I saw that everything I was trying to do was in some way derived from the *Commedia dell' Arte.* Charlie was a shabby Pierrot. The more I studied the *Commedia dell' Arte,* the more I realised that Charlie was in existence long before I invented him.'

Pierrot, of course, took many forms. He could be sentimentalised almost out of existence. Under the name of Gilles he decorates the canvases of Watteau, but Gilles is hardly more than a gentle wraith, Pierrot at the vanishing point. There was sterner stuff in Pagliaccio, who also derived from Pedrolino. He, too, was simple, awkward and heedless, and like Pulcinella he wore a mask covering all of his face except his mouth and chin, but the mask was painted white, and he had, as Pierrot had, the virtues of a tumbler and of a savage. The ancient ambiguity runs through him also. He was lightfooted, graceful, gentle, but suddenly he would break out into ribald laughter and bawdry, and Montaigne complained of the savagery of his grimaces while admiring the delicacy of his acrobatics. The early Pierrot was all effeminate delicacy and sweetness; it was of this stupid Pierrot that eighteenth century France sang:

> *Au clair de la lune,*
> *Mon ami Pierrot,*
> *Prête-moi ta plume*
> *Pour écrire un mot:*

and the song demonstrated that Pierrot was hardly more than the complaisant confidant of the lovers, the butt of Harlequin, the ingenious and beneficent nurse in male costume. He was the peasant prinked up to serve his masters, always loyal, never asking for more money, devoutly humble until his masters' backs were turned, when he would mimic them to his heart's content. Columbine marries Harlequin, and Pierrot contents himself with a few discreet tears, a witty jest, a little giggle. He grew with the times. Gradually the tears vanished, and he became the emblematic figure of the giggle, the man cast in adversity who laughs triumphantly at fate. At this point one of the great master-strokes occurred: his sleeves lengthened, so that he appeared to be without hands, and those long flapping sleeves, like the wings of an ungainly bird, conveyed his emotions. In the early plays he spoke. Now he had no need to speak: it was enough if he raised a protesting sleeve, smiled, shook his poor dumb head, uttered the faintest of protesting sighs. Poor Pierrot! Everyone loved him. Columbine on her way to be married would kiss him tenderly, even fondle him, while a blissful smile crossed the face of Pierrot; then it was enough to leave him alone on the empty stage, the candles of the footlights shining up at him as he gazed straight at the audience, while a thousand passions and frustrations marched across his face. He begged for sympathy, and no one ever received so much; and what Columbine refused, the audience offered in double measure. Out of this Pierrot emerged the wonderfully distinctive Pierrot invented around 1835 by one of the greatest clowns who ever lived.

Jean-Gaspard Deburau was born in 1796, somewhere in Bohemia. His father was a soldier of fortune who came originally from Amiens; his mother seems to have been Czech. Part of his childhood was spent near Warsaw, and he sometimes spoke of himself as a Pole. He was the youngest of five children. He might never have become a clown at all if his father had not fallen on evil times. There was hope of a living on an ancestral property in the north of France, but how to reach France? To live, the father turned himself and his five children into tight-rope walkers, and so clowning and tightrope-walking they made their way back to France, two young girls, three boys, the old soldier and his wife. The ancestral property turned out to be a half-acre of briars near Amiens.

There followed lean years. It was winter when they reached Amiens, and there was something wintry about Deburau to the end. For eighteen francs the father bought a pack-horse, placed his family in the panniers, and they journeyed from village to village, from town to town. The boys concentrated on walking the tightrope piggy-back. Jean-Gaspard was usually ill, often stumbled, hated tightrope walking and was remarkable only for his extraordinary leanness. No flesh grew on him. His second name was Baptiste: he was as spindly as the desert-wandering saint. In Paris, where they settled for a while, Jean-Gaspard was forgotten, left at home when the others acted, given crumbs for comfort, while his brothers and sisters acquired new clothes, good food and *noms du théâtre*.

Occasionally, dressed in rags, he followed them to the theatre, and years later he recounted how, when he was performing in an act known as 'the Egyptian Pyramid', he was given the topmost position. His brothers were drunk, and his brothers formed the feet of the pyramid. The pyramid was six or seven men high, and when the drunken brothers collapsed, the boy was thrown headlong. He landed with a crash, broke twelve bones, and lay bleeding. The audience rocked with applause. At another time, when they were in Constantinople, he climbed on top of a ladder and looked through the veil which concealed the watching concubines of the Sultan. No one noticed him, otherwise he would have been thrown into a sack and drowned in the Bosphorus. When Deburau came to maturity, the distant vision of the sultan's odalisques, the briar-patch in Amiens, the fall from the pyramid, the long years of wandering through France, Germany and Italy, all these had their proper place in his characterisation of the part of Pierrot, the creature of invincible *sang-froid* who seemed always about to open a curtain upon an enchanting display of amorous women, who suggested with all the arts of mimicry that such displays were for the asking, and then with a little flap of his empty sleeves showed that he was still lying in the briar-patch. He was gay with a desperate gaiety, the master of acrobatic horseplay and a dancer of eccentric genius. He had only to make a couple of steps on the stage for everyone in the audience to be aware of his complex mood, and more wonderful than anything else was the strange mingling of extreme joy and extreme sadness which streamed from his face.

But this was for the future. Deburau was thirty-four before he first acted on the stage in the Funambules Theatre in the Boulevard du Temple in the part of Pierrot. This part was previously played by Felix Charigny, who had accepted the existing tradition. Deburau changed it entirely, beginning with the costume. He removed the conical hat and replaced it with a black velvet skull-piece. He removed the immense ruffle entirely, saying that it threw too many shadows on his face. He wore a loose, ill-fitting white cotton coat, white cotton trousers and white shoes with buckles, the only decoration being the *pompoms* he wore down the middle of his coat. He was now Pierrot reduced to its essentials and stripped for action. Previously, Pierrot had been a comparatively minor figure. Deburau, who wrote his own mimes, made him the central character, giving him that air of desperation which was his own, for often enough he had been near suicide and all his life he was poverty-stricken. Once, he was about to cut his own throat when he overheard some people in a café discussing the art of the great tragedian Talma, and the thought that it was possible to become an artist had kept him alive. But the battle was waged every night on the boards of the Funambules Theatre.

This theatre was no larger and no better than the little tumble-down theatres in the East End of London called the Penny Gaffs. Wedged between two other theatres, it never seated more than two or three hundred people. The patrons were generally poor workmen, who hung their coats over the gallery rails and smelt of garlic and stamped their feet, loud-mouthed and jubilant. Deburau played for them, not for the famous and fastidious men of the world who occasionally occupied the boxes in the *avant-scène*. Balzac, George Sand, Baudelaire, Gérard de Nerval, Théophile Gautier, a host of others equally celebrated, attended frequently, and sometimes afterwards Deburau would welcome them in his little underground dressing-room, so dank that mushrooms grew on the bare walls, but it was not for them that he created the rôle of Pierrot. He played for the people and was of the people. He drew his strength from them. He knew their joys, and he could provoke them to out-bursts of terrifying joy or grief. The simple folk of the *quartier* saw him as one of themselves, only larger and more luminous; and like them he saw that victory would come only when the last was first, as in *Cinderella*. At no time in his life did he earn more than fifty francs a week.

What was the secret of Deburau? Partly, of course, it was the secret of intimacy, which all great actors possess, his power of communicating across that vast abyss which separates a per-former from his audience, but many remarked on the fascination that derived from the sense of danger which surrounded him.

When, in one of his most famous comedies, his head was cut off, the groan that travelled through the audience was frightening. There was something wholly reckless about him. 'The good comedian,' said Riccoboni, the authority on the *Commedia dell' Arte*, 'marches in the middle of the road; the great comedian wanders along the edge of a precipice.' Deburau wandered along precipices, and everyone in the audience was attempting to prevent his fall.

Like Chaplin, he invented plays which were largely auto-biographical. He told his own life *sub specie aeternae commediae*. The briar-patch, the visions of a hungry boy as he presses his nose against shop-windows, the donkey loaded with panniers which later died of hunger, the miseries of acrobats, the girls who offer their love and then run away, these were the staples of his comedy. He begins one play as a hungry clown in front of a pastry-cook's shop. At last, summoning all his strength, sniffing eagerly, he enters the shop, but at that moment the shop turns into a milliner's establishment; the pastry shop has suddenly swung to the other side of the road. Pierrot is offered bonnets. He refuses, runs to the pastry-cook's, and once again finds himself in the presence of the milliner. The shops perform a fantastic *chassé-croisée*, with Pierrot running backwards and forwards between them, his tongue hanging out. Then he does what Charlie does in the same circumstances. He tries gentleness, coaxing, pleading. He becomes exceptionally sweet-tempered, almost coy, but still the shops swing round and still the pastries are out of his reach. There comes a time when he snaps, becomes incoherent, begins to rave. He offers to fight everybody. The shops are still wheeling round him, he clamps his hand to his head, pretends to be thinking calmly, but suddenly he erupts, making his attack in a direction no one had anticipated. With a dozen broomsticks in his hands he holds off his embattled opponents, and the first scene ends with Pierrot flaying every-one, even the beautiful Léandre whom he can no longer recognise – in those days the broomstick was the equivalent of a custard pie with the added advantage that it could suggest the ultimate of indecencies.

The first scene described Pierrot's hunger; when we see him again he is dressed in the clothes of a wandering mountebank, beating a drum as if he wanted to burst it. The villagers dance, but suddenly it is the villagers who go berserk, for Pierrot's drumming has sent them mad. This drumming has the effect of Pan's shriek in the woodlands. The villagers run madly away, and leave not a penny behind for poor Pierrot. Miserably, Pierrot continues his wanderings. An English milord offers to let Pierrot do his laundry. Pierrot assents. He has come to the stage where he will do anything, even the laundry of a red-headed Englishman. He begins to work. Gradually he becomes infuriated with his work. The clothes are ugly, they smell too much, who is this Englishman who can make him work? When the Englishman returns to ask how the work is progressing, Pierrot indignantly throws him into the tub. Himself dirty, Pierrot attempts to enter a bath-house, but he can only find a bath-house reserved for women. He disguises himself with a bonnet and skirt, jumps with joy at the thought of the naked odalisques who will soon be his companions in the bath, but the women penetrate his disguise, invite him in, say the sweetest imaginable things to him, and secretly arrange that the water should be scalding hot. Pierrot, without clothes and red as a lobster, is thrown headlong into the street.

The beauty of Deburau's acting lay, then, in his nonchalance, his simple joy in defeat, his sudden rages, the little scamperings of the feet which announced his momentary triumphs. There was a prodigious grace in him. Jules Janin, who wrote his biography, spoke of him as 'an actor without words, without passion and almost without countenance; one who says every-thing, expresses everything, mocks everything; capable of playing, without uttering a word, all the comedies of Molière; a man informed of all the follies of his day, and who reproduces them to the life.' Baudelaire described him as 'pale as the moon, mysterious as silence, supple and mute as the serpent, straight and tall as the gallows.' Even while he was alive he belonged to legend.

As he grew older, Deburau suffered one misfortune after another. The damp dressing-room made him tubercular, and in addition he suffered from asthma. He fell through a trap-door, which opened too quickly, and cracked his head. The stage manager came forward, explained the accident and asked the audience to leave the theatre, but at that moment Deburau appeared, smiling his odd smile, mysteriously silent, and without any movement of his lips, with a single gesture, he conveyed that the play would go on. When George Sand, who was present at the performance, having seen the look of sickness on his face when he was standing in the wings and how suddenly the look had disappeared, wrote to congratulate him, he answered with a letter saying that she had exaggerated his accomplishments, and added: 'My pen is like my voice on the stage, but my heart is like my countenance, and I pray you will accept its sincere expression.' 'My heart is like my countenance.' In such simple phrases did he describe himself more accurately than the writers who wrote so learnedly about him.

Deburau died of asthma at the age of fifty. Shortly before his death he played in one of his favourite comedies, *Les Noces de Pierrot*. The little candle-lit Funambules Theatre was crowded with well-wishers. The curtain rose slowly. There was Deburau in the centre of the stage with a pretty girl on his arm, a flower in his buttonhole. Ordinarily, he would have executed one of those dramatic little dances which often began his plays, a queer high-flinging mixture of the *cancan* and the sedate dances of the Directoire. Someone shouted out for the dance, but the voice was drowned. Instead, very slowly, forgetting the dance, Deburau walked to the back of the stage and the comedy began now, as it always did, with a kiss bestowed on Columbine. There was silence throughout the play. In the end there was an ovation, and when he appeared at the stage door he still wore his clown's costume and the flower in his buttonhole. He was dead in less than a week.

With the death of Deburau there were some who said that all clowning was dead. Deburau's delicacy and insolence, his terrible power over the audience, the way he would crane forward over the footlights and hold them all in his hollow hand, his extraordinary beauty, these had perished, but other clowns arose to follow in his footsteps. His son took his place. Paul Legrand, Louis Rouffe, the great Séverin who added *provençal* fire to the original, and who died barely twenty years ago, these followed, and all of them spoke of Deburau with reverence, and all imitated him. More recently Jean-Louis Barrault, having made Jean-Gaspard luminously familiar in *Les Enfants du Paradis*, has set himself the task of inventing him afresh.

Pierrot did not die. For a few more years, until Baron Haussmann's workmen pulled down the Boulevard du Temple to make way for the Boulevard Voltaire, the small patchwork theatre showed the further adventures of Pierrot. Champfleury and Théophile Gautier wrote the scenarios. It was observed that as Pierrot grew older, his themes grew more terrifying. Deburau had played with death at a remove; Paul Legrand appeared in plays where death was actually present. In one of these plays, called *Pierrot, Valet de la Mort*, there is a scene where three coffins descend towards Death who sits quietly on his throne. The first is a very small coffin, containing a child, and Death is displeased, for he desired something larger. The second coffin contains a doctor. Death is highly amused to receive a visitor so faithful to himself. The third coffin contains Pierrot, stretched out white and motionless in his clown's clothes. There is a thunderclap, blue lights shine over the stage, and Pierrot is allowed to descend from the coffin. Death amuses himself in the presence of Pierrot, asks him whether he likes the underworld, reminds him that he must return to the coffin. Thereupon Pierrot begs to be allowed to serve his new master. As what? A valet, if necessary. Death agrees, provided that Pierrot will also amuse him. There follows a terrible dance with all Hell's minions, and Death himself taking part, and while Death cracks with laughter and jumps up and down on his throne, Pierrot succeeds in escaping.[1] It is a strange story, written as a kind of tribute to the great Deburau shortly after his death; and Champfleury, who knew Deburau and wrote an epitaph for him, deliberately includes in *Pierrot, Valet de la Mort*, some lines which he wrote for the clown, saying that his white clothes were always a

[1] The story is taken from Champfleury, *Souvenir des Funambules*, Paris, 1859. Champfleury may have had in mind the extraordinary story which Dio Cassius tells of the Emperor Domitian, who would invite his friends into a room draped from floor to ceiling in black. At the head of the couches were pillars like tombstones with the guests' names written on them. Naked boys, painted black, danced among them, and while the terror-stricken guests looked on, the death-like silence was broken by the ageing Emperor recounting savage stories of blood and torture.

shroud, and from the very beginning the narrow stage of the Funambules Theatre had been his coffin. It was partly true. Some death-like quality hung about Deburau. The white-faced clown lived close to the skeleton. He had known death, stared it in the face and returned triumphant, but he knew that death was always waiting for him, knew it with the abandoned knowledge of a man who has seen Death plain and made no effort to hide his knowledge. 'Everything which touches upon death,' said Champfleury, 'is of an astounding gaiety.' In later years this knowledge was to be employed with incredible tact and finesse by Monsieur Verdoux.

Chaplin descends from Deburau, but he also descends from the English clowns, as we shall see. Outwardly the French and English clowns have little in common, as Baudelaire remarked long ago, finding himself at a loss to explain what the English find amusing in their clowning. He found in the English a taste for exaggeration beyond all understanding, yet somehow convincing. He wrote:

> The English Pierrot comes running in like a tempest, falls down like a sack of coal and shakes the house with his laughter. His laughter is like a happy thunderstorm. He is a short thick fellow who has increased his bulk with a costume loaded with ribbons which serve the same office as the feathers and down of a bird or the fur of a Persian cat. Over his face he has painted, without any delicacy, two enormous scarlet circles, and his mouth is made wider by dabs of carmine, so that when he laughs his mouth seems to stretch from ear to ear. As for his behaviour, watch what he does with the tarts. Where Deburau would simply stretch out an inoffensive finger and lick the tart, your English Pierrot jumps into the tarts with both feet: he suffers from the vertigo of exaggeration. Watch him as he passes a woman scrubbing her doorstep. He empties her pockets and takes everything she has on her, then he proceeds to steal her sponge, the broom, the soap, even the water in the bucket.

> I remember seeing an English Pierrot being guillotined. Why in England he should suffer death by the guillotine rather than the hangman's rope I have no way of knowing.

Pierrot is led to the slaughter. He cries out, like a cow with the smell of the abattoir in his nostrils. He yells at the top of his lungs. Then the knife drops on that head which is all scarlet and white, and you see the head rolling across the stage, the bleeding neck and the broken vertebrae. Then suddenly, moved by the unquenchable egotism which is the hallmark of the English clown, Pierrot goes running wildly after his own head, with exactly the same gestures as previously he had run after a ham or a bottle of wine, and he proudly puts his head in his own pocket. The English must possess a special gift for exaggeration, for I found these monstrous farces took on the air of a strangely convincing reality.

Baudelaire found himself incapable of explaining that 'strangely convincing reality'. It puzzled him that Deburau should have convinced by gentleness where the English clown convinces by ribald farce; he would have been more than ever puzzled if he had seen Charlie, who combines the two traditions.

The Vagabond, 1916

One A.M., 1916

The Cure, 1917

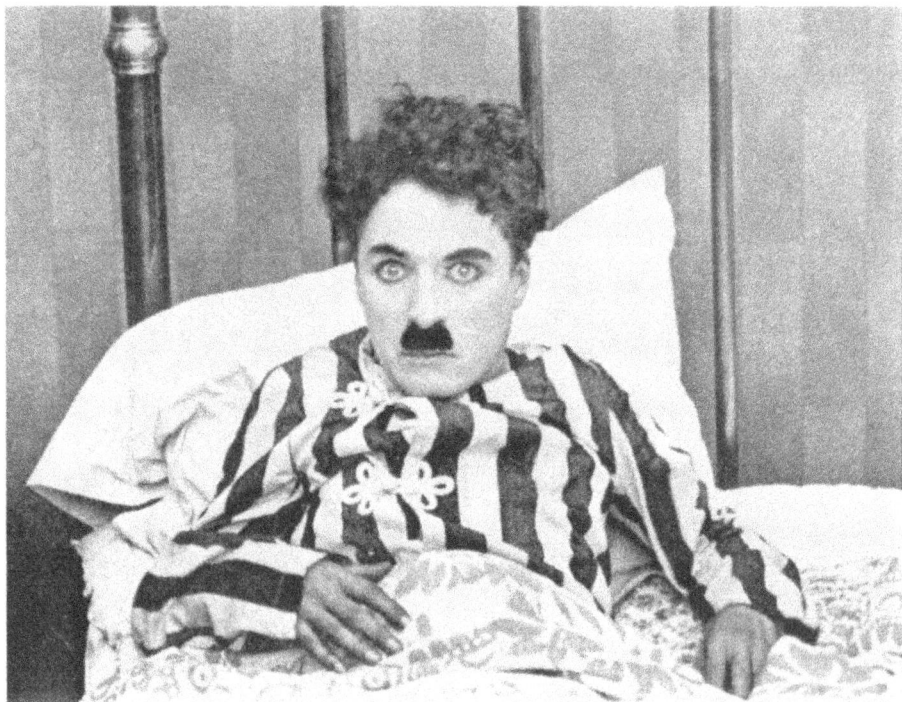

The Adventurer, 1917

CHAPTER VI

THE FUNNY OLD MAN WITH THE DRIPPING PAN

FRENCH comedy was gay and gentle from the beginning, even in those early beginnings when the Lucifer in Arnoul Gréban's *Le Vrai Mystère de la Passion* was gently laughed away, his fierce song of death and damnation being turned against him by the children who sing the same words as a roundelay. English comedy was of fiercer stuff. Shakespeare's clowns rant on the edge of madness, themselves heroic figures caught up into the heights of tragedy. The clowns of the English mystery plays began their lives by being the devils who thrust the sinners into Hell's flames – hence the red-hot pokers, the death-gleam in their eyes, the way they are always harried and out of breath, poor devils roasting too close to the flames.

About the time of Shakespeare or a little later Punch emerged. An old clown, weary of roasting sinners, he sets himself against all authority, even the devil's. He has a merry shrewish wife, a hunchback, a hook nose and a murderous rage which is aroused the moment the dog Toby appears and bites his nose. Very sensitive about his nose, he appeals to Toby's master Scaramouch, and when Scaramouch gives him no satisfaction, he knocks the old man's head clean off his shoulders and immediately afterwards comforts himself by showering affection on the dog. He calls his wife to bring the baby. The baby screams, and when Judy has left the stage, having pressed the baby into Punch's arms, Punch wearies of the whole business of baby tending and throws it out of the window. Judy returns and remonstrates. Punch decides she is behaving unreasonably, knocks her on the head and throws her out of the window after the baby, and it occurs to him to go in search of Pretty Polly, who will shower him with

C   65

the affection which can no longer be showered on him because he has massacred all those who might have had any regard for him.

So far Punch is nothing more than a portrait of the ribald murderer, cousin to Sweeney Todd, the barber of Fleet Street who amused himself by cutting his customer's throats, and cousin, too, to the stern parents who appear in Harry Graham's ruthless rhymes:

> *Father heard the children scream.*
> *So he threw them in the stream,*
> *Saying, as he drowned the third:*
> *'Children should be seen, not heard.'*

But in the second scene of the puppet show complications begin. Punch complains of his loneliness and misery, and riding his horse Hector he goes in pursuit of Pretty Polly and a haven of safety; but there is no safety anywhere in the world, the most ferocious dragons attack him, and though he succeeds in administering punishment to the dragons, he is himself punished by three fierce virgins. He escapes from them, but as he goes singing happily on his way he is thrown by Hector. Punch, declaring that he is a dead man, cries out for a doctor, and when the doctor comes and examines the wounds, Punch kicks him in the eye and leaps up. The doctor applies a dose of his stick, but Punch is deathless and the doctor succumbs with a broken skull. Thereupon, ringing a sheepbell, Punch performs a giddy dance and proclaims that he is lord of everyone. A lackey who comes to complain of the noise is immediately set upon and killed. There ends the second scene, compounded of a whole medley of legends, for the three fierce virgins are evidently stolen from the chaste females in Spenser's Squire of Dames (*Faerie Queene*, III, 7), the dance of the sheepbells is evidently the dance of Pan, and the lonely wanderer has something of the aspect of a murderous Parsifal.

When the third scene opens we are mysteriously back in London Town. Punch, walking down the street, meets a blind beggar dressed as a friar. Punch decides he is an impostor, beats him off, and when he comes running back again, kills him. Thereupon the Constable, a formidable figure, enters with a warrant for Punch's arrest. Punch has killed at least four people, excluding the dragons, but only the name of Scaramouch appears on the warrant. Punch knocks the Constable down, and the still more formidable Officer who arrives to rescue him. The executioner, Jack Ketch, at last succeeds in pinioning Punch and marching him off to prison with the help of considerable assistance. A curtain opens at the back. We see Punch rubbing his nose against the bars, quite content with himself, while he openly declares that no prison bars can hold him. Enter a gibbet and a coffin. Punch laughs at them, tricks Jack Ketch into hanging himself and laughs gleefully when the hangman is placed in the coffin and carried out. While he is laughing the Devil appears, with horns and long claws and a tail. There is a wild rampageous struggle between them, but at last the Devil, who is dressed in a black skin and looks remarkably like a goat, is slain. The puppet-show ends with Punch whirling madly with the Devil on the end of a stick, shouting: 'Huzza! Huzza! The Devil's dead!'

It is all, of course, terribly confused, with any number of legends intermingled. The incident of the blind friar dates from the time of Henry VIII. Scaramouch is the little cowardly skirmisher, Scarramuccia, of the *Commedia dell' Arte*, and clearly he is an insertion. Punch himself has some of the physical characteristics of the Italian Pulcinella, but his irony, his cold-blooded ferocity, his seductions (according to an eighteenth century ballad he needed twenty-two women to keep him satisfied), even his wars with the dragons derive from English sources. He is all the clowns rolled into one – Harlequin, Pulcinella, Robin Goodfellow, Tom o' Bedlam. As for the scene with the hangman, it is stolen straight out of the *Commedia dell' Arte*, for an exactly similar scene occurs at the end of the mime called *Pulcinella the Brigand Chief*. There Pulcinella is caught at last, after having taken a windmill by storm and threatened the mill-owner's wife. He is led to the scaffold. When the rope is placed round his neck, he plays with it and explains that he doesn't understand what it is for. The hangman cries: 'You fool! This is how it is done!' Thereupon he slips his own head through the noose, and Pulcinella seizes his opportunity; he pulls on the rope and strangles the hangman, crying: 'Who's a fool now?'

Punch, however, remains a complex creature, and though in

his outward appearance he resembles Pulcinella most of all, his behaviour is nearer to the behaviour of the devils in the miracle plays who staked their wits on their cunning as they pushed the sinners into hell's flames. There is a Beelzebub in one of the mystery plays who comes running on the stage, shouting:

> *In comes I, Beelzebub:*
> *In my hands I carries club,*
> *On my head a dripping pan.*
> *Don't you think I'm a funny old man?*

Of course we do, but one of the reasons why we think he is funny is because he is shovelling sinners into hell. Punch is funny for a very contrary reason: he shoves the Devil into hell, and is not in the least bashful about his accomplishments. Yet they have the same gusto, the same rudeness and coarseness.

This rudeness, this coarseness, this play with death and damnation are part of English comedy from the beginning. The Italians would provide excellent reasons for Pulcinella's crimes; the English laugh at reasons. Punch starts his holocaust of murders because he is irritated when Toby bites his nose. The English also laugh at plot and dramatic shape. Professor Francis Cornford has tried to show that the story of Punch follows the outlines of a classic Greek drama, beginning with the unknown crime, advancing to the contest between the forces of good and evil, then ending with the formal announcement of the heavenly victory. This is nonsense. The story of Punch is as inconsequential as the dreams of Alice in Wonderland, and is nearly as terrible. Today in the market-places of England the enraptured children still laugh at the terrible deeds of Punch, for the same reason that they laugh at the adventures of Gulliver, the lonely misery of Crusoe and the graveyard adventures of Alice, and would if they could hold even Long John Silver to their breasts.

We have seen the goat-footed god in many of his disguises. Punch is one of them. Another is Robin Goodfellow, who is even closer to the tradition of the English clown, less complex, far more elemental. He was called Robin Goodfellow for the excellent reason that he was not a good fellow except on rare occasions. Shaggy, goat-footed, goat-horned, always naked, he had the world at his mercy. He would come when you least expected him. He liked to turn the milk sour, and get under your bed, and shout in the middle of the night. He liked to meddle with maids. You could propitiate him with a dish of cream, but not for long. Grim the Collier of Croydon described him as 'the honestest merry devil that ever I saw', but there were others who were not so certain of his honesty. Shakespeare was gentle with him. It was Robin Goodfellow who contrived the episode concerning Bottom the Weaver and the ass's head in *Midsummer Night's Dream*, and Pistol played him in *The Merrie Wives of Windsor*. He was the embodiment of English clowning, and to see him in all his finery bursting on the English stage we must go to the astonishing figure of Joseph Grimaldi, whose Italian name disguises the most English of Charlie's spiritual ancestors.

Grimaldi was born in 1779, and he was at his height during the Napoleonic wars. He was the son of one of those wandering *Commedianti dell' Arte* who invaded France from Italy. The old man was once an accomplished dancer, and he was called 'Iron Legs', because on a famous occasion in Paris he had while dancing kicked a chandelier hanging far above the stage into the face of the Turkish ambassador. Then the dancer, wearying of his trade, came to England and became, of all things, chief dentist to the Queen, but he seems to have been easily wearied of dentistry, for he returned to the stage and became a famous clown, with Joseph as his chief assistant. Once, when the boy was disguised as a monkey on a chain, the father swung him so forcefully that the chain broke, and the boy would have been killed if he had not landed on a particularly plump spectator. At another time he was given a beating, and then went weeping and howling across the stage, to the delight of the audience, who insisted that the boy should always make his entry howling. His childhood was miserable, he was called 'Grim-all-day' and he was famous for his look of unconcealed misery when he was off the stage. On the stage, when he grew older, he was the fiery spirit of mocking laughter, the purest of clowns – he invented the part of the Clown in the Harlequinade – and there were critics like Coleridge and Leigh Hunt who regarded a single wink, the intonation of a single monosyllable from Grimaldi as the highest form of comic art.

What was he like? We can only guess. Cruikshank's drawings

make him resemble a devilish kind of monkey, with a monkey face and a monkey manner, and this hardly helps us, for all the other evidence goes to show that he was remarkably human. He wrote his own memoirs, which Dickens edited, but they were written during the last years of his life and there comes from them no more than a warm ember glow. We see him more clearly through the eyes of Coleridge and Leigh Hunt, those avid watchers of pantomimes. They noted his elemental fury, his animal spirits, the way he immediately established contact with his audience, the deadliness of his mimicry. When put to the torture, he would say 'Don't' in a way which sent a wild shudder of delight through the audience. He would gaze at the moon and say 'Nice' with the same effect. He would say 'May I?' to the cakeman as he pilfered from a tray, and the audience became hysterical with joy. At this late date no one quite knows how it was done. He would dip the white trousers of a dandy into a mixture labelled 'Raspberry Jam' or put a policeman through the mangle, so that he came out completely flat, and the rafters shook, and it was the same when he sang a duet with a mammoth oyster that had been crossed in love. Perhaps the explanation lay in the quality of his timing and the excellence of his mimicry.

He had a voice like no one else: one moment it squeaked, the next it broke out into ribald laughter, and it was the joyful cavernous rumbling of that laughter which people remember, saying like Coleridge that it sounded like the laughter of Robin Goodfellow, who was only the great god Pan under an English name. He employed a paddle and used it to good effect on the backside of Pantaloon; Coleridge noted that in the hands of Grimaldi the paddle was 'as lissom as a cane'. He was brutal, clownish, wonderfully dexterous in his obscenity, so that he never gave offence to the women in the audience, and he could contrive to make anything out of anything. Out of a beadle's hat, a milliner's box, a salmon's head and a pair of boots he deftly fashioned something that resembled a clown, and suddenly this clown came to life, and then the very foundations of the theatre were shaken by the whirlwind of laughter. He had a famous song called 'Hot Codlins' about a little old woman who sold hot codlins for a living, but though the codlins were hot, she was cold and to warm herself thought it no sin to fetch herself a quartern of —— At this point Grimaldi would pause and gaze innocently up at the gallery, and suddenly, with a sound like the roaring of an avalanche, there would come the cry: 'Gin!' followed by an insane, meaningless chorus:

> Ri-tol-id-dy, id-dy, id-dy
> Ri-tol idy-dy, ri tol-lay.

There were many verses to the song, and Grimaldi would extemporise on the theme of an old woman drinking gin until it would seem that there was nothing left to say, but he always succeeded in giving a new shape to the comical old woman. Mostly, he was Clown in the Harlequinade, a gross figure who usurped the place of Harlequin and stole Columbine from under the eyes of her old father, Pantaloon, and knocked Harlequin straight out of the window. He would knock old Pantaloon to the floor and listen happily while the old fellow's skull cracked like a dropped egg. According to tradition Harlequin was something of a daredevil, but the clown was now more mocking, insolent, clownish and obscene than Harlequin had ever dared to be.

Some prodigious power drove Grimaldi, and long before his death he burned himself out. Wasted and ill, he visited a doctor who took one look at the sick face of the clown and said: 'I would recommend that you see Grimaldi.' The clown replied: 'I am Grimaldi.' The story is true, and Chaplin holds it to be the best of all the stories ever told of clowns. Something of Grimaldi's mood during those last days can be seen in the letter he wrote to a friend, declining an invitation:

Dear old friend,

I shall not be able to come – Poor Joey's laid up in lavender, this cold weather, and will never again make Christmas folk grin with his anticks, his buffooneries, and his quips and cranks.

No more concealment of sausages in his capacious trucks pockets – no more bottles stored away – no more merry songs, sayings and gibes.

O my heart grieves! Well, there must be an end to every-

thing mortal, and, as poor Palmer said (his last words):
'There is another and a better world.' I wonder if I shall be
able to 'clown' it THERE! Well, *adsum*.

Yours as ever,

Joey Grimaldi

('Grim-all-day')

The letter was written in December 1836, when his savings had
melted away and when his only child, a gifted clown, had died in
a roaring delirium after a fling of vicious dissipation. He lived
on charity, a man who looked much older than his years, suffering from creeping paralysis, haunted by the thought that he was
completely forgotten. He need not have worried. His hilarious
shadow dominated the pantomime until nearly the end of the
century.

Grimaldi's death left a gap which no single clown could fill.
This man who hurled himself upon the stage with something of
the elemental fury of a drunken Hercules had changed the shape
of English humour. The man who put together a lady's muff, a
pocket-watch, a bell-rope, a pair of coal-scuttles and a red-hot
poker, and somehow contrived to make out of these odds and
ends a hussar of the line was not altogether capable of dying. He
had two successors. One was Dan Leno, the other was Charles
Chaplin.

Dan Leno was the product of the pantomime, the music-hall
and the Penny Gaffs. The Penny Gaffs were theatres where poor
people spent a penny for an evening's entertainment in the thirties
and forties of the last century. Nearly all of them were in the
East End of London, in the Commercial Road, the Mile-End
Road and the villainous Ratcliffe Highway, which was the scene
of some of the adventures of Oliver Twist. There were others
around King's Cross, Marylebone and Paddington. These
theatres were in the mews, barns, cowsheds or stables, with
only a miniature stage for the players and rough benches for the
audience. The performances consisted of two short plays with a
song in between, which the audience sang with the players.
There was almost no scenery, and the costumes served many
purposes. Usually, the performance lasted a bare forty-five
minutes, and was repeated later in the evening. The actors

starved, rarely getting more than a shilling a night, and most of them got less. They put on pantomimes at Christmas, where they guyed the great displays at Drury Lane, and though no great actors ever came from the Penny Gaffs they established the tradition which introduced the music-hall.

The music-hall was slightly more decorous, and far more comfortable. Noisy, ill-ventilated, reeking of beer and sex, the music-halls paid higher salaries, transformed the two violent plays into a number of comic or sentimental acts, introduced the earnest monologue and the lady harpist, and provided adequate contrasts in buffoonery and horseplay. Like the Penny Gaffs they began in the East End of London. The first was the Canterbury, erected on the site of a public saloon in 1837. There was Gilbert's in Whitechapel, the Rodney, the Lord Nelson, the Cambridge in Shoreditch, the Foresters in the Cambridge Road. Later there was the New Canterbury Hall at the junction of the Westminster Bridge Road and the Upper Marsh, which young Chaplin attended assiduously. The English in the reign of Queen Victoria possessed boisterous passions which they concealed with difficulty; the music-halls provided the safety-valve. Usually it was some little devil of a sharp-witted Cockney who was responsible for allowing the steam to escape.

The pantomimes were performed at Christmas and followed rigorous patterns. So did the Penny Gaffs. The music-halls broke the patterns, borrowed from both, and erected Grimaldi's Clown into the place of honour, for the acts were always announced by a clown whose ribald comments held them together and maintained a sense of continuity.

The clown, however, did not wear the uniform of Grimaldi. Grimaldi's uniform consisted of a wig with three black tufts in imitation of the dandy of Napoleonic days who wore his wig brushed down the back and tied the ends in a silk bag. Then there was a lace collar, a white tunic embroidered with scarlet circles or roses, silk hose with clocks and scarlet shoes and bright red garters at the knees. The face was painted dead white with here and there a few scarlet smears. Grimaldi explained that the scarlet smears and the large scarlet mouth were designed to give the effect of a boy who had been caught smearing his face with jam. It was a costume perfectly appropriate for the times, but Dan Leno, living in an industrial age, abandoned the costume, keeping the dead white face and three black tufts. For the rest he wore whatever it was necessary to wear. He would play the clown or the dame in a pantomime, but on the music-hall stage he usually wore a seedy morning coat, long baggy trousers and enormous long boots. A man of prodigious nervous energy, he was known to leap backwards six feet and come to rest on the points of the boots. Like Grimaldi he was no more than five foot four in height, and he even possessed a physical resemblance to his great predecessor, but where Grimaldi was the leaping spirit of the earthly comedy, Dan Leno hinted at tragedy. He had frightening large eyes, a wide grin with a twist at the corners of the mouth and high arched eyebrows set in a perpetual expression of surprise. His face was emaciated, and as though to make himself even more emaciated, he usually painted two black lines stretching from the bridge of his nose to his forehead. He was a new Grimaldi who had blundered into an industrial age, shopworn, perpetually exhausted. Where Grimaldi grimaced, Dan Leno leered. Where Grimaldi was all fire and thunder, Dan Leno was all nerves. He had once been a champion clog-dancer. The tired mask concealed enormous physical vitality, and those sudden unaccountable and altogether unreasonable leaps across the stage were to become as famous as Nijinsky's. But it was observed that all his actions, even these extraordinary leaps, seemed to be dictated by a sense of rhythm, and his pathos was no more than a mimicking of his audience.

It is impossible to avoid the association of Dan Leno with Charlie Chaplin. There were physical and psychological resemblances. Both came from the London streets, both were born with a fantastic power of mimicry, and they possessed the mysterious power of being able to conjure up whole landscapes. Wearing a spiky moustache and a soiled napkin on his arm, Dan Leno imitated a waiter on an empty stage. There were no tables, no guests, no mirrors, no candelabras, but the stage had suddenly became a vast restaurant and Dan Leno was weaving among the tables, to fall at last upon some luckless guest complaining of the food. In a dry husky voice, in a huge rush of words, he would argue with the guest, and you would almost hear the guest shrivelling up when Dan Leno explained:

'Change your chop, sir? I couldn't do that, sir. You've stuck your fork in and let the steam out.' Or else he was a travelling show-man and he would recite a long history of miserable travelling, how they changed their trains and got lost and how a child was left behind, but they found the child somehow, and in the end they all sat down to enjoy a feast, the clowns, the fat woman of the circus, the child, the showman, everyone glad the journey was over. 'So then we all 'ad tea, and the fat woman sat down on a pound of butter. Lord, I never saw a pound of butter go so far in my life.' He would puff out his chest and become a Beefeater in the Tower of London, luring a party to the refreshment rooms – 'You want everything to be ancient, do you? Well, look inside. Look at our sandwiches and our barmaids.'

It was corny, but it was magnificent, and he would repeat the same gags night after night, but somehow they had changed. He was born in St Pancras, which is in sound of the bells of Bow Church, and therefore by definition he was a Cockney, and there was a Cockney insolence in his demeanour; and at the same time there was that gallery of humble characters he created with the lift of an eyebrow and with the simplest props, an old squashed bonnet if he was imitating a charwoman, the butcher boy's blue-and-white striped apron, an imaginary bicycle if he was a cyclist, and two bicycles if he was a boy and a girl going out into the country on a Saturday afternoon. These humble characters were never caricatures. He chose his imaginary backgrounds carefully. A bar, a street corner, the entrance of a house where three or four people have met on the way back from fetching the supper beer. He would make breathless confidences in a patter so fast that it seemed impossible that he would be able to go on without pausing for breath, but the patter continued, every word in place, and suddenly he would break out into a ribald song. As he grew older, thin as a lamp-post, with an uncanny gleam in his eyes, he became more boisterous and a little shriller. He played ping-pong with a frying pan and potatoes, or burlesqued a young girl at her harp lessons, and it was noticed that there was an added savagery and petulance in his performances. He expostu-lated, as always, with an irrational world, himself the only rational being in it, but the great grey London *Times* remarked that he was growing thoughtful and there was more than a touch of philosophical resignation in that remorseless stream of patter. 'If he goes on in this way,' thundered *The Times*, 'criticism will have to rank him among the "thoughtful" and that may be an honour embarrassing to him as "taking silk" is to some members of the outer Bar. It would hardly do for Mr Leno to be regarded merely as an intellectual treat.' The progress was probably inevitable: the line which separates the very comic from the tragic is thin as a hair, and in the end Dan Leno went mad. Just before he went mad he wrote a brief account of his life. There he discussed some of the same problems which fascinated Kierkegaard, and speaking of his childhood at No. 4 East Court, St Pancras, he said:

> Here I spent my happy childhood hours. Ah! What is man? Wherefore does he why? Whence did he whence? Whither is he whithering? . . . Then the guard yelled out: Leicester, Derby, Nottingham, Manchester, Liverpool!

Perhaps, he seemed to be saying, the blast of the guard's whistle and the recital of the towns of England was sufficient explanation for life.

Though he went mad, there were intervals when sanity returned, long periods when he walked the music-halls or played the dame part in pantomimes. Gentleness had descended on him. He was a wraith of a man, but with grease paint the ghost could be made to assume flesh and blood. He still hurried on to the stage with an air of wild determination, but the fire had gone. There were moments when he would pause in his lines and smile sweetly at the audience, and no one knew whether to laugh or cry, or whether he had forgotten his lines, or what the smile meant. When he died in the autumn of 1904, chiefly of grief over the death of one of his stage companions, *The Times* commented that no one had ever seen his like before and it would be necessary to go back to the *Commedia dell' Arte* to see his like again.

The music-halls continue in England, shorn of their former magnificence, but the great days were over long before Dan Leno died. The pantomime, too, remains, but it has become a thing of processions and bare-legged girls and the dame has usurped the role of Harlequin and a mechanical glitter has taken the place of the broad comedy of the nineties. No longer does the Clown go right through the pantomime as in the days of Grimaldi. In those days the pantomime began with a Transformation Scene where the veils lifted to reveal an earthly paradise of young women reclining among strange rocks and rose-leaves and lotuses. Then Clown, Pantaloon, Columbine and Harlequin appeared, and the Clown jumped to the footlights with the famous old greeting derived from the Miracle Plays: 'Here we are again!' He threw crackers to all the children in the audience, and sometimes he hurled them casually as far as the dress circle. There followed a street scene against the front-cloth, with the Clown wielding his sword and stealing a string of sausages from a butcher's shop and the Policeman had his trousers burned and Columbine pirouetted happily and Pantaloon fell flat on his face. The front-cloth lifted, and you saw Harlequin thrown ten feet in the air through a star-trap, and so the Harlequinade went on, and all the rest of the pantomime was constructed around them. By the early nineties the street scene, which set the pace, had vanished, and the others followed one by one. When Harry Payne, the last of the Harlequinade clowns of the Drury Lane pantomime, with his white face, vermilion cheeks, tufted white wig and scarlet-and-white tunic, died in 1895, the tradition was coming to an end. Today the Harlequinade is extinct; it had almost perished while Dan Leno was playing his charwomen on the music-hall stage.

When Chaplin emerged there were only the fag-ends of a dying tradition. By 1900 the great days were over. The century died, and the spirit of comedy died with it. The wave of hilarious comedy, which began with Grimaldi during the Napoleonic Wars, died with the Boer War and was not to rise again until Charlie flashed on the screen in 1914.

CHAPTER VII

THE DARK CITY

OUT of royal London came those immense choruses of laughter which rolled across the whole of England and then rolled back again, a strange wild laughter with devilry in it, and some malice, a laughter which grew out of the sodden poverty-stricken alleyways. The sources of that laughter were mostly in the East End and along the Embankment. It was the laughter of the poor, touched with craziness and the happiness of drinking gin which Londoners called 'strip-me-naked'. Dickens had his drunks, but they are apt to be seen at their convivial pleasures. It was the laughter of the poor devil drinking alone which spilt over on the music-hall stage.

At the end of the century London was still recognisably the same place which produced Hogarth's haunting picture of Gin Lane with its drunken half-naked women and carousing men. The pawnbroker's shops are overflowing, a steady stream of people flock to the gin-mills and no one pays any attention to the man who has hanged himself in full view of the street. On the steps beneath the pawnbroker's shop Hogarth shows a girl laughing at the top of her lungs, having just tossed her baby down an alleyway.

The poverty of London, the welling misery of it, struck Dickens like a crushing blow. He never quite recovered from that gaping sore. Henry Mayhew, in his monumental study of *London Labour and the London Poor*, could suggest the misery in a single phrase, where Dickens used several thousands. He once asked an eight-year-old girl selling watercress whether she had seen children crying. 'It's no use,' the girl said. He did not always touch that raw nerve. He asked a whelkman boiling whelks whether they suffered. 'No,' answered the whelkman reflectively. 'Lobsters and crabs kick, but whelks never. They take it gently. Why, I've suffered more with a toothache than the whole of a measure of whelks has in a boiling.' But the Londoners of the East End did not take it quiet; they rebelled, and their rebellion took the form of laughter. It was mostly healthy, but there were insane glints in it.

Today, there is little left of the primitive horror which boiled over the East End even fifty years ago. The horror had been boiling for a long time. There are hints of it in the Elizabethan playwrights, Lamb cursed against it mightily, and Blake raged against it in *Auguries of Innocence*:

> *The beggar's rags, fluttering in air,*
> *Does to rags the heavens tear.*

Unfortunately, there is always something comic in a beggar's rags, if only because we can see his flesh within the rags, and ever since clowning began, the clown has worn the livery of beggardom. The East End was full of beggars, criminals, poverty-stricken Poles in the factories, poor Jews coughing up their lungs in steaming laundries, as well as Cockneys, who were dock-workers or costermongers, and all were ragged, and all struggled for existence on the fringes of a seedy respectability heavy with the fumes of hot gin and greasy lumps of nameless food. It was a place where murder ripened and grew fat, and cut-throats were legion. 'At last I shall present you with real criminals,' says Dickens in the introduction to *Oliver Twist*. He knew them well, for at the age of twelve he was thrust into Warren's blacking factory at Hungerford Stairs, and in that rat-ridden warehouse by the Thames he was conscious, he tells us, of 'a deep sense of abandonment'. He was not the only one. Abandonment was in the air. It was something people fed on, while the yellowish mists gathered over the river and the garish gas lamps on the riverside were like fruit growing from no tree. Dickens spoke of 'that black tree, of which I am the ripened fruit', but sometimes, as he knew well enough, he would shut his eyes and see the tree flourishing like a flurry of rockets, all gold and green and blue, and then the dreams came, and when he woke up he was still a snot-nosed awkward boy lost among the rats of the blacking factory. For the rest of his life he wrote novels which made the ugliness absurd, so that he could laugh at it, but it was still ugliness when he had finished laughing, and on his own showing the horror drove him into moments of madness, all the world turning against him, the blackness coming out of the river and chasing him through the dark alleys.

Nowadays they say Dickens was not a realistic novelist; some fantastical imp, they say, was dancing in his brain when he invented those fantastical characters. But it was not so. London was full of dark, straggling, savage, comic characters, and there was only a little caricature in his drawing of them. The thieves' kitchens were real enough; so was the sour taste in the air, the misery of the shreds of fog, the loneliness of a London street at twilight. Dickens speaks once of a servant 'pale and *polite* with fear', which describes one of the moods of Charlie well enough. The fear welled up from the river, from the dark streets where all the houses were the same, all crumbling in the same way, with their small whitewashed stone steps, lace curtains turning yellow and glossy aspidistras – there was something terrible even in that desperate desire for respectability. The streets were like the streets in nightmares, always empty, every house like every other house, and somewhere at the end of the street a small boy is running away from an invisible dread. One day in Italy Dickens found himself pursued by the nightmare, and suddenly out of nowhere there came to him the memory of 'a road like some byway in Whitechapel – or – I look again – like Wych Street, down by the little baker's shop on the same side of the way as Holywell Street – or – I look again – as like Holywell Street itself – as ever street was like a street, or ever will be in this world'. The horror of it tormented him, a nameless horror like that which came to him when he saw the words MOOR-EEFFOC one day in St Martin's Lane and thought the devil had spoken from the plate-glass window of a coffee-shop.

Dickens wrote the mark of London on all his novels, and spent his last hours entangled in a story of a London murder so dark, so mysterious, so filled with the heaviness of river-fog, that no one has yet been able to penetrate into that last unfinished work of his. London held him by the throat. He went away to America, but London drew him back again, for the hand stretching round his throat reached all the way across the Atlantic and

he was conscious of it even when he was standing below Niagara
Falls. And he was all his characters except Pickwick, the fruit of
a youthful exuberance. He was Uriah Heep as well as David
Copperfield. David hates Uriah, and so does Dickens, but Uriah
Heep talks in the accents of Dickens. Listen to him discussing
humility:

> Father and me was both brought up at a foundation school
> for boys; and mother, she was likewise brought up at a
> public, sort of charitable establishment. They taught us a
> deal of umbleness. . . . We was to be umble to this person,
> and umble to that; and to pull off our caps here, and to make
> bows there; and always to know our place and abase ourselves
> before our betters; Father got the monitor medal for being
> umble. . . . 'Be umble, Uriah,' says father to me, 'and you'll
> get on.' It was what was always being dinned into you and
> me at school; it's what goes down best. 'Be umble,' says
> father, 'and you'll do.' And really it aint done bad. . . . I'm
> very umble to the present moment, Master Copperfield, but
> I've got a little power.

So, to the very end, Dickens demonstrated his tormented
humility, and showed that he possessed a little power. But the
power came later. In his childhood there was only torment,
humility, the blacking factory, Marshalsea Prison, the smell of
death in the air.

Dickens was so affected by the spirit of his lost childhood that
he never spoke of it to his wife and children, and they only
learned that he had been a slave in a factory and a prisoner in a
debtor's prison from Forster's biography, long after his death.
Here are two passages describing the crushed hopes of people
lost in the maze of London:

> No words can express the secret agony of my soul as I
> sunk into this companionship; compared these every day
> associates with those of my happier childhood; and felt my
> early hopes of growing up to be a learned and distinguished
> man crushed in my breast. The deep remembrance of the
> sense I had of being utterly neglected and hopeless; of the
> shame I felt in my position; of the misery it was to my young

heart to believe that, day by day, what I had learned, and thought, and delighted in, and raised my fancy and my emulation up by, was passing away from me, never to be brought back any more; cannot be written. My whole nature was so penetrated with the grief and humiliation of such considerations, that even now, famous and caressed and happy, I often forget in my dreams that I have a dear wife and children; even that I am a man; and wander desolately back to that time of my life.

* * *

I can picture the old derelict as he first appeared to me beside his round cart heaped with tomatoes, his greasy clothes shiny in their unkemptness, the rather glassy single eye that had looked from one side of his face staring at nothing in particular, but giving you the feeling that it was seeing all. His method never varied. There was a sudden twitching convulsion, and he leaned to one side, trying to straighten out the other as he did so, and then, taking into his one good lung all the air it would stand, he would let forth a clattering, gargling, asthmatic, high-pitched wheeze, a series of sounds which defied interpretation. Somewhere in the explosion there could be detected 'ripe tomatoes'.

The first of the passages is by Dickens; the second was written by Chaplin after his return to London; but how similar they are in their evocation of a mood of frustrated hope and longing, of hurt and helpless misery. Their origins were in the same dark corners of London; both struggled to get away; both received the shocks of fame too young; both relied on the arts of mimicry and caricature, and tortured themselves with memories of London, as though they thought they could exorcise the evil by staring it in the face, and both possessed a wonderful power of describing incidents without the least command over plot or situation. They saw things in blinding flashes, in sudden spurts of intuition, catching the model on the wing in an attitude so characteristic that the rest of him could be deduced by an exercise of the imagination; the result is a rapid, boldly executed impressionistic sketch, masterly in its contours, unbelievably accurate, but often without depth. Mr E. M. Forster has observed of

Micawber that 'at any moment we may look at him edgewise
and find him no thicker than a gramophone record'. So it is with
the early films of Chaplin. We are convinced of the reality of the
clown, but we are not wholly convinced that if we stuck him with
a pin he would bleed. As for Pickwick, stuck with a pin, that
fantastic monster clearly has no blood in him; there would
bubble out of him good gravy and English beer.

There is nothing in the least strange in the fact that the art of
Chaplin approximates so closely to the art of Dickens; nor is it
surprising that Chaplin regards *Great Expectations* as one of
the greatest of all books and one of the greatest of all films, for
here, with the fewest possible subterfuges, Dickens recounted
his own life, not quite as accurately as he recounted it in some
portions of *David Copperfield*, but with greater breadth and with
a terrible insistence on the graveyard images that haunted him,
and with a closer feeling for the genuine nobility of the child.
Dickens was a man, as Edmund Wilson has shown in *Dickens:
the Two Scrooges*, who was sorely divided from childhood, and as
he grew older the chasm in his soul grew wider. Part of him
remained the Victorian gentleman; part of him was a guilty
outcast with a contempt for the law and an eternal horror of
prison. There was nothing unusual in this dichotomy of the
Victorian soul. There are moments when even Browning, the
apostle of God's goodness, shows a Manichee's belief in Satan's
victory over the world; there are passages in *Pippa Passes* and
The Ring and the Book which show a guilty delight in the knowledge of evil, the sense of some crime never wholly concealed, of
some beautiful and lost face murdered among the ormolu clocks
and the antimacassars.

We shall never know why the age of Queen Victoria, so
tranquil, timid and adventurous, introduced a sense of guilt;
nothing like it existed in Elizabethan times. It came, perhaps,
out of the smoke of industrialism, out of the knowledge that
huge powers were placed in men's hands – the power to scale
continents, to disembowel the earth of its treasures, to move as
quick as lightning. The guilt of Dickens arose from the misery
of the rat-ridden warehouse and the debtor's prison, but it had
other origins. It was in the air men breathed; and Browning,
living in France or Italy, breathed it there as well as in London.

Perhaps men knew instinctively that a murder had been committed on the human person when he was compelled to attend to machines, and another murder was committed when justice became bureaucratic. At some period during the reign of Queen Victoria, or perhaps a little earlier, there occurred a fall from grace, a sense of the degradation of the whole human family. The revolutions failed. The dreams of paradise were seen to be no more than dreams. Out of that failure come the shabby, carefree, mutilated creatures of Dickens; and from the same failure comes Charlie, who may be Pan in disguise, but he wears the cutaway of a Victorian dandy. Once, before he grew lean with misery and imprisonment, he may have been Pickwick – how else can one explain those trousers five sizes too big for him?

The Victorian misery was real and urgent; out of that misery Marx constructed his desperate visions of an enthroned proletariat, and we are paying dearly for the sins of our great-grandfathers. We think of the Victorian age in terms of gewgaws and mahogany tables, bead curtains and monstrous monuments to German princes; but the proper symbols of that age are the debtors' prisons and Sweeney Todd, the Demon Barber of Fleet Street, who had a habit of cutting throats with the precision of a machine and whose performances were completely arbitrary. One should not despise Sweeney Todd, the first of the cutting machines. He was well known to Dickens; he appears at considerable length in the longest of James Joyce's works, and T. S. Eliot has discussed him without irony in *Sweeney Agonistes*, where he announces himself as a cannibal and boasts of knowing a man who 'did a girl in', as though it was not obvious that the murderer was the cannibal himself. He appears in *Sweeney Among the Nightingales:*

> *Apeneck Sweeney spread his knees*
> *Letting his arms hang down to laugh . . .*

He is all the horror of brute force and all the malevolence of industrialism. He is what made Dickens' characters become what they are. He is the enemy who 'sang within the bloody wood when Agamemnon cried aloud', and he is everything which Charlie and Dickens' characters, or most of them, are not. He is the baboon behind the face of the Queen, and if we sometimes fail to recognise him, it is because the Queen gets in his way. Victorian decorum concealed the crime; but invisible, known to everyone, like some Grendel emerging from the swamps, the shaggy baboon with the razor between his teeth ruled the roost. There are times when the Victorian age seems to be one of shuddering terror, even more fearful than our own. At such times we see the ape-like figures stalking like the apaches through the fog-laden streets, determined to kill or punish or imprison for no better reason than the lust in their blood, that diseased blood which had grown rotten from the acid-smells of the mud-swamps of London river. Shakespeare knew those mud-swamps well; so did Dickens who described them at length; Chaplin lived among them, and breathed the same foetid air. Shakespeare lived in Shoreditch, Dickens in the shadow of Hungerford Bridge, and saw the gibbets on the marshes at low-tide – the names Shoreditch and Hunger-ford described the landscape. But worse than even the clammy shores of the East End were the prisons where men rotted.

Dickens knew prison well enough, because he had been in one; and the prison is one of the central symbols of his work, the inescapable symbol of dread and death, or worse. Listen to Mr Jingle, once a grinning Punchinello, now a grimacing prisoner huddled in the darkness and the shadows of the Fleet:

> Lie in bed – starve – die – Inquest – little bone-house – poor prisoner – common necessaries – hush it up – gentlemen of the jury – warden's tradesmen – keep it snug – natural death – coroner's orders – workhouse funeral – serve him right – all over – drop the curtain.

The strange thing is that we regard *Pickwick* as a happy book, yet it is crowded with characters as menacing as Mr Jingle when he contemplates an inevitable death in prison. *Pickwick* winds its way inevitably to the Fleet Prison; the shadows are present even at moments of the highest comedy. They could hardly avoid being present, because they are a part of Dickens, as they are a part of Chaplin, whose tramp, shrugging his shoulders and going down a country lane, is bound for the county jail. In the Fleet, Mr Pickwick hears the pathetic cry: 'Pray, remember the poor debtors.' Dickens and Chaplin remembered them; and it is a part of their genius that they remembered honestly and well.

The human comedy, as men live it, is played out in minute shadings from white to black. Dickens, retaining his child-like vision, forever remembering the brutal gin-soaked horrors of Regency London, sees a world of crude contrasting primary colours inhabited by people at once mysterious, simple and faintly grotesque. His blacks are as black as pitch; his whites are floating bridal veils, crowns of blossoms, plains of virgin snow. It could hardly be otherwise, for his passions were acute; but passion injects strange dyes into the colours of the world we see, and both Dickens and Chaplin found it necessary to caricature the world, and for the same reason. Within the wide limits of their vision, the world as they see it is perfectly rendered. But occasionally they both surrender to a merciless delight in carica-ture, and with hoots of ecstatic joy they describe the meaningless gestures and tics with which even the most noble of men pass through the world. The early Keystone and Essanay shorts are full of caricatures; there are almost none in *The Kid* and *Monsieur Verdoux*, while *The Great Dictator* is brimming over with them.

With caricature goes facetiousness, the same kind of facetious-ness which led Chaplin to call his characters Lord de Boko and Count Chloride de Lime, and Dickens to invent a whole gallery of improbable names like Mr Gradgrind, Mrs Gamp and Lord Verisopht, which belongs to the same order of things as Adenoid Hynkel. This facetiousness was traditional; in nineteenth century English fiction half the doctors are incomprehensibly born with names like Slasher, Carver and Fillgrave. But facetiousness is not a good basis for comedy, and we are appalled when Dickens writes in the first chapter of one of his greatest books: 'Madame Mantalini wrung her hands for grief and rung the bell for her husband; which done, she fell into a chair and a fainting fit simultaneously.' There are a few, a very few, moments in Chaplin's films when an exactly similar parody occurs. As for Madame Mantalini, she never wholly recovers from this assault on her dignity, for it is clear that she did none of these things; she could not; some owlish schoolboy has assumed the place of Dickens; and the precociously witty schoolboy is soon put away. Gissing has suggested that these farcical extravagances were employed to soften the bitterness of truth. It is a nice phrase, but Dickens was rarely concerned to soften bitterness of any kind, and it is more likely that his facetiousness arose when he stepped beyond caricature into farce. Farce hovers over his novels, never far removed though rarely present in the substance of the novels themselves. It is the same with Chaplin. The slightest twist of the micrometer, the slightest faltering of focus, and all the films would evaporate into farce, so close are high tragedy and high comedy to the farcical.

Chaplin's childhood in Lambeth was farce, tragedy, comedy and utter boredom. Born in Fontainebleau near Paris, he was less than a year old when he was brought to live in Chester Street which runs between Kennington Road and Lower Kennington Lane. Until he went on tour the shabby side-streets of Kennington were his home. His mother was half-French, there was some Spanish blood in her, and there may have been gypsy blood as well. Her grandfather was a French general who may have fought under Napoleon. His father, a cobbler's son, was a baritone and a 'cellist, and well known in the music-halls. A photograph reproduced on the music-sheets of a song he popularised shows him to have had a debonair expression, his hair thick and curly, his eyes very large and his lips rather feminine, but the whole face suggests a carefree extravert and a man of the world. He was about twenty-five when he married his half-French wife in 1888. In the early morning of 16 April in the following year, the first and only son of the marriage was born. Three months before his birth an obscure photographer called Friese Greene had taken at the corner of Hyde Park the first moving pictures ever made.

The early years of the marriage were hard torture for the young parents, both of whom had children from previous marriages to support. They went on tour, but music-halls provided them with a bare living, and they were often in debt. They were gifted performers, and if they had found a good manager they might have made a decent living, but mostly they were reduced to singing ballads on the stage and they were never at the top of the bill. The father was proud of his comic singing, the mother of her Gilbert and Sullivan repertoire and her knowledge of French ballads. The boy was barely two when he learned to be a clog dancer and to sing from their repertoire. He was taken with them on their travels. Bright and well-formed, with his mother's sensitivity and his father's features, he was appealing when he was led out on to the stage; like Grimaldi he was an actor almost before he could walk. There were constant visits to France to escape creditors, then long dismal days in London while the two music-hall veterans searched for jobs, and the jobs came rarely, and gradually they drifted apart. At the age of four or five young Charles took his mother's place on the stage at Croydon and sang the rowdy old coster song, *Jack Jones*. His mother was ill. Out of desperation the boy gave a performance which brought the house down. Like many children he had the power of total recall, and therefore, imitating his mother, he sang with all the requisite nuances, all her fire. Pennies were rained down on the stage, and he would have gone on singing all night if his father had not dragged him away.

He was seeing the world as it is. Fascinated, he watched the drunks and derelicts shambling along the Embankment; the small world which stretched between Kennington Road and the Thames was to haunt him all his life. The doss-houses he knew, for he wandered into them. He remembered the costers with their round carts heaped with tomatoes, their greasy clothes shining in the light of kerosene lamps, and he remembered particularly one coster with a glass eye which stared at nothing in particular, but gave you the feeling that he was seeing everything. He had a large bottled nose with a net of red veins on it. There is something of that majestic all-seeing coster in the portrait of Charlie, but it was the old blind man with the ear-muffs and clothes green with age who left the greatest mark on the boy. Sitting under Westminster Bridge with his back against the damp wall, the blind man read the dirty embossed Bible in his hands, and all the while his lips moved silently. His beard was grey and matted, and the eyes with their stark sightless stare filled Charles with utter misery. Blindness haunted him, and the pure horror of these blind old men was to become transformed into the quiet horror of the blind girl in *City Lights*.

London was full of deformed men, victims of an outrageous social system. They were not men who were crippled in the wars; they were crippled by disease, by poverty, by the cold London winters. There was the old cabman in Kennington Road with his

bad feet and boots of immense size, who slithered along the road
in a kind of hobbling crawl. Unknown, he was to provide the
world with that wonderful marionette-like walk which Chaplin
brought to perfection. The evil was turned into a kind of dancing
humour. There were innumerable monsters, and Charles
watched them all, taking comfort in mimicking them, and sometimes he would put on his mimicking acts in the pubs. With the
money he would wander off to Baxter Hall, where he could see
magic lantern shows for a penny, or to Kennington Baths where
you could swim in the second-class bath for threepence if you
brought your own swimming costume. His father died of
alcoholism at St Thomas's Hospital and was buried at Tooting,
and for years afterwards the boy remembered watching the light
in the unshuttered window of the ward where his father was
lying. It was the first hard blow, and there were more to come.

Penniless or almost penniless, making an occasional living by
dressmaking, or sewing on buttons, the mother tried to keep her
family together. There was another son, Sidney, the child of an
earlier marriage. Sidney attended a merchant seaman's training
school, while Charles stayed at home, himself the main provider.
Before Sidney went to sea he helped to cut suits for his brother
out of the mother's theatrical wardrobe. On wet days Charles
could be seen wearing a green plush mantle cut to the shape of
an overcoat, and he went to school in a pair of his mother's
cut-down tights. This was the time when he sold newspapers at
Ludgate Circus and danced barefoot when he heard a barrel-
organ playing, and he would collect some coppers for his dancing,
to run laughing away when the organ-grinder chased him. His
mother's mind was already clouding with despair. Sometimes
she would hold him up to the window, and there the boy watched
with her the passing scene. With terrifying accuracy his mother
could mimic the appearance of people as they came down the
street: the school-teacher, the minister, the justice who crept
past with his hands in his pockets and his face bent down to the
earth.

They were living then a stone's throw from Chester Street,
where they lived before. It was a small street called Pownall
Terrace, and they lived in a single top room. Down three flights
of narrow stairs Charles would wander to remove the slops, or

to go to Heeley's, the greengrocer in Chester Street, for a penn'orth of pot herbs. Then there was Waghorn, the butcher, across the way, who supplied a pound of tuppenny pieces. A little coal, some stale cake from the grocers, some over-ripe eggs: it was on this kind of fare that they lived.

One day, Charles returned home to find that the ambulance had come, and there were a crowd of children gathered round the house. The boy rushed up the stairs to find his mother gone. He learned that while he was away she had gone to all the neighbours with a little piece of coal in her hands. To them all she said: 'I have brought you a pretty present.'

That was the end of Charles's stay in Lambeth for a while. He disappeared to an orphanage at Hanwell. There he passed the most miserable year of his life, completely alone, detesting the loneliness. At Christmas the children were given an orange and a bag of sweets. By sucking the sweets very gently he could make two of them last a fortnight; when autumn came, he still had some sweets left. Here he fed regularly, and no policemen came to remove his possessions for debt – once the police had taken everything except the mattress at Pownall Terrace, but there was nothing to do, no way of earning money, and in the end he could bear it no longer. He fled into the forest of London, slept on park benches, and at the age of eight he succeeded in joining a music-hall act called 'The Eight Lancashire Lads'. When this folded, he went to Hern Boys School for two years, and then ran away again, taking a small part in a play called *Giddy Ostend* at the London Hippodrome in January 1900. There followed three years of touring in a play based on one of the stories of Sherlock Holmes, with William Gillette in the lead and Charles Chaplin at the bottom of the list acting the part of Billy the office boy. In December 1904 he was one of the wolves in the first performance of Barrie's *Peter Pan* at the Duke of York's Theatre in St Martin's Lane. He was now fifteen. His mother had recovered, and still occupied the horrible little room in Pownall Terrace. The boy was not always affluent. In the intervals of acting he took odd jobs. For a while he was a lather boy. Later he took a job in a printing press. The first morning he came into the press wearing a second-hand morning coat and a wavy black tie. The Cockneys stopped the presses as .

soon as they saw him and shouted, 'Morning, me lord!' The boy was furious. He had simply got together the best clothes he could put his hands on, because he had been told to wear good clothes, but instead of showing his fury – he was white with shame and anger – he began to strut like a toff, and this pleased the printers. Out of that proud little strut and the shambling walk of an old cabman came Charlie's well-known walk.

By the spring of 1906 Charles was already an experienced actor. He had acted up and down the country. For a brief while he had been an acrobat, till a heavy fall decided him against joining a circus. He had played in at least three different plays performed at the Duke of York's Theatre, and he was beginning to be something of a success at the music-halls. His brother Sidney had returned from South Africa and was now his guardian. On 26 May 1906, Sidney Chaplin signed a contract for him, which read:

> I, the guardian of Charles Chaplin, agree for him to appear in *Casey's Court* wherever it may be booked in the British Isles only, the agreement to commence 14 May 1906, at a salary weekly of £2-5-0 (two pounds five shillings) increasing to £2-10s. the week commencing July 1906.

It was the first contract ever signed for him, and it led him to a mode of living far superior to anything he had known. *Casey's Court* brought him no more money than he had received when he was acting the part of Billy, for he earned exactly £2–10s. in the Sherlock Holmes play, but now there was a steady income and the possibility of going abroad: it was not for nothing that Sidney Chaplin had inserted the words 'in the British Isles only'. *Casey's Court* consisted of a number of slap-happy imitations of public favourites, a kind of walking waxworks, and in this Chaplin was in his element. He could mimic anyone to perfection, and in any language, and by the spring of 1907 he was already clowning at the Cigale, the Folies-Bergère and Olympia in Paris, and there he saw some of the early films of Max Linder. He was deeply impressed, but he had no intention of being a film actor.

He returned to England, met Mrs Madge Kendal who invited him to her house and offered him an engagement for thirty-eight weeks but kept him waiting so long that he decided to

punish her by refusing the engagement. Afterwards he was glad
he refused. He had the makings of a straight actor and a reverence
for the legitimate stage. He was proud and cocky. He bought
carpets and lanterns for his lodgings in Kennington, and began
to read Schopenhauer. Blaise Cendrars, then a juggler, later a
novelist, lived in the same lodging-house for a while and
remembered him as a sallow youth with a ferocious quietness
about him, who talked of making a career of medicine and
explained that 'everything is contained in Schopenhauer', and
in the evenings they would appear on the same bill, Cendrars
with his coloured balls, Chaplin in his top-hat and jaunty tails.
He noted that Chaplin became an entirely different person when
he stepped on the stage. Gone was the world-weariness and the
biting tongue. He was all action, and, said Cendrars, 'he had a
way of kicking people which was wonderful to behold'. There
was a quickness in the stage Chaplin which reminded the
Frenchman of the tongue of a chameleon.

By this time Chaplin had already joined Fred Karno's troupe
of knockabout comedians. Karno was busy mechanising the
music-halls. There were about fifty music-halls altogether in
London, and Karno pressed motor-cars into his service and sent
his actors to make four or five different turns on as many stages.
There was very little of the *Commedia dell' Arte* in the Fred
Karno comic tradition. His *forte* was farce, played at immense
speed and with innumerable props; and Chaplin, who looked
when he was off the stage rather like a modest student of
medicine, did not resemble a knockabout comedian. At first Karno
refused to employ him, but Sidney was already a member of the
troupe, and on Sidney's advice he was given a few small parts.
His first big part was in a skit called *The Football Match*.
Fast-paced, the skit called for a villain to bribe a goalkeeper to
throw the game. The villain was Charles in a slouch hat and a
small moustache. *Jimmy the Fearless* followed. Jimmy was a boy
who dreamed of unimaginable feats of conquest. He woke up
only when his father came in with a razor-strop and gave him a
hiding. The feats of conquest were all mimicked, and Charles
played it to the hilt, clowning through a whole series of
imaginary adventures with cowboys and rescued princesses. He
played in twenty or thirty skits, but the one he liked best was

Mumming Birds, where he played the part of a drunken dude who continually interfered in the performances, went upon the stage, argued with the performers, insulted the musicians, the stage manager, the audience and the stage hands, always calm and self-possessed, with his cigarette dangling from the corner of his lips and his top-hat at an angle, and sometimes blowing his nose on an immense handkerchief which he would wave with something of the effect of a matador waving a red flag to a bull. He played the part deadpan, with fastidious taste and incredible assurance, for he remained calm even when the audience was in a state of riot. Under the title *A Night at an English Music-Hall* he played the same part during his first tour of America in 1910–11, he played it in France and in the Channel Islands in 1912, and he was still playing it in America when he returned in the late autumn of 1912. When he set out for America for the second time he had some faint inkling that it would be many years before he would return. The boy who had been a barefoot gutter-rat in the slums of Kennington, who had slept in half the doss-houses of London and would never be able to forget their terrible smell, who read Schopenhauer until the inanity of the world seemed to creep up at him from the printed pages, was determined to conquer America. 'I give you warning,' he announced to the Statue of Liberty, 'I have come to conquer America.' Four years later he had conquered the world.

CHAPTER VIII

THE COMING OF THE CUSTARD PIE

W H E N Chaplin announced that he was about to conquer America he was uttering a prayer, the same prayer which has been whispered by a million other immigrants as they catch sight of New York, for there is something about those towering pinnacles on the water's edge which summons a man to assume the attitude of a conqueror. But Chaplin's prayer was remarkable in that it was spoken against all the evidence. In New York he was faced with one fact of quite exceptional importance: everything he represented, his whole conception of comedy, the vast traditions going back to Grimaldi, Deburau and the *Commedia dell' Arte,* all these were hopelessly at odds with the American comic tradition.

In America the pantomime never took root, and there was no equivalent to the music-hall. There was vaudeville, but vaudeville was an exotic plant which had grown feverishly and would soon die. There was slapstick and Negro minstrels and comic monologues. These were indigenous, but they had little in common with the complexities of the English comic stage. Vaudeville, which was born in 1883 and died of a lingering affliction in 1932 during the depression, originated with Benjamin Keith who was one of Barnum's assistants. He knew circus life, freak shows and some actors. Why not combine them all? So he opened the Gaiety Theatre in Boston with a midget weighing one and a half pounds, a stuffed mermaid, and a few 'turns', and prayed that this singular mixture would take care of his fortune. It did. Within five years there were vaudevilles in half the towns of America, and Barnum grew fearful of their popularity. To the very end vaudeville showed that freaks were as important as 'turns'.

American vaudeville was garish, boisterous, friendly, exuberant; the shadow of Barnum hung over it; and it was a world away from the music-hall, with slapstick instead of Cockney wit to drive the fuse. The closest to the English tradition was probably Joe Cook who invented a bewildering kind of nonsensical double-talk and took the part of the master of ceremonies, wandering in and out of the 'turns', bestowing fatuous and irrelevant remarks about the state of the weather or the skills of the performers. He was the master of the completely irrelevant statement. He would take a pack of cards, fumble with it behind his back for five minutes while his fingers searched helplessly for the ace of spades, but the ace of spades never appeared; and while he fumbled he would explain at enormous length, in a patter as fast as an express train, that he absolutely refused to imitate four Hawaiians playing the ukelele for the very good reason that the four Hawaiians—— 'How are you?' he would shout. 'Well, how are *you?* Fine, how's yourself? Good. And you? Splendid? How's your uncle? I haven't got an uncle? Fine, how is he?' He was trigger-happy and wonderful, but when he left the stage you felt drained of energy, and there was something inhuman in the massive irrelevance of the man.

Nat Wills was inhuman in another way. He played the part of the tramp, and something of his insane hilarity went into the picture which Chaplin finally drew of Charlie. He was a bum with a red nose, a slit mouth, a battered hat and baggy pants which he held together with a string; from this waist-string hung a tomato can, the most sacred of his possessions. His boots were cracked, and his immense toes resembled bell-hammers: at the least provocation the toes would dance a jig of their own. His specialty was a tramp monologue, recounting his glorious thirsts, his joy in lying. He was splendid in his arrogance – the arrogance of a Wild Bill Hickok or a Paul Bunyan.

There was more tenderness in Joe Jackson, who gravely took a bicycle to pieces and still more gravely attempted to put it together again. He patiently dissected the anatomy of a bicycle and held up for our astonished admiration the strange animated creatures who lurked within it. He could do more with a bicycle pump than anyone ever believed possible. He had Jimmy Durante's mania for destruction, but with a slower fuse.

Easy Street, 1917

Shoulder Arms, 1918

The greatest of the clowns, though, was W. C. Fields whose bottle nose was not yet developed, and who tended towards elegance and liked being photographed leaning negligently on his billiard cue: the 'turn' for which he first became famous was a hilarious game of billiards where he made up the rules as he went along. Jimmy Durante tore a piano to pieces; W. C. Fields would have regarded the destruction of so small a thing as a piano as beneath his dignity. He was malice personified, pretended to no dignity and clearly loved no one but himself. His ambition was to be a juggler. In his early days he practised juggling assiduously, until he perfected his masterpiece, which was a trick of juggling twenty-four cigar-boxes on end with a little rubber ball on top. The cost was terrible. He practised till his shins were bleeding and the tears were streaming down his face, and some of the anguish of those early years marked him still when he had achieved a place in the Hollywood sun, drinking his two quarts of gin a day, bullying everyone on the set, reserving his greatest malice for defenceless children and incompetent starlets: the black malice showed even when he wore checkered trousers and a morning coat. But the force of his comic malice was such that he acquired a perfection in the art of mime which raised him above his fellows. Of the comics of his time he alone deserves to be ranked with Chaplin.

Fields was the son of an English immigrant, and to the very end there was an English sense of intimacy in his performances. He had no mastery of wisecracks. It was the manner of the man, the blustering, boisterous charm of his idiocy, the senile twitch in his face, the resemblance to an over-ripe fruit, which attracted people to him. He was a throwback to Regency times, a shrivelled Beau Brummell with a dew-lap and little taste for shaving, roaring his perpetual complaints against the weather and the interference of people, always accusing the world of malice, though it was clear enough that he contained in his own person enough black bile to drown the world. Where Groucho Marx was purely synthetic, Fields was a natural, and his behaviour off the stage was often indistinguishable from his behaviour on it, so providing one more proof (if any was needed) that his malice arose from his experience of the world, the conjured enemies who filled his dreams and against whom he waged an

D

unceasing war. There was something devilish in Fields, as there
was in Charlie. It is the absence of the devil which makes the
modern stage so tame.

When Chaplin came to America the great days of vaudeville
were nearly over. He appeared at the old Hammerstein's
Theatre in New York in *A Night at an English Music-Hall*, but
he was not wildly successful. He went on tour. He was adored in
Brooklyn and tolerated in Kansas. He went through the whole
Karno repertoire, but his *forte* was the dude who lolls just below·
the stage and interrupts the performance with a wild contempt
for performers and audience alike, forever scrambling with the
musicians in the orchestra pit, the actors, the stage· manager,
the lady with the boa, smoking continually – he could suggest
his massive contempt of the world with a single puff of his
cigarette, a wiggle of his finger, and when he marched on the
stage the welling anger on the pale face assumed the proportions
of the unearthly anger of the Greek tragic heroes.

A refined version of *A Night at an English Music-Hall*
appeared in the two-part Essanay comedy, *A Night at the Show*.
In this film, as in *The Great Dictator*, he deliberately split himself in two, becoming the contemptuous dude near the orchestra
rail and the besotted rowdy with the walrus moustache in the
gallery whose loathing leads him to turn the fire-hose on the
whole assembly. But all this came later.

Chaplin on tour maintained the tradition of the English
music-hall, and saw no reason to change it for an American
audience. There were appreciative notices, but there was no
outpouring of praise. He earned fifty dollars a week, which was
considerably more than the three pounds a week he earned in
England. When Mack Sennett telegraphed to his eastern repre-
sentative: 'Get in touch with a fellow called Chapman or
Chamberlain – something like that – playing second circuit,' no
one knew where he was, and it was some time before the agent
caught up with him and found him playing in Oil City, Penn-
sylvania. Mack Sennett had seen *A Night at an English Music-
Hall* in New York, and he was impressed with the unruly actor
who defied the conventions of the theatre. The telegram
reached Chaplin in May 1913. He immediately went to New
York where he was interviewed by Adam Kessel and explained

that he was on contract and would not be able to leave his company before the end of the year. He was offered seventy-five dollars a week, the usual salary for an unknown comedian on the Keystone lot. Chaplin demurred. There was not so very much difference between his salary in vaudeville and the salary offered by Keystone. They offered a year's contract. To go to Keystone meant cutting himself off from Karno's troupe. He knew nothing about films. He had never known such security as he received during his vaudeville tour before. Why go to Los Angeles? He possessed absolutely no assurance that he had the makings of a film comedian, and what would happen when the year was over? In the end he accepted the offer only because Adam Kessel, outraged by Chaplin's I-don't-care-whether-I-do attitude, offered him a year's contract at one hundred and twenty-five dollars a week. It was the highest price Mack Sennett had ever paid to a beginner, and afterwards he confessed: 'I don't know why I did it. I wasn't too hopeful. He was English all the way through, but he could make you laugh till you cried.'

Mack Sennett in 1913 was at the height of his powers. It was the time of Roscoe Arbuckle, Hank Mann, Chester Conklin, Rube Miller and Ford Sterling. They were superb mimes, comedians by instinct, incapable of lowering themselves to whatever is the pantomime equivalent of a wisecrack, the arch gesture or the calculated applause. The humour was physical and robust. They went out after it like happy warriors. They had no tidy props, no big budgets, no elaborate sets; the scripts were very apt to be written down on someone's cuffs, though Mack Sennett has confessed to writing scripts eight or nine pages long. The scripts were usually torn up halfway through. The theme of all the Keystone comedies – altogether there were about nine hundred of them – was simple. Out of whatever props and actors lay at hand, the utmost confusion was made to flower. The aim was a mounting crescendo of madness. The theory behind it all was the same theory which produced the vaudeville: if you mix up a circus, a freak-show and a number of comic turns you get a Keystone comedy. A little later the bathing belles were added. They arrived by accident. Mack Sennett decided that the presence of bathing belles close to the comedians inspired the newspapers to reproduce more photographs from his films. The fabulous mad rush in which cops, comedians and bathing belles all contributed was equally accidental. It had simply happened one day during a street scene that the police interfered. They began to chase the actors and directors who had roped off a part of Hollywood Boulevard, and the camera-man had continued to photograph the chase with a hidden camera. Afterwards, when the film was run through, the chase by the cops was seen to be more amusing than the original street scene. From that moment the Keystone Cops were invented. If Mabel Normand had not rushed out into the street with a doll in her arms and thrust it into the arms of a total stranger, if an excited mob had not then gathered, if the cops had not thought that the crowd was menacing the safety of Hollywood Boulevard, and if at that moment a parade had not passed down the street, so adding to the resulting confusion, it is likely that there never would have been the Keystone Cops. They were born out of the confusion of those early days when films were still taken by a photographer who turned a crank and Hollywood Boulevard was thought to be as good a stage as any other.

The crowning accident, the most beautiful and the most accidental of accidents, was the discovery of the custard pie. The coming of the custard pie gave an added dimension to comedy and entailed a complete revision of the comic standards of the time. Henceforward whenever the comedy lagged there was always the possibility of keeping it in motion by a well-aimed pie.

The coming of the custard pie occurred early in 1913. No one remembers the precise date, which is a pity, for it is a date of considerable significance in the history of the cinema. But the circumstances are well-known. It happened that Ben Turpin, whose walrus moustache and insignificant cross eyes were merely the outward decorations of a refined and resourceful comedian, was ordered by Mack Sennett to thrust his head through a door.

'You're not funny,' Mack Sennett objected.

'Shall I uncross my eyes?' Ben Turpin asked, unhelpfully.

'No, just be funny. Do your damndest to be funny.'

Ben Turpin tried. He glared, he opened his mouth, he closed

his mouth, he wiggled his walrus moustache, but he was a signal failure. In desperation he rolled his cross eyes, but the director only groaned. They worked until late afternoon, their tempers fraying. Suddenly from out of nowhere a custard pie sailed over the camera to land squarely on Ben Turpin's face. The camera crew and everyone on the set howled. It was funny enough when Ben Turpin was smacked by the custard pie, but it was funnier still when he attempted to unstick the thing from his face and blinked pitifully through the mess.

'Who sent the custard pie?' Mack Sennett asked.

'I, with my little pie,' Mabel Normand answered. 'I threw the pie.'

The subtle refinements inherent in pie-throwing remained to be explored. Considerable advances were made that evening. It was decided that the beauty of the throwing resulted from the softness of the dough, the large amplitude of the pie, the firm stance and careful aim of the thrower. Roscoe Arbuckle was on the set. He had the strength and accuracy of a good baseball player; he became the acknowledged master. Even Chaplin, who possessed an excellent stance and considerable stamina, failed to rival him; nor could Chaplin like Arbuckle throw a pie with unerring aim in two directions at once or round corners. Chaplin had chosen the time of his arrival in Los Angeles well. He came in the full tide of the custard pies.

Though Mack Sennett could not claim that he invented the custard pie or the Keystone Cops, he could claim a fair share in inventing the forms of film comedy. An ex-boiler-maker and a former actor (he once played the hind legs of a horse), he was himself the most reckless of men, expending his own and every-one else's energies at a furious pace. He had one, and only one basic tenet: 'Always keep the comic on the wrong end of the gun.' He meant, of course, the right end, the end the bullet comes out of. The process of comedy was a simple one: the comedian must be shot to pieces, and everyone else in sight must be shot to pieces with him. He could appraise lucidly the exact speed, the exact stance for a stern skid – Mabel Normand, who was adept at all forms of comedy, was particularly adept at the stern skid; and he possessed a clairvoyant's tact in arranging that the accidental should be put to the service of comedy. He had a Russian cameraman who hoped to save film by turning the crank slowly. The effect was magnificent, for when the film was screened, the slow paces of the heavy, blundering Ford Sterling were transformed into quick dancing steps. Sennett was the first to manipulate camera speeds, and the first to introduce the manoeuvre known as 'the zig-zag rally', which is like nothing which has ever existed on earth. 'The zig-zag rally' is the technical name of the scene in which cops, children, animals, lumbering old men, bathing belles and everyone else who happens to be on the set takes part in a mad chase. The Keystone chase is not naturalistic. It follows a prescribed pattern. As the mob flees from the camera it is seen to sway from side to side. In the Keystone comedies no posse of policemen running down a road is ever seen to run in a straight line. They must move sideways as well, like billiard balls smacking off the cushions, in a bouncing motion which reflected something of Mack Sennett's own zest for comedy. Also, he was vulgar. He like to have his comedians paddle the backsides of bathing belles. He called all pretty girls 'girlie', and he had a pleasant habit of smacking his lips as he said the word.

Partly, it was the vulgarity of his time, a time of leers and winks and ferocious sexual appetites. Lovers were expected to tumble in bed, not to lie down gracefully beside a prop fireplace. Since the players had to act with their bodies, and every gesture had to be driven home, there was no need for subtle shadings. The cops for the most part were portly Irishmen; Mack Sennett made them more portly, larger than life. The contrast between evil and innocence was assured by giving the comedians light-coloured clothes while the cops were always dressed in padded black. It was the time before the gag-man and the light verbal charades were invented. Where Gregory Peck expresses his emotions through a quiver of his Adam's apple, those pre-war actors expressed emotions by a wild flailing of the arms, and if they were asked why they behaved in this way, they would have answered: 'What are arms for?' But while the bit players were taught to underscore emotions, the truly great clowns like Harry Langdon and Buster Keaton preserved a fatuous deadpan. Nothing ever surprised them. They were drained of emotion, callous, untouched. To them was given the power of passing through all emotions undisturbed. It was the same with Roscoe Arbuckle and Ben Turpin, for though there were occasions when they expressed their emotions emphatically, they were capable of long withdrawn silences as they gazed entranced upon a world whose orgies they never shared. Roscoe Arbuckle, in particular, possessed a Chinese suavity, and he rarely showed more emotion than is shown on the face of a trained seal. Ben Turpin might be tortured on a pirate ship, thrown overboard, picked out of the water with grappling irons; at most there would be a faint stirring of some of the hairs of his precocious walrus moustache. A whole gallery of fastidious palefaced heroes was invented, all demonstrating that they were impervious to harm, and Chaplin merely followed the accepted tradition. By emphasising the heroic calm of the chief comedian Sennett had hit upon one of his most resourceful tricks. The idea was not new. It may not have been new even when Deburau was walking the *Théâtre des Funambules*, giving the impression that he alone had invented absolute silence and immobility, a god-like untouchability. The deadpan face was a commonplace among comic recitals on the vaudeville stage, but it was the cinema which first exploited the possibilities of deadpan in all its complexity, for the close shot provided another dimension. A close shot of Harry Langdon or Charlie gave them the appearance of marble. They were beyond the reach of this world, yet partakers in its joys. They were more like marionettes than men. But while their faces were impassive, their arms flailed and their bodies remained in feverish movement. From a study of those faces shining with a god-like calm, it would be reasonable to deduce that the ancient Greeks were right when they insisted that their comic actors should wear masks.

For these intoxicated white-faced clowns, descendants of Deburau, their remoteness giving their smallest gesture the impact of a steam-hammer, words were a hindrance. They found their humour in situation, in posture, in sudden leaps, in improbable adventures, in madcap rallies and furious explosions of temper. The dexterity was physical and spiritual, not verbal. The words were left to the idiots who wrote the captions. They were rarely brilliant, and mostly they were downright careless. 'Came the dawn' is almost the worst, but Mack Sennett

perpetrated a number of equally childish captions, and unbelievably childish titles. He called one film *The Battle of Who
Run* and another *Uncle Tom without the Cabin*. Such heavy verbal
by-play was characteristic of the times; and the captions of
Chaplin's early films, and some of his later ones, full of atrocious
puns and *double-entendres*, were no worse than Sennett's. Concerned with comic action, not with words, they fumbled when
they came to captions, but they were not entirely responsible for
their errors. The times demanded that kind of word-play.
Today, you can still see at Venice, California, in one of the
exhibits on the fair-ground, those crazy notices which reflect
the passing of an era:

DIGEM DEPER AND PLANTEM: UNDERTAKER

BALD HEADS WAXED FREE

MR I. P. FREELY

HUNG FA TOO LO

CHINESE LAUNDRY

There are many more of these relics of an age which has passed.
The most boorish of us can hardly be expected to take any fun
in these things now, perhaps because the headlines with the
flames and the smoke pouring out of them have given us a
new respect for words, or simply because the fashion has
changed. It was the time of the mutascope and the hour-glass
figure, of waxed moustaches and the bathing costume shaped
like a miniature tent. The heavy-handed verbal play was no
more than decoration. The heart of the mystery was something
very simple and recognisable: a pale-faced impassive clown
teetering on the edge of nowhere.

In Mack Sennett's films produced before the arrival of
Chaplin, the chief clown was played by Ford Sterling. How
Sterling came to be accepted as a comic, or why anyone thought
him to be amusing, is a question best left unsettled. Heavily
built, pompous, Germanic to the roots, his face resembled a
knuckle of beef. He had none of Ben Turpin's steady defiance of
the laws of gravity, but he possessed a certain dexterity, the
same kind of dexterity which was employed by King Kong on
the Empire State building. He belonged to the age of Prince
Albert hats and guffaws and HUNG FA TOO LO, and he was

gradually losing his popularity, for the age was changing. Sennett hardly knew which way the wind was blowing. He progressed by a series of accidents, but the accidental was beginning to follow a fixed pattern. The pale, the dapper, the gentle clowns were beginning to take the place of raw beef. There was Max Linder, whose delicacy and tact owed much to Deburau. There was the young Frank Capra, already a director. There were Raymond Griffith, Mai St Clair, Harold Lloyd, Eddie Sutherland, George Marshall, all names to be reckoned with. Above all there was Mack Sennett, a man who regarded custard pies and crowds of flat-footed cops with the deadly earnestness they deserved. Then in one fabulous year Chaplin was to take the established tradition and mould it into something closer to his heart. From the dark roads of London and the guttersnipes who haunted Lambeth and Kennington; from the huge derision of Grimaldi; from the silence of Deburau; from the ferocious battles of the Keystone comics – there emerged Charlie.

CHAPTER IX

THE FABULOUS YEAR

DURING 1914 Chaplin performed in thirty-five films. Twenty-two or twenty-three he directed himself. Such huge output was never to be reached again. It was as though, in the first burst of enthusiasm for the new medium, he was determined to explore all the possibilities of the strange character he had invented, to see him in all lights and to follow him through all conceivable adventures. As we look back on those thirty-five films we see them haunted with the shapes of Monsieur Verdoux, the Great Dictator and the gold-miner of the Alaskan adventure, and we can even discern the ghostly features of the Kid. After the Keystone comedies, the rest is decoration.

The world as Charlie sees it in the Keystone comedies has one central point of reference – the ashcan, which is always near by, straight in front or just round the corner. Charlie half adores ashcans. He will sleep in them, hide in them, jump in them, and he knows his way all round them. Later he will take to sleeping in dog-kennels and even in doss-houses, but this is clearly only a temporary measure – the ashcan waits him at the end of the road. As he wanders from one ashcan to another with an immortal patience, he intends to extract as much amusement as possible from life, and he will even occasionally interrupt his wanderings to take a temporary job. He has learned patience in a hard school; it never leaves him. Watch how slowly, how patiently, he climbs the innumerable stairs from his pigeon-hole to the skyscraper office in *The New Janitor*. A bell has rung. Charlie must trudge up the stairs with his mop and pail. He puts one foot forward, and then the other, but he is in no hurry. Only when he sees the robber does he move with lightning speed. Then he is all fire! Pan awakes from his dream, twists the revolver from the man's

107

hand and frightens him into submission by suddenly turning his back and threatening the man with a revolver pointed through his legs. Faced with the strange spectacle of Charlie bending down with a revolver between his knees, the robber surrenders. In all this Charlie resembles the gay conquistador Astolfo in Boiardo's *Orlando Innamorato*, eternally surprised by his own accomplishments.

Boiardo's immense epic is rarely read nowadays. It is a pity, for the strait-laced octets of this fifteenth-century verse drama have a chivalric sweep and they march with precise gusto through a wonderfully embroidered tale of heroism. Astolfo is an English carpet-knight, with nothing of the look of the hero about him. He is weak, gentle, polite to everyone. He has no special skill, but he possesses an abiding love for danger and plunges recklessly where even the giants fear to tread, with never-failing humour and dauntless courage. Everyone is sorry for him, and everyone admires him. By accident the enchanted lance of Argalia falls into his hands just before he is sent out to fight the giant Grandonio. No one expected him to survive. Astolfo did not know he possessed the magic sword. As he went out to take part in the tournament, everyone expected him to be brought back dead, and everyone acknowledged that in offering to sacrifice his life he was only showing his loyalty to Charlemagne. 'Let someone else come to his aid,' they cried. Then, to Astolfo's intense surprise, he unseats the enemy and wins the victory, and immediately afterwards he is saying that this was exactly what he expected, it was the most natural thing in the world, it would be absurd if a Christian knight could not kill a mere paynim. Without rancour to anyone, light-hearted always, conscious of his own powers, Astolfo goes jauntily through the whole epic; and even when he is thrust into prison by Charlemagne or surrounded by treacherous knights, he refuses to indulge in recriminations. Nothing quite like this figure of the happy knight appears in the *Morte D'Arthur*. Astolfo is only a minor character in the *Orlando Innamorato*, but on that dancing figure Boiardo has cast the gentle light of grace and high adventure. There is a deep kinship between Charlie and Astolfo, though Charlie's lance may be no more than his twitching bamboo cane.

As for Charlie's private life, there are few secrets. The lonely knight of the faith wanders from doss-house to doss-house. In love with Mabel Normand, he will never possess her any more than the mediæval knight possesses the princess to whom he dedicates his life. She will drop him a *billet-doux*, flirt with him, even kiss him occasionally, but she will never run away with him. In the pitiless world where he lives few rewards are offered for heroism. It is true that in *The New Janitor* Charlie receives a wad of bank-notes, which he counts excessively carefully, but the bank-notes are hardly more than stage props, and he will be back with his mop and slop-bucket the next day. The true and unattainable prize is Miss Normand, who is all youth and gaiety. A year later, in *The Jitney Elopement*, he rides off with her in a dilapidated Ford pursued by her father and the inevitable Count Chloride de Lime, who had been offered her hand. The film ends in a mad chase, with Charlie throwing brickbats at the pursuing car, but we know that the father will catch up with them, and the woman will remain unattainable and virgin, the world's enchantress, as Charlie is the world's imp, beholden neither to Charlie nor to Count Chloride de Lime.

Though there are no secrets concerning Charlie, there are occasional red herrings. Once he is depicted as being married to Mabel Normand. He even has a child which he forgets to feed and carries by the scruff of his rompers. Miss Normand scolds him when he returns from a restaurant after finding in his coat a letter which reads: 'My dearest Snooky Ookums, meet me at 3 a.m.' There is a great to-do about the letter and the coat which Charlie picked up by accident in the restaurant, and after a wild chase in the park he is thrown into an ashcan, to emerge in time for the park photographer to take a photograph of him smiling on the bench with Mabel Normand beside him and the child on his shoulder. It is a pleasing photograph, but we are permitted to doubt whether the marriage was more than a dream-marriage. We suspect there is subterfuge somewhere. The film is called *His Trysting Place*, but there is no tryst except the eternal tryst with the ashcan. Charlie is at home in the empty streets and the crowded doss-houses; most of all he is at home when he has a mop and pail in his hand, and goes about his business. He was born to be a nightwatchman or a janitor. He is happy with his sweepings, the oily water in the pail, the forgotten things lumped together and thrown down the chute. Erratic as a chauffeur, incompetent as a boxing referee, awkward as a lover, a perverse scene-shifter, he is at his full powers as a janitor.

Halfway through that fabulous year, in a film called *Laughing Gas*, Charlie appears as a kind of janitor to Dr Pain, the Dentist. Now it happens that dentistry is a subject which has long haunted clowns, and Charlie has always desired to practise the art. The task of the dentist is a suitably intimate one; he has the patient at his mercy; what more could he desire? The dentist appears in a script by Flaminio Scala written for the *Commedia dell' Arte*. The story begins with a mad fight between Pedrolino and Pantalone. Pedrolino is bitten in the arm. The arm swells. To take his mind from the swelling arm he is told that the cause of all his worries is his bad breath, and to this Pedrolino weakly assents, for he discovers that everyone is complaining of his breath. With complete seriousness he goes up to all his acquaintances, asking them if it is true that his breath is so bad. They all peer into his mouth and expound on his halitosis. They want to help him. He wants to be helped. They suggest remedies. Pedrolino begs them not to reveal his plight to his daughter, but when he returns to his house his daughter is the first to tell him that he is evil-smelling, and so he finally consents to go to the dentist. There, of course, four good teeth are pulled out, and Pantalone is the dentist disguised with a wig and the scene ends as they fight, with all the furniture broken, and they scream at each other like cats, while Pedrolino waves the wig and hops on one foot and holds his hand to his broken mouth.

The dentist in the *Commedia dell' Arte* is a savage; so he is in *Laughing Gas*. But there are important differences. In the *Commedia dell' Arte* the movement of the comedy is towards a predetermined end. There is a slow fuse, and a final explosion. In *Laughing Gas* the fuse is continually spluttering and behaving a little like a Chinese cracker, and though the end is a free-for-all, the end is the least important thing about the story, and indeed seems to have been added as an afterthought or in obedience to Mack Sennett's wishes.

Laughing Gas begins with Charlie entering the dentist's office. He is very sprightly, impeccably dressed, though a little battered. He seems to be the dentist or at least the dentist's chief assistant, for he looks sadly at the patients, counts them, removes his gloves, bows, rubs his hands and then picks up the cuspidor. His exact position in the dentist's chambers is never made quite clear. He is 'the man who picks up the cuspidor', a general factotum, a man with a grievance. We are never told exactly what the grievance is. He picks a quarrel with the dentist's assistant, fights with him and at the moment after they have shaken hands, Charlie clips him over the head. He is called in when one of the dentist's patients falls unconscious from the gas. Charlie picks up the man's foot and listens to the heartbeats, then picks up a mallet and taps the man on the skull. Immediately the patient has a laughing jag. Charlie is thereupon sent out with a prescription, but he forgets the prescription in admiration of the dentist's wife, who loses her skirt and reveals her balloony bloomers when she rushes up some steps to avoid Charlie. The dentist is summoned home. The patient is still having a laughing jag. Charlie returns with the prescription, or he has failed to find it – the prescription was, after all, no more than an excuse to get Charlie out of the dentist's office – and now the patients are all crowding to be attended to, and inevitably Charlie must choose the most handsome and delightful of them all. Meanwhile the dentist's wife is still bewailing the loss of her skirt and refuses to be comforted by the dentist. There must be retribution. Charlie must be punished for the indignity she has suffered. She does not know that Charlie can never be punished, and that if there is ever any question of indignities, he is more capable of making other people suffer them than of suffering them himself. He is charming to his new patient, lifts up her chair, cleans her boots, throws one foot over her lap and peers into her mouth. Heaven has sent him a magnificent gift. He is almost crazy with happiness. He trips over a spittoon, but the patient is still there, smiling, leaning back in the chair, waiting for his attentions. He lifts the pair of pincers, studies them, ponders what to do with them and at last hits on the true, the incontrovertible solution – he will use them to hold her nose while he kisses her mouth. Afterwards the dentist returns, and there is the battle royal.

As in so many of the Keystone films there are only moments

when Charlie is fully alive. The moment when he enters the dentist's office and picks up the cuspidor, the long moments when he gazes lovingly into the patient's mouth, the moment when he returns to the dentist's office and looks at the assembled patients with arch surprise, bewildered by that blossoming of beards and cadaverous freaks. But with what explicit understanding of the world's ways does he demonstrate that he is not himself a freak, with what abandon does he choose his patient and with what sly hints of amatory experience does he wield his forceps!

Laughing Gas is atrociously put together. All the scenes in which Charlie and Slim Summerville hurl brickbats at one another might have been taken from another film. There is no rhyme or reason in them. The scene sags whenever Charlie is off the stage; it sometimes sags when he is on the stage, for there are moments when the slapstick is beyond control; there are odd experiments in brutality, inexplicable contortions which do not spring from the untrammelled soul of the clown but from the American slapstick tradition, that rough and ready tradition which encouraged everything explosive in life. But the charm of Charlie is that he refuses generally to partake in uncontrolled explosions. He has his own explosiveness to contend with. At such moments he is like the winking eye of the hurricane, calm in the midst of turbulence, impatient only for more calm, for a greater safety from the intolerance and turbulence of things.

Shortly after *Laughing Gas* there appeared a film in which Charlie's turbulence was at its height. This film was called *The Face on the Bar-Room Floor*, and was based on H. Antoine D'Arcy's bromidic elegy which begins:

> *'Twas a balmy summer's evening and a goodly crowd was there,*
> *Which well-nigh filled Joe's bar-room on the corner of the square:*
> *And as songs and witty ditties came through the open door,*
> *A vagabond crept slowly in and posed upon the floor.*

The miserable vagabond, who seems to come in like the drift of leaves, is given a drink and asked for a song, but instead he offers to tell the story of his lovelorn life. He was an artist, by his own account a good artist who once painted a picture called *The Chase of Fame* which he sold for fifteen hundred pounds.

Most of the money was squandered on a woman called Madeline. Then, one afternoon in May, when he was painting 'a fair-haired boy, a friend of mine, who lived across the way', Madeline entered the studio, and within a year she had run away with the fair-haired boy. The bar-room guests are deeply affected, wipe their tears away and watch attentively when the vagabond draws Madeline's face on the bar-room floor:

Another drink and with chalk in hand, the vagabond began
To sketch a face that might buy the soul of any man,
Then, as he placed another lock upon the shapely head,
With a fearful shriek he leaped and fell across the picture – dead.

Such is the story, and six or seven generations have either wept or laughed themselves sick over the fate of the nameless vagabond. Today, there are more rooms in Colorado and New Mexico bearing the genuine imprint of 'the face on the bar-room floor' than there are beds in New England that Washington slept in.

Chaplin, of course, turns the whole story upside down. Charlie is the homeless waif with the sob-story. He is given his drink. He leans drunkenly over the bar-counter and tells the story in flashbacks, and when the girl leaves him he is overwhelmed by her parting words: 'Goodbye, you great hunk of a man, and remember not to fall on your feet.' Yes, this is what hurt him. If only she had said farewell tenderly! She had no regard for his sensibilities. Back in the bar, he chokes out his sobs and gravely commands the bartender to give him more drinks. Then we flash back to Charlie's chance meeting with the couple some years later in a park, both of them harassed now, a typical unhappy middle-class couple with four unruly children, and Charlie gazes after them with the expression of celestial bliss which a fly offers to a spider after escaping from the web. But in the bar he is still choking with sobs. Offered a chalk he begins to draw the face of the beloved on the floor at the moment when a violent brawl breaks out. But what he draws is not a face. Desperately, urgently, savagely, crawling all over the floor like an enormous insect, Charlie draws a whole series of noughts and crosses. It is the first of the great daemonic moments. Suddenly the comedy stops still on the tracks. It is a moment unbearable in its intensity. There is Charlie's quiet calculated savagery as he depicts the zero faces of Madeline, and all round him there is the hurricane. But it is the hard winking eye at the centre of the hurricane, the remorseless drunk reducing all the faces of the world to an irresponsible zero, which hurts. It is not tragedy nor is it comedy. Some new, remorseless element has entered into the pattern. *Suddenly Pan has shrieked.* If we ask ourselves why he has shrieked there is no explanation. It is not contempt for the world or lovesickness or drunkenness; it was simply that it had to be; and though the shriek is never heard so loud again, and Charlie is an adept at muffling it, we are always aware that it may break out; it is the threat he hangs over the world.

Charlie's capacity to imitate the absolute dead centre of the hurricane was repeated in *The Rounders*, which appeared in September. It begins harmlessly enough with two couples in confronting hotel bedrooms arguing bitterly. Doors burst open, the screaming continues and each couple attempts to out-scream the other. Charlie's wife is a haggard fish-jawed matron. Charlie knocks her down, but she throws him on the bed – Charlie's prodigious leap into the bed, ending with a sudden twist and twirl of his feet round the bedrail is a masterpiece of sudden and unexpected clowning comparable with his leap up the curtains in *The Great Dictator*. This is no longer slapstick, but the purest of fantastic inventions, and all the more wonderful because immediately afterwards the slapstick resumes. Eventually the two harassed husbands – the other is Roscoe Arbuckle – teeter off to escape from their wives, Charlie having first purloined the money in his wife's purse. They are weary of the world's indignities. They come to a restaurant, and the faces of the guests merely have the effect of increasing their weariness. They discuss what they will do. The band plays. Some of the guests are dancing. Clearly, one should join the dance. So they dance together for a while, falling in each other's arms, and suddenly they will dance no longer; they lie down on the floor, pull the table-cloths over them and go to sleep, that deep sleep which is permitted to clowns alone, and they would have continued to sleep on for ever at the dead centre of the hurricane if their wives had not arrived. The chase is resumed. Always in search of rest, they find themselves on the shores of a lake. A canoe is waiting. They jump into it. Along the bank come the screaming hordes of people they have annoyed at the restaurant. They laugh. They are out of harm's way. They throw the oars away with a careless gesture of disdain for all mechanical implements and all progress, and lie down happily in the bottom of the boat, only rising occasionally to mock the people on the bank. The boat springs a leak. They are quite untroubled. Above all they must find the rest which has been promised to them. They lie down peacefully while the water rises, but the rising water disturbs them not at all. Finally, they sink below the surface of the lake and there is only Charlie's battered top-hat floating on the waves to mark their graves.

Not all the Keystone films were so magnificently centred upon great and tragic themes. *Caught in a Cabaret*, the twelfth film, was largely concerned with exploring the world of facetiousness. It is difficult to believe that a film could be more facetious, more concerned with a deadly sequence of puns. Punning was part of the English tradition, and the English have always been adepts at it, and Chaplin has encouraged them to his heart's content. If the worst of his puns occurs in the opening title of the comparatively late *Pay Day*, where the screen title is immediately followed by the words: 'Hard-Shirking Man', the puns in *Caught in a Cabaret* are nearly as ferocious.

The film opens with Charlie walking his dog near a pavement fountain tumbling over rocks into a gutter. Charlie gently edges the dog's backside into the stream of water, explaining: 'I have to cool him off. He is built too near the hot pavements'. The explanation fools nobody. When he is asked about the pedigree of the dog, he answers: 'Spitz!' Soon afterwards the dog is caught in a fight with another dog, and Charlie finds himself fighting a bully in defence of Mabel Normand, who invites him to her house for a *tête-à- tête*. Charlie says: 'Certainly, if you have any on ice,' and offers his card which bears armorial bearings with the inscription: *Ad lib moritorium sub rosa* and identifies him as 'Ambassador for Greece, O. T. Axle'. Mabel Normand invites him to her forthcoming garden-party, delighted with her discovery. 'Fancy a real ambassador,' she explains, holding the visiting card to her breast. 'He must be the man all the hotels are named after.' All this is bad enough, and there is worse to come. Charlie arrives late at the garden-party wearing a top-hat. He apologises for his late arrival, saying his Rolls Royce has unfortunately broken down. For a brief moment the whole unhappy mess of puns and facetiousness is jettisoned while Charlie, having led Mabel Normand to a secluded part of the garden, makes frantic love to her. It is a beautiful scene. Charlie takes full advantage of her innocence, grins shyly to himself, rests his elbow on her bosom, throws one leg over her, smiles as he has never smiled before, lights a cigarette, chokes, takes the whole wine-bottle when the servant brings the wine-cups, and finally hurries away with the explanation that 'nothing but the affairs of Greece would take me away from you tonight'. This small scene is magisterially performed, but the extraordinary air of reality which is conjured around the bench where Charlie makes his impassioned declarations of love vanishes when the camera turns to observe the guests at the garden-party. Most of them are freaks. All of them are wildly alarmed by Charlie's behaviour. Only Mabel Normand is charmed. 'Isn't he wonderful,' she comments. 'So full of stagger and swagger.' As a description of Charlie's behaviour the statement is untrue, and about as misleading as the statement that the garden is 'redolent with the perfume of roses and home brew'. We are not to be misled by these heavy verbal intrusions. They reach depths of unhappy inanity which one would have thought unreachable. When Charlie says: 'I'll kick him so hard he'll need shock absorbers in his auto-suggestion,' we know that there is no limit to inanity. But inanity is not comedy.

The comedy is resumed when we discover Charlie at work as an unhappy drudge and waiter in a cheap restaurant. This explains, if we needed any explanation, the references to Greece. Charlie had offended Mabel's suitor, who has the brilliant idea of taking all the guests at the garden-party slumming 'to see the great unwashed'. Providentially they arrive at the restaurant where Charlie is working. They take their places. Charlie, against his wishes, is ordered to serve them. He spills everything he is carrying over the suitor, and accidentally knocks Mabel down. The battle royal begins. Custard pies are thrown, someone fires a gun, everyone is running in all directions, and in the end Charlie finds himself in Mabel's arms. 'I may be only a waiter,' he explains, 'but remember Bismarck was only a herring.'

Caught in a Cabaret was followed immediately by *Caught in the Rain*. Once again we are confronted with the incredible mixture of slapstick and something so quiet, so terrifying that it belongs to genius. Charlie meets a lady in the park, and is delighted with her. He smiles, primps himself, invites her to a park bench, and is thrown into the shrubbery by the irate husband for his pains. In his battered hat, he returns to his hotel so absentmindedly that he is nearly run over. Equally absentmindedly he enters the lady's bedroom, and once more he is thrown out. In the comfort of his own bedroom, fully dressed, he lies under the sheets thumbing his nose at the couple in the next room. He has not bargained with the lady who comes sleepwalking into his room, her arms outstretched like another Lady Macbeth. Charlie is puzzled. He gazes down at her with mingled fear, desire and derision, and as he sits beside her, her hand gropes in his pockets for his wallet. Then the husband finds her, and Charlie is thrown out into the rain and the story ends with the inevitable 'rally' with the cops in full pursuit.

This is the bare bones of the story, conveying nothing of what Laurence Sterne once called 'the vile errantry of the man', his ruined elegance, his gentle promptings and beckonings of the woman even when she is sleepwalking, his total *insouciance* before the spectacle of her thieving hands, for he merely assumes that this is what she would be doing, and calmly removes the wallet the moment she takes hold of it. There is a horror here which goes beyond the horror of *Macbeth*, for the sleepwalker is both wide awake and walking at the same time, and the settings, more terrifying than any Scottish castle, are smeared with the desolate wallpaper, the infinite ugliness and disorder of a cheap lodging-house in Los Angeles. Chaplin knew his lodging-houses. He lived by choice in an obscure rooming house at the western end of the Third Street Tunnel in Los Angeles, which was the nearest thing to the Kennington slums he ever found in America. The operative word in both these films was 'caught'.

The Keystone films possessed a devilish sobriety. In them men acted like drunks when they were cold sober, and by force of acting like sober drunks they endowed themselves with complex reactions. It was the time of the great stone faces, the godlike immobility, the falling bricks, the exaggerated wallops and the immense pratfalls. We talk of the early Keystone comedies as being soundless. They were not. You heard the agonising thwacks of the cops' truncheons, you heard the smack of a custard pie and the crack of a chair-leg on an unoffending head, the clatter of bricks falling and the rush of a hundred boots in pursuit. In all this hurricane of noise you were deafened into sharing the emotions of the protagonists on the screen. You could not think. You were caught up in that perpetual wave perpetually crashing against rock. It was a technique which Hitler employed with surprising effect. As for the emotions of the protagonists, they belonged to two easily defined classes: they were wildly negative or wildly positive. There was Mack Swain, who was a vast monument of exaggerated emotion, and there were brilliant actors like Chester Conklin who concealed all their emotions behind the protective colouring of a walrus moustache. They were deadpan.

The term had originated with the gold-diggers in '49, but it was an oddly revealing word. Webster defines pan as the hollow part of a gunlock which receives the priming, and then goes on to say that it can also mean a hollow depression containing water or mud. The definitions were appropriate. The one thing it did not mean was dead Pan.

The deadpan face was a wonderful invention, and Charlie seems often of a mind to employ it. Yet he rarely does, for the good reason that it would be excessively difficult for him to be a mask. He flirts with it. He will keep his lips still, but the ever-rolling eyes betray him, and so does his unruly hair and the expression of his chin. Even his ears speak. Buster Keaton with his crushed pork-pie hat could keep everything so still that even when he opened his mouth you were not aware that anything had moved. Before Chaplin, war was declared between the deadpan faces and the faces of the freaks: the war which Roscoe Arbuckle fought with Chester Conklin was continued by Hardy in his adventures with Laurel. The war between the freaks and the deadpans was not however entirely convincing. There were no explosions: only the imitated effects of explosions, the shock waves, the smoke (which was really flour) and the flames (which were strips of ribbon rising from an electric fan). We know the garrulous adventures of Laurel and Hardy, but we are only rarely aware of the incandescent spirit of comedy. The hooves of the god do not strike sparks from the earth. When the sparks fly, and only then, do we know we are in the presence of high comedy.

It is worth while to linger a little with the deadpan face, for Charlie employs it at times in the early Keystone comedies and continues to employ it at intervals throughout his life. There is precision in that expression. It hints at subtleties which are beyond us. A man praying will often have that expression, and so will a girl in love. It is a thing of abstractions; and in its hardest and most brutal form you will see it on the faces of conquering generals conscious of the admiration of their audience, while teetering on the edge of the wildest self-applause. Marcellinus Ammianus tells of the young Emperor Constantius II entering Rome in his triumphal chariot to the plaudits of the people, 'his countenance remaining unchanged, while he gazed straight in front of him, looking neither to the left nor to the right, as though his neck were fixed; and like a statue he never moved his head or hands even when the wheels of his chariot shook him, nor was he observed to spit or rub his nose or wipe his mouth'. It is a brilliant picture of the proud man, fit to be put beside St Gregory's description of the man 'who walks with himself along the broad spaces of his thought and silently utters his own praises'. Aristotle, describing the *megalopsychos*, the man of great soul, speaks of his fastidious and unchanging expression. It is part of the aristocratic tradition that emotions should be buried under slip-covers, and when Lord Chesterfield reminded his son that a gentleman should never laugh, he was hinting that a gentleman should never weep as well; by definition a gentleman is deadpan.

This, as we have seen, is precisely what Charlie is not. He is Pan alive, calling upon the earth and heavens to witness that he is alive and kicking. Half bird, half elephant, he lives in a universe which grows, as does Blake's, according to the acts of his imagination and in no other way. He is one of God's elect, but that disturbs him less than his knowledge of the evil of the

world, and the folly of it, yet he goes out to encounter folly with
the divine grace of a Don Quixote. 'He is chasing folly, and he
knows it,' Chaplin said once. 'He is trying to meet the world
bravely, to put up a bluff, and he knows that too.' So he does,
but the game is played unfairly, for he hides up his sleeve an
armament of cards which he can snap upon the table whenever
the eternal poker game goes in his disfavour. Those who
pretended to see him as the little man baffled by the world's
authority forgot the hidden cards, the knowledge that he will
always win.

None of this, of course, is made entirely clear by the Keystone
comedies. We have the advantage of hindsight. The figure of
Charlie was to grow rounded; the sketch became a painting, and
then a sculpture, and then something that walked. The picture
at the beginning of the year was still fuzzy, and there was his
almost insuperable tendency to rail, to grimace, to mock whatever his eyes alighted upon, an attitude which may have arisen
as a result of playing *A Night at an English Music-Hall*, where
he was the pure spirit of mockery and nothing else. There was
tenderness in the short scene at the edge of *His Trysting Place*,
where he knelt in prayer beside an ashcan, and in *Tillie's
Punctured Romance*, which appeared in November 1914, the
tenderness returns in the brief interlude where he makes love to
Marie Dressler while sitting on a high fence, balancing himself
with the delicacy of a drunken tightrope-walker, and those brief
smiles of unalloyed happiness each time he regains his balance
foretell the future of Charlie.

Tillie's Punctured Romance, the first of the feature-length
films in which Charlie appeared, followed a pattern which
possessed classic proportions. It progresses furiously in one
direction, beginning in the country where Charlie runs off with
Marie Dressler, who plays the part of a farm-girl, the daughter
of a rich farmer and the niece of a millionaire. With stolen
money they run to the city, where they both acquire the latest
fashions. From a bum Charlie becomes a toff, from a farm-girl
Marie becomes a lady of fashion. Both have violent tempers, and
they are otherwise ill-matched, and when Charlie finds Mabel
Normand waiting for him in the city, he is prepared to run
away from the preposterously ugly Marie, but the city claims

him, and when Charlie and Mabel innocently enter a restaurant, they find Marie working there as a waitress. They have taken her money. There is no escape. There will be a battle royal, or so it seems, but mercifully Marie faints away, and the two are able to escape. Thereupon we see some extraordinarily realistic shots of Marie's rich uncle, Charles Bennett, climbing in the moutains. The rope breaks. He falls into a snow crevasse, and we see him lying there, stretched out in death, and the film, which has been wandering on the edge of comedy, rarely amusing, suddenly grows sharp and clear. A very dead man is lying there, and the comedy has turned into stark tragedy. The trick has not been used often, but it is a surprisingly successful one, and when Chaplin employed it later in *Carmen*, where the death-scene is unbearably cruel on the audience, he was following a tradition established by the single lingering shot in *Tillie's Punctured Romance* where we see the millionaire stiff and ugly in death.

The millionaire's death changes the fortunes of Marie. She inherits the estate and the precocious hilltop mansion filled with preposterous tapestries, knick-knacks and overgrown vases. Charlie, reading in the newspaper that Marie has inherited the fortune and surmising that she is still unaware of the news, slips away from Mabel and marries her. The marriage ceremony is performed before Marie has time to get her breath back. They celebrate by throwing a party in the hilltop mansion. Mabel comes as an uninvited guest. But the party, which provides an excuse for a sustained chase up and down the stairs and through all the gaudy over-decorated rooms, threatens to blow the film apart by a process akin to the inertia of a centrifugal force. The party, with Marie shooting wildly at Charlie because she has caught him kissing Mabel, is Mack Sennett at his dizzy best, but it is Marie who wins the laurels.

Chaplin's scene comes earlier. He has arrived with Marie on his arm after the wedding. Marie is coy and simpering, and she leans gently on his arm, as gently as any woman can when she weighs twice as much as her husband. Two rows of butlers in full livery, with buckled shoes, knee-breeches and powdered wigs, stand stiffly at attention in the long gallery to greet them. Charlie gazes upon them as he would gaze upon a row of cigar-store Indians. He hangs his hat and cane on them, bawls them out, trips over their feet, flicks cigarette-ash into their faces and has the time of his life parading up and down in front of these stony sentinels of his newly acquired palace; we shall not see such a scene again until Chaplin revived it, with suitable alterations, in *The Great Dictator*. For the rest it is largely Marie Dressler's play. She blazes away with her pistol and her piecrusts, tears up and down the stairs, dances a drunken tango, and when her uncle revives from his snow crevasse and turns her out of her house, she chases Charlie and Mabel all over the seafront and up and down Venice pier. In the end Charlie is left alone, while the two women commiserate with one another, complaining: 'He ain't no good to neither of us.' The statement is not strictly true. He was very good to both of them, but he was kindest to Marie, for he made love to her from a high fence and amused her with his play with flunkeys. These two scenes were memorable for other reasons: they showed the emergence of a sense of style, a talent for sustained invention. Previously, Charlie had been able to invent anything he liked provided the invention did not last more than thirty seconds, and he had never possessed a single style; he is at least three different people in *Laughing Gas*, and his changes of mood in *His Trysting Place* were excessively bewildering. In *Tillie's Punctured Romance* these moods are kept under control.

The last film Chaplin composed for Keystone was *His Prehistoric Past*, where Mack Swain, appearing as Lord Lowbrow, a giant in a bearskin attended by a host of concubines, succeeds at times in stealing Charlie's thunder. The most sustained of Mack Swain's performances occurred in *The Gold Rush* more than ten years later, where he was drowned in furs against an Alaskan winter. Now it is summer, and he wears only sufficient clothes to conceal his modesty. Charlie who has wandered into his prehistoric encampment finds him congenial, and lunges out at the concubines. He does it with *expertise*, with cunning, with as much flamboyance as a man can muster when he wears only a bowler hat and a thin strip of bearskin. It is the world of Pan and the Arcadian forests, and now for a brief interval Charlie is all goat, trembling in the excitement of the chase and sometimes warning himself not to tremble with such evident relish for his quarry. He follows one of these Arcadian

nymphs round a rock – all his slow cunning is manifest in that
pursuit which ends, in the proper manner of a Keystone comedy,
with Mack Swain and Charlie stealthily making their way round
the rock and then meeting, or rather their posteriors meet
Charlie merely lifts his bowler. He is good at maintaining the
civilities in the age of the dinosaurs. When Lord Lowbrow tells
a joke, Charlie digs him in the ribs with a battle-axe. On the
whole the battle-axe is rather too much in evidence; we do not
want to be clubbed into laughing. Yet the style is there, without
archness, and his huge thirst for life is at once caricatured and
underscored when he calmly walks over a carpet of Mack Swain's
women. He walks on them with gentleness, as though he did it
every day of his life, with the faintest of apologetic shrugs of the
shoulders. And in the end, when he wakes up from the dream,
the memory of Arcadia is so sharp that there are tears in his
eyes. But it was not a dream. To Chaplin's astonishment, Charlie
had become a thing of flesh and blood.

CHAPTER X

THE TRAGIC MASK

W H E N Chaplin left Keystone at the end of the year and joined the Essanay Company in Chicago his technique was already worked out. The bones were there; he could now clothe them in flesh, add trimmings and decorations, give himself a wider canvas. Mack Sennett had always insisted on an absence of studio props; he would use a real road and a real park, and care not a fig for the lighting. With the Essanay films we are made aware of props, of cardboard rooms, of careful planning. The tempo slows down, the bar room fights are rare, and the devil of self-consciousness occasionally enters the picture. Instead of thirty-five pictures a year, Chaplin performed in fourteen pictures in nearly as many months.

Attempts have been made to distinguish between the Keystone, Essanay and Mutual periods, very much as art critics distinguish between the blue and pink periods of Picasso, but in fact there were no sudden changes of technique, no furious discoveries, no quiet emergence of pathos or tenderness, for all these were there from the beginning. All that we can discern is an increase in depth, a sustained effort to broaden the extent of comedy and the devil of self-consciousness growing apace, until in *Monsieur Verdoux* self-consciousness drove the actor to the wall and the brilliance of the performance derived as much from desperation as from the natural ability of the born clown.

Self-consciousness was a problem to be grappled with, and Chaplin attacked it in his own way. About this time in a discussion on the nature of comedy he said:

Comedy is a thing which has developed up to a certain point, retrograded and come back to that point again. It has

125

never progressed. We think it has developed all through the
ages. We get this illusion of its development from its fluctua-
tions, its characteristics as it has been preferred by the various
generations and nationalities. The comedy that amuses the
world today is identical with that which brought laughter to
the Babylonians, the Greeks and the Romans. Every age in
history is eaten up by the egotism of men. Every age thinks
that the world has reached the highest point in the development in itself. That is because the man of this age sees himself
at the centre of the picture.

I have a theory that comedy increases in refinement in
inverse proportion to the refinement of the world in which
it appears. I mean that the more intellectual the world is, the
more boisterous will be the successful comedy of that world.
Look for example at the poor misshapen jester of the middle
ages, that 'end man in the world's minstrel show'. There he
is, clever and calculated, surrounded by the evidence of
power and wealth, himself powerless and poverty-stricken,
the jester who played on words and mimicked the great
people of the court, and poured scorn on those who were out
of favour with the King.

It was a good theory, but it left some ragged ends. There are
no yardsticks by which comedy and refinement can be measured;
there is no way of knowing for certain whether the Babylonians
laughed at the same jokes we laugh at; and the implied theory that
boisterous comedy will compensate for an over-intellectualised
world, that there is always a kind of balance between comedy
and refinement, is incapable of proof, and there is some reason
for believing it to be untrue. During the reign of Tiberius
Caesar the great mime of the time came on the stage, imitated
Caesar, and suddenly spewed blood from his mouth. More actors
came on the stage and spewed blood, with the result that the
whole stage was swimming in blood. This was taken by Caesar
as a deliberate pantomiming of his own death. Apparently it was
hilariously funny. The jester was mocking the King, and we
imagine that he skidded on the blood and fell flat on his face in
it and swam in it, and the audience applauded. This joke,
typical of the time, occurred during a period which might be

regarded as refined; certainly the extent and wealth of the Roman Empire were never greater. The joke could be described as boisterous, but it was not comic; nor is there any reason to believe that the clown as we know him today existed in ancient Europe. His descent must be traced through the gods, by way of Pan and Hercules, and though the minor gods were freely acted on the stage, their purpose was to guy the other gods; the purpose of the clown is to guy the whole world of men, and at the same time to enrich them with the gifts he brings. Unlike the humorist or the comic, the clown bears the weight of the world's destiny and walks within the inner circle where great and terrifying decisions are made and things eternal weigh down his soul. Dante's second circle is his habitation; in its shady pathways he knows each stone of the road. As for the humorist and the comic they are all-too-human. They gag or tell funny stories. The tremendous things are not for them. They enchant us with tales from way back, tell stories in dialect, sing and dance, or they are smart at repartee. They have no god-like strength in them, nor have they the bitterness of the court jester, that 'end man in the world's minstrel show' who scorns the poor though he is poverty-stricken, and scorns the King as well, though the King grants him favours.

At his best Charlie is the pure clown; at his worst he is gagman, comedian, humorist, bore. In *His New Job*, the first film produced for Essanay, he is all these. Charlie is a stagehand for the Lockstone Studio, which must be some kind of pun on Henry Lehrman's L-Ko, or Lehrman-Knockout Studio. He is not a very efficient stagehand. He argues with his assistant, thrusts the mop into his face, trips over everything. The male lead in a film to be called *The King's Ransom* is late. Charlie is invited to take the part. Dressed up in a hussar's costume, the coat tails reaching to the ground, the embroidered coat five sizes too large for him, wearing an enormous shako, looking like a monkey in tails, Charlie abandons himself to a life of mayhem. While the cameraman turns the crank, the director orders him to escort the queen up the stairway. Charlie treads on her hem, and half her skirt falls away. Interrupted in a crap game behind a screen, he lunges out with his prop sword through the curtain. The film is played fast, and this prevents it from being a complete disaster.

The Jitney Elopement which followed was hardly better, though it opens with a scene which was later to become classic – Charlie in the street twirling a daffodil as he serenades his beloved in a Spanish balcony. She drops a note, declaring her love and inviting him into the house. At the same time he learns he must impersonate Count Chloride de Lime, the suitor her father is expecting. Charlie impersonates the count and receives a royal welcome and is invited to dine, but someone has sprinkled pepper in the dinner and soon they are all coughing, and then the real Chloride de Lime arrives and the trouble starts. Eventually the count succeeds in enticing the girl into his car. Charlie gives chase, and they all come to an abrupt halt near a park, where Charlie manifests his talents for horseplay. By this time the story has become farce. Policemen pop unaccountably out of the bushes, give chase, disappear, return from the other side of the stage and pounce on Chloride de Lime to Charlie's enormous amusement. Only once does Charlie show his characteristic delicacy. This is when he feels a great need to light a cigarette. With the utmost care he extracts cigarette paper and tobacco, rolls the tobacco neatly into the paper, puts the finished cigarette to his lips and lights it, but what he lights is only the paper, for the tobacco has dribbled out. Charlie's insouciance as he accomplishes the feat of lighting a cigarette that isn't there is wonderful, but it has nothing to do with the story and could have been inserted at any place he pleased. The first five Essanays are shapeless and repetitious. With *The Tramp* Charlie comes into his own.

Chaplin has recounted how *The Tramp* came about. Quite accidentally he met a hobo in San Francisco. The man was down and out, hungry and thirsty. Chaplin offered him food and drink, and asked which he would like to have first.

'Why,' the man said, 'if I am hungry enough, I can eat grass. But what am I going to do for this thirst of mine? You know what water does to iron? Well, try to think what it will do for your insides?'

Chaplin took him into the bar room for a drink and some food, and suddenly the man began to talk of his own irresponsible joy in living the life of a hobo. It was life lived to the uttermost. You saw the countryside, you travelled in exclusive freight-trains, you were greeted by the kindliness of farmers. Chaplin was

Sunnyside, 1919

The Kid, 1921

delighted with the man, with his gestures, his expressions, his good talk. 'He was rather surprised when we parted, because I thanked him so much,' Chaplin said later. 'But he had given me a good deal more than I had given him, though he didn't know it.'

The two-reel comedy was completed in three weeks. Out of the hobo's wanderings in the countryside, his life on the farm, and an imaginary girl who befriends him the comedy was constructed. Chaplin was determined upon perfection. In *The Jitney Elopement* the direction had gone to pieces; this time Chaplin was determined that all the actors should know their parts. Some of the minor situations were rehearsed fifty times. They spent hours working on problems like the exact weight of a bag of meal falling on a man's head, and exactly how it should fall. A little thing like the twist of a foot on a ladder might be the work of a whole day. The result was a masterpiece. He simply told the story of the tramp hobbling in the countryside. He comes upon some thieves, bundles them up and reduces the fiery farmer to tears of gratitude. Wounded in the struggle with the thieves, Charlie is looked after by the farmer's daughter. He is all hope and gaiety. He never expected that anyone could be so kind to him. He cavorts about the farm, doing all the work, and he works with incomparable grace, even when he is pumping the cow by employing the tail as a handle. He makes outrageous love to the girl and pretends not to be aware that she has another suitor. Such things cannot be! He not only refuses to believe in the presence of the suitor, but he cavalierly dismisses the thoughts of all suitors from his mind. Destiny would never play such a cavalier trick. Finally, the existence of the suitor becomes only too evident, Charlie wraps up his little bundle, writes a sad note and goes quietly on his way. When we last see him he is walking sorrowfully down an empty road with the bundle on his shoulder, and the sorrow is unbearable until he suddenly takes it into his head to do a little dance, square his shoulders and go dancing to the horizon.

This was the first of the films to possess a rounded story, the first to include the long road leading nowhere, the first to demonstrate the tenderness of Charlie to women. Previously he had played with them, and if sometimes he had gazed at them with the consummate eagerness of a soulful puppy, this

E

was as much as one could demand. Slapstick, too great an entanglement with props, a wit so keen that it tore the film apart, all these were dangers he had to contend with. None of the Keystone comedies was better than his first wonderful appearance during the kid auto races. There were hints towards another dimension – the love scene in *Caught in a Cabaret*, the nightmarish scenes in *Caught in the Rain* and *The Face on the Bar Room Floor*, a hundred other minor miracles. In *The Tramp* Charlie began to perform his greatest miracle: out of the water of comedy he would produce the wine of undiluted joy.

So it was in *The Tramp*; so it was again in *Work* (which became more widely known as *The Paperhanger*), *The Bank*, *Shanghaied*, *A Night at the Show*, *Carmen*, and that strange incoherent piece called *Triple Trouble*, a title which indicated only too obviously that three separate comedies, each unfinished, had somehow been strung together into a single comedy, which made no sense at all, though it contained some passages of the most consummate artistry.

Work is only incidentally about work; it has far more to do with the delirious joys of a paperhanger. The idea of the opening scene came to Chaplin when he saw a painter's assistant pushing a two-wheeled barrow loaded with material up a hill, while the weight of the barrow kept pulling him into the air and then letting him down again, so that he was carried in a half-circle over his barrow-wheel and the contents were all spilled out on the road. It was not funny for the painter's assistant; it was laughable for the onlookers; and it provided the needed curtain scene with which Chaplin has nearly always begun his films, as though he felt an overriding desire to set a mood by some comic business which has little or nothing to do with the ensuing comedy.

The opening of *Work* belongs to the lunatic heights of Charlie's imagination. Nothing could be simpler. There is Charlie, the patient work-horse, between the thin shafts of the paperhanger's cart, which is piled high with buckets, brooms and a particularly nauseating ladder. Seated among all these things, like an emperor on his throne, is the boss, who flicks a whip, shouts out orders, pays not the least attention to Charlie's difficulties when the weight of the cart brings him flying into the air. A tramcar

comes out of nowhere and narrowly misses them. Charlie is
upbraided by the boss, mops his face with a handkerchief and
once more goes shooting into the air. When we see him again
he is climbing a hill inclined at forty-five degrees. Uncomplain-
ing as an ant, Charlie is forever sliding back, digging in, moving
forward three paces to retreat ten paces. Some of these trick
shots are taken in silhouette, and because the whole scene is then
reduced to its simplest proportions, they are remarkably effective: you can hear Charlie's grunting as he labours in his toil.
He lives in the world of Samson, eyeless at Gaza, blind to
everything except his own suffering, and we no longer laugh;
we merely admire his grace as he leaps up and down between
the shafts, for ever incapable of subduing the mechanical monster
of buckets and pails and wheels behind him. So he remains on the
hill for ever; and if, during the next shots we see him already at
the top of the hill, while someone else, a friend of the boss's,
crawls on to the cart, this is merely a trick performed by the
cameras for our benefit: one cannot watch those cavortings
between the shafts for ever.

At the gates of the house where the wallpaper is to be
solemnly unwrapped and placed on the wall, Charlie's difficulties
begin. Somehow he must escape from the shafts, disentangle
himself from these monsters. The beast gives one further grunt,
the whole edifice of buckets and ladders falls down – the ladder
falls on to Charlie's shoulders and neatly imprisons him – and
the boss leaves Charlie to struggle as best he can with the
untamable monster.

The house is a small replica of the hilltop mansion in *Tillie's
Punctured Romance*. It has nothing to commend it except the
grotesque frivolity of the taste of its owner. There are bear-rugs,
bronze heroic statues of St George, the inevitable cast of
Pomona and Apollo on the upright piano. A nude performs the
office of support for a lampshade. Weary beyond endurance,
Charlie finds comfort in playing with the shade. He removes the
shade, leers at the nude, quickly replaces the shade when he
finds someone looking, and he is still wholly immersed in contemplating the shade when the paperhanger orders him to set to
work. A servant enters, sweeps up all the valuables in the room
and places them in a safe. Charlie gathers his own valuables,

contemplates them avidly and decides to hang them with safety-pins on his trousers. In this way he can keep an eye on them. But the nude distracts him. A pretty servant-girl is sitting on the stairs. Seeing her, Charlie decides to wiggle the shade a little less voluptuously, and then, forgetting her or in the overwhelming desire to attract her attention, he wiggles it lustily. Meanwhile the decks are cleared, all the preparations for the paperhanging are over, and the boss merely sits down at the piano and diverts himself with the young wife, whose appearance throughout the film provides an inexplicable commentary on the necessity of complicating a plot which will become far too complicated to be followed with any exactitude. The work of paperhanging at last begins.

The boss, who bears an unhappy resemblance to Flaubert, becomes the prey of Charlie's wildest fancies. Charlie trips him up, catches him on the head with a board, and knocks him clean out with a bucket of paste when the servant-girl enters the room and Charlie's attention is distracted. Paste is everywhere. Charlie has one horrified glance at the girl and then throws water all over the boss in the hope of removing the great smears of paste in which he is choking. The scene where Charlie frantically attempts at the same time to revive the boss and to drown him is accomplished with wonderful finesse, and the boss, sitting on the floor, only his eyes visible, looking for all the world like a more robust image of Charlie himself, shaking water and paste out of his ears and nose, is an image of the slap-stick tradition at its best. Charlie's giggling ineptitude as he throws the buckets of water on his enemy, the way he slips in the puddles and leers at his own efforts, his complaisant and humble devotion to the task of cleaning up the mess while at the same time further increasing it belong to high comedy; and the mood, once established, is maintained through the three following scenes.

We see Charlie at work alone. All the ambiguities which result from concerted effort are put away. Charlie will paper the wall by his own unaided efforts. No one shall interfere. He calmly surveys a roll of paper, unwinds it, jabs it with paste, sticks it on the wall. Part of the paper sticks to his hand. In an effort to disentangle himself he manages to wrap himself up in the wallpaper. The maid-servant enters at the moment when he is being nearly choked by the paper which fastens itself in soft coils all over him, a boa-constrictor in no mood for surrender. At this moment the scene ends, and when we see Charlie again he is sitting on the bed beside the maid-servant, dangling a paste-brush. The scene is joyously bawdy. The significance of the paste-brush is never obscured. Charlie sits there, his face a mask, gazing dumbly in front of him. Evidently he has been rebuffed. When he turns towards her again his mind is made up. He will make one last determined effort to win her. He jabs the air disconsolately with the brush, and then, like wine poured into an empty skin, the face assumes a wonderful array of meanings. Words, desperate pleas, these are unnecessary; the face tells all. It was said of Garrick that he had only to put his head between two folding doors in front of an audience for a few minutes for everyone to be aware of high drama. In the course of those brief minutes Garrick's expression would change successively from wild delight to temperate pleasure, and then to tranquillity and surprise and blank astonishment and fear and horror. The drama was played before your eyes. There were no words, but the stage (the little gap between the door) was crowded. So it is in the scene where Charlie makes impassioned love to the maid, beginning with wistful pleadings, gentle admonitions, encouraging sighs, then drawing closer to her, imagining assent only to find that his imagination cannot tolerate her assent; he must plead his case with abandon; he must dare himself to perform feats of love which will shake her soul. He moves closer to her. He very nearly jabs her with the paste-brush. He is all fire. He tells her, without any use of words, the most intimate things about himself, about this flowering of his love for her, and at the moment when she seems about to surrender, she stands up and strides out of the room. Charlie returns to his wall, to the venomous little scraps of wallpaper which refuse to adhere to anything except his brush, or to his clothes, and in his fury he tears the wallpaper into little pieces.

The best is now over. Slapstick takes command the moment the wife's lover appears with flowers, mounts the over-decorated staircase and charges to greet the beloved. He is soon daubed with paste. In no time the whole house is an inferno of paste.

Alone with his dripping brush Charlie faces the world, a lion at bay, and when everybody is milling around, when every permutation and combination of chance meeting has been completed, when everyone is smeared with paste, when the boss has fallen into the bath and the maid is hysterical, someone fires a gun and the stove explodes, and the last we see of Charlie is the impish face emerging, wreathed with smiles, out of the stove. He makes one terrifying leer of triumph, and then, when someone throws a lump of plaster at him, he disappears beneath the stove-grating like a god vanishing below the surface of the waves.

Work belongs to the main canon of Chaplin's films. With the exception of the concluding passages of slapstick it explores with subtle irrelevance the whole contour of Charlie. We see him at play, at work, in love and in the full panoply of his rage, his lust for action. Nothing in *The Tramp* ever quite approached this quiet mastery of the materials. When Charlie exercises the tail of a cow, thinking in some strange way that it serves the purpose of a pump and a teat, we are aware of a conscious manipulation of incident. Such things are invented. Nothing in *Work* is invented, except perhaps the last apotheosis of Charlie as he appears through the stove-grating against a ruined landscape, grinning devilishly, and there it is not the devilish grin nor the stove-grating which is invented – what he has invented is the particular relevance of the incident in a story about a paper-hanger's assistant. It has nothing to do with the story. It could come at the end of any of these films, and in fact when *Triple Trouble* was put together out of existing odds and ends, the same explosions, the same rain of plaster, the same stove and the same Charlie were introduced to provide an ending to the film. It is the classic ending. In a sense it is the ending of all Charlie's films, and we shall see the same look of mingled triumph and awareness of disaster at the end of *The Kid, City Lights* and at least twenty other films, and if sometimes Charlie prefers not to show his face but turns his back in contempt upon the audience and the world, we are not misled; on his face, as the curtain falls, there must be the expression of an angel who has fallen from a cloud and is still dazed by his fall.

Work, with its classic use of the paste-brush, was also the most bawdy of all Chaplin's comedies. In other films Charlie will hint at bawdiness, and the hint is enough. The most wonderful passages in the two-reeler are concerned with his desperate encounter with the maid on the bed, where the utmost tenderness is combined with the utmost bawdry. Intoxicating prospects open out. Deliberate and unalloyed obscenity has very little to commend it, but obscenity transformed into poetry is rare, desirable and only too difficult to achieve, though Shakespeare was an accomplished master. Schoolgirls reading *Romeo and Juliet* are usually unaware of the multitudinous obscenities with which the lovers address one another, but Elizabethan audiences were only too well aware of these poetic jests, this play with the generation of the world's fruit and flowers. And this is as it should be. Obscenity made poetry is a proper part of our lives. We do not love a woman the less because she assumes hilarious postures in bed; we know that in her eyes we are assuming equally hilarious postures, and we hope we are equally lovable. So it is in *Work* where the very name of the comedy is more appropriate to the delicate handling of the paste-brush than to the trials of a paperhanger caught between the shafts. With what elegance, what tortured frivolity, what cunning he wields his brush! We knew, and guessed long ago, that the red-hot pokers and inflated sausage-shaped balloons of the pantomime descended from the raw and scarlet phalluses, three feet long, worn by the comedians on the Attic stage. We thought them indecorous. Perhaps they were; but in the hands of a genius with what gentle insistence can they be made to perform their dance. Perhaps, after all, the Athenians were not so indecorous as we thought.

But if *Work* is important for its rejoicing in love, it was important for other reasons. That love scene is a thing to ponder, to see again and again. Here, for the first time there emerges the tragic mask in its full splendour. When the maid rejects Charlie and he turns away to contemplate a wall littered with scraps of paper, all of different sizes, reaching from the door to the bed, all of them coiling away from the wall, we become aware that the wall resembles the noughts and crosses he inscribed madly on the floor in *The Face on the Bar Room Floor*. The horror of emptiness and the emptiness of horror are both revealed. Here Charlie is at his last gasp. He can suffer no more. Like the clown in *He Who Gets Slapped*, Charlie has received his 'fifty-two slaps a day, all of them of crystal purity', and beyond these there is nothing: nothing to be suffered, nothing to be lost, nothing to gain. But as we are told so often by those who have never suffered, it is darkest before the dawn, the vision of God follows 'the dark night of the soul', out of the depths come the soaring hopes. Sometimes they do. With Charlie, when grief has penetrated so deep, there is only one way of escape: he escapes into a tornado of action, splashing everybody with that miraculous brush which never has to be dipped into the paste-bucket, but is replenished the moment he has daubed the paste on someone's protesting face.

The love scene and its final conclusions should be taken as a text for how a love scene is played by a consummate actor. The hesitations of the lover, the way his mind works by aposiopesis, his incalculable hesitations and mental sleights of hand are admirably depicted. The thin line between the wildest joy and the most unutterable grief are explored. 'I laugh till I cry,' wrote Laurence Sterne in one of his letters, 'and in some tender moments *cry till I laugh.*' It is that world which is explored, with an enviable matter-of-factness and a certain disdain for easy solutions, but it is necessary to insist that they are tears of the wildest grief and the laughter of the wildest joy, and the whole scene is played without forcing a note. Anyone who has carefully observed a love scene in a modern film is usually made aware of the absence of the essential quality which the director intended to depict – love. In *Work* the quality of love is frighteningly apparent.

Here it is necessary to make a distinction. We are accustomed to regard the early Chaplin comedies as dated. We speak of their abominable lighting, their lack of structure, the impossible situations in which Charlie finds himself. All this is true enough, though the defective lighting proves to be an advantage, the lack of structure is essential to the comedy and the situations are impossible only in the sense that they are possible to no one except Charlie. He is talking about eternal truths, or rather he is being silent in a hundred languages about eternal truths. He speaks of love, and it is real love. He speaks of joy, and it is real joy. He speaks of grief, and it is the kind that can find consolation only in miracles. He is no comedian or tragedian: he sees the world as comedy and tragedy at once, instantaneously both. There is a moment in *King Lear* which may be considered the highest point ever reached by the English drama. It occurs when the raging King stumbles into the presence of Kent, Edgar and Albany while bearing Cordelia in his arms. 'I know when one is dead, and when one lives,' Lear declaims. 'She's dead as earth. Lend me a looking-glass.' He holds the mirror over her mouth, and there follows an intolerable pause weighty with mortality; then one by one, in three short lyrical phrases, Kent, Edgar and Albany startle us with poetry which possesses the purity of unexpected perfection:

> *Is this the promis'd end?*
> *Or image of that horror?*
> *Fall, and cease!*

That is all; and it more than enough, more than we can bear, and when we ask ourselves what it means we realise that 'promis'd end' can only refer to the Day of Judgment, and the last line spoken by Albany can refer only to the 'dissolution of all the bonds that bind us'. Now listen to poor mad Miss Flite as she contends with the unpaid rent and the avarice of lawyers in *Dombey and Sons.* She says: 'I expect a judgment. Shortly. On the Day of Judgment.' Isn't this the same horror, the same perception of horror, stated more obliquely, and with a kind of desolate wit, the wit of one who refuses to be intimidated, who refuses to bend? Or compare Hamlet's 'To be or not to be' soliloquy with Sam Weller's resolute attempt to prove 'the great principle that crumpets wos wholesome':

'How many crumpets, at a sittin', do you think 'ud kill me off at once?' said the patient. 'I don't know,' says the doctor. 'Do you think half-a-crown's worth 'ud do it?' says the patient. 'I think it might,' says the doctor. 'Three shillin's' worth 'ud be sure to do it I s'pose?' says the patient. 'Certainly,' says the doctor. 'Wery good,' says the patient, 'goodnight.' Next mornin' he gets up, has a fire lit, orders in three shillin's worth o' crumpets, toasts 'em all, eats 'em all, and blows his brains out.

This is, of course, unexplored territory, and there is no certainty that we will ever be able to explore it adequately, yet on this territory we live and breathe and have our being. On this territory the clowns throw sometimes a greater light than the tragic actors, and here the mad Miss Flite and the unknown patient with the fondness for crumpets march together with Hamlet and the courtiers of King Lear.

The great passages in the tragic comedy of Charlie belong to poetry, and should be regarded as poetry.

There is poetry and to spare in *The Bank*, which followed shortly after *Work*. The love passages, the moments of dream and resignation and joy, are here diluted, perhaps because the marble bank itself, with its mad manager, its enormous vault, its continual comings and goings, tends to overshadow the clown. Here Chaplin was faced on another level with the same problem he contended with in *The Great Dictator*. You cannot parody a large city bank, for however much you exaggerate its inanity, it is still remarkably like a bank, with its pompous managers, its queues of eager worshippers, its cages which resemble prisons where the prisoners disburse life and death, and the vault which provides the sacramental mystery, taking the place of an altar, unhallowed but nevertheless veiled. Charlie does the best he can.

He enters the bank, having unwound himself from the revolving door, with a sense of his own importance. He marches grandly to the vault and when he has reached it he examines his cuffs at intervals to remind himself of the complicated combinations. On the outside of the vault there is a wheel, like a ship's wheel, which he spins with *brio*. He is evidently the bank manager who has spent the weekend on his yacht. But as soon as the immense vault opens, he simply hangs up his coat and from somewhere in the dark recess of the vault he brings out a bucket, and inside the bucket is his coat and his office cap. The operation has evidently taken a long time, for when he entered the bank it was nearly empty and when he returns with his mop and pail it is crowded, so crowded indeed that he is able to slop everyone in sight, and the wet mop he holds over his shoulders swipes the bank manager and his client in the face, and goes on blissfully swiping people in the face, and there are puddles everywhere, and Charlie steps on the client's top-hat, and every conceivable permutation and combination arising from a wet mop's attacks on personal dignity are investigated, and even then he has not done with it, for the last drop must be squeezed out. This last drop falls when Charlie is thrown out of the main building and finds himself alone with another janitor, whereupon he calmly arranges that water from the mop should spill into the other janitor's tea. All this is excellent folly; it is not comedy. Charlie is merely displaying some of the things he can do with a mop. The mop is registered in our minds as something indissolubly connected with Charlie. In the end, when Charlie wakes up from his dream and drowsily kisses the mop, we shall have our reward, but not till then.

The uses of mops are limited, and soon the mop is abandoned for some delightful play with a wastepaper basket. As we have seen, Charlie is in his element with garbage cans; he is only a little less in his element with wastepaper baskets. Wastepaper provokes the devil in him. The other janitor, beautifully played by Billy Armstrong, has carefully swept vast quantities of loose paper away just outside the office which Charlie has been ordered to sweep up. Charlie has no real desire to sweep the office up. He toys with the little pieces that lie about, gently entices them into the basket, surveys them with anguish and seems to be waiting for them to jump in the basket of their own accord. This they refuse to do, and finally Charlie sweeps them all out into the hallway. Billy Armstrong, pushing one white wave of paper away, is confronted with the spectacle of another wave following on his heels. Finally all the paper is swept back into the original office, and when the bank manager complains, Charlie simply turns on the electric fan. Then the paper is everywhere, and all we see of Charlie is a grinning face in a wild rain of paper.

So far Charlie is seen to be playing with the utmost elegance as a funny man. We are even amused when the two janitors' pails get stuck together and Charlie offers to fight Billy. This he does in characteristic fashion, for he removes his coat, hands it to Billy who quietly accepts the privilege of holding it, and is surprised when Charlie knocks him on the jaw. But all this is preliminary fencing. The real drama is concerned with the

cashier's tie. In the stenographer's little cubbyhole of an office
Charlie comes upon a birthday parcel, and a little note reading:
To Charles with love from Edna. Charlie has always loved Edna
from a distance. He gazes at the parcel with an expression of
rapturous delight. He is so delighted that he starts to spin the
handle of the hand-press and he only stops spinning when one of
his hands becomes dreadfully mangled. He blows a tragic kiss
towards her typewriter, assumes the postures of a lover, inflates
his chest with a quiet pride, and then steals out of her office to
gather (God knows where from) some roses for her. He places
them on her typewriter and kisses the keys, and adds a note: *To
Edna with love from Charles.* Deliriously happy, he is next seen
in the company of a preoccupied bond salesman. Charlie feels his
pulse, orders him to stick out his tongue and then proceeds to
moisten a stamp for a letter. The letter is too large to be put into
the mailbox, and so Charlie simply tears the letter up into little
pieces. Satisfied with himself, he goes to see what Edna is doing.
She is giving the birthday present to one of the cashiers, a thin
balding young man who possesses no presence, no gift for
comedy. Edna tells him about the roses she found on her typewriter. The cashier denies that he gave them to her. Then who is
the donor? There can be only one explanation, and when Edna
returns to her office she calmly throws the flowers and the little
note into the wastepaper basket – that infallible wastepaper
basket which receives all human joys and sorrows. When Edna
leaves the room, Charlie tiptoes in, removes the flowers, buries
them under his coat and then pauses. Once more we see the mask
of tragedy, such a mask as an Athenian sculptor might have
conceived, a thing that snaps the heartstrings, dreadful to contemplate. This is not a man suffering, nor an actor mimicking;
this is Pan at the moment of the terrible delirium, the moment
before he shrieks, in his rage of love and grief. Wandering away
Charlie sees the cashier prinking himself with his new tie. He
looks on with contempt, smiling his odd bewildered smile, then
he runs off to the corner where the other janitor is similarly
prinking himself. Charlie gazes at the flowers, as one might gaze
at one's own bleeding heart. It occurs to him that they might
find their home in the ashcan.

The bank has now closed, and Charlie rests wearily on a

bench. The bank president is still at work. The time has come
for the cashier and Edna to take the day's takings to the safe.
Under the marble stairs the thugs are waiting. The cashier and
Edna smile at one another in the blissful awakening of their only
too tawdry love. Charlie looks on. There is nothing he can do,
nothing he cares to do, and then the thugs emerge from their
hiding place, throw themselves on Edna, gag her, force her into
the safe which they make her open, while the cashier takes to his
heels. Soon the thugs have the whole bank at their mercy. They
have not counted on Charlie. Alone he confronts them. He
releases Edna, wallops one of the thugs with a sack of gold, goes
like a whirlwind through the marble halls of the bank, kicking,
shoving, blundering his way to victory. The bank president is
menaced by the thugs. Charlie storms into the bank president's
office. He is Walter Mitty, all hero, seven times larger than life.
No head is raised, but he must smack it down. The police come,
and from his hiding place under the president's desk the cowardly
cashier emerges like a tamed octopus, all legs and saucer eyes,
and Charlie mocks at him – 'Those things I have done, thou
couldst have done.' It is the time for the *dénouement*. Charlie
removes the flowers from inside his coat, those flowers which
had been his token of victory, and now he gazes at them, lets
them drop gently on the floor, unable to see them any more, his
eyes brimming with tears. Edna picks them up and puts her
head against his shoulder. It is a moment of the utmost poignancy,
Charlie and Edna coming together at last, and it hardly matters
that the cashier is being removed by the police: this is not the
victory desired by the lovers. Then very slowly Charlie turns to
kiss the beloved. At that moment he wakes up, and finds himself
kissing the mop, and there in front of him are Edna and Charles
coyly kissing one another. Charlie rises, kicks the flowers away
with the back of his sausage-shaped boots, and goes – nowhere.

Such is the outline of the story, and even from the outline it
should be clear that the whole gamut of comedy from farce to the
highest reaches of the comic spirit are explored. The film has
become the vehicle of all Chaplin's astonishing gifts. When he is
not on the screen, the film dies. The poet Nonnus, who wrote at
the time of Theodosius, speaks of 'the gestures that are language,
the hands that are mouths, the fingers that are voices'. So it is in

The Bank. The dexterity by which Charlie conveys words that
are in no known vocabulary and cannot be spoken, the way he
speaks with the inclination of his little finger, his amazing sense
of the charity of the space in which he wanders, how all things aid
and abet him, his luminous face, perpetually alive while everything around him is touched with decay, these are beyond
criticism. There is a scene in *The Tramp* where the hobo gazes
through the window of a cheap restaurant at a fat man being
served a huge steak. The hobo has forgotten the taste of a steak,
but watching the fat man he subtly imitates the movements of
the man. He does not do this broadly. He does not lift up imaginary
forks and knives to his mouth. He makes the minute gestures,
and all the time he yearns towards the steak, and there comes
from the corner of his mouth a little stream of saliva. This is not
great art, thought Charlie performs admirably. But imagine that
the steak gives way to something infinitely more valuable – the
secret of the universe, whatever is most desirable, a girl, or
simply an understanding of life. Imagine that he desires this
with all the powers of his soul, and knows that the desire will
never be fulfilled, and yet finds himself compelled to yearn for
these things against all the obstacles that the world sets before
him. Then imagine that by continually adoring these things
which are beyond one's reach, as a nun perpetually adores the
body of Christ, a vision is given to him, no more than a blinding
flash, the lightning-lit landscape of heaven lying before him: such
is the expression on his face. We shall see it many times, but it
is never quite the same. Charlie has known heaven, and therefore
his fall is greater. When he is rejected by Edna, when he stands
outside her door shuddering with the violence of rejection, when
he recognises the mop as a mop, when he sees the world as it is
in all its insane complications, a world where there is no joy and
little comfort, he has come to the end and can go no further – and
at this moment the miracle occurs, for he *does* go further – there
is always the little goat-like skip, which is as much a sign of his
authority as the flowers which he wears against his heart,
buttoned up under the janitor's uniform.

  The Bank was followed by *Shanghaied* and *A Night at the
Show. Shanghaied* is farce, and *A Night at the Show* is a careful
recapitulation of the act which brought him into prominence

when he was a member of Fred Karno's troupe. There is very little to be said about *Shanghaied* except that it maintains a precarious balance on a lunatic tightrope. Charlie is offered three dollars if he will help the ship's captain get three men on board. He is given a mallet, squats in a tub and hits the three men over the head, and for good measure he hits the captain. Finally, Charlie is also hit over the head, and finds himself appointed assistant to the cook, with the onerous task of seeing that everyone is fed. The best scenes occur when Charlie succeeds magnificently in keeping his balance while the ship teeters from side to side. He carries his trays with superb aplomb, slides backwards and forwards across the deck, fools with pieces of soap which are mistaken for pastry, and dances a hornpipe with a mop. He places the plates on the table, but they slide across the whole length of the ship and he neatly catches them when they return. It is, of course, the trapeze-like world he has known from the beginning, and he shows not the least signs of astonishment until he discovers that there is dynamite on board – the captain intends to blow up the ship for the insurance money by means of a time fuse. He also discovers that the shipowner's daughter is a stowaway. There is some mild lunacy in the hold where Charlie, covered in flour, pretends to be a ghost and frightens everyone, and Edna is equally frightening in her ghostly sackcloth. The captain, who has no idea that Edna is on board, sets light to the fuse, and the shipowner, who has only just learnt that his daughter is on the ship, arrives in a fast motorboat at the moment that Charlie throws the dynamite overboard. There is one magnificently ironic moment at the end when he finds himself with the shipowner on the motorboat and declares that he has nothing left to live for, he will commit suicide; and so he promptly jumps off the boat, being careful however to pinch his nose, and he shoots up on the other side of the boat and kicks the shipowner off. But this is small beer. Charlie plays the rôles given to him with charm and spirit, but he is not playing the parts with an air of desperation or with any intention of employing his gifts to the uttermost. In *A Night at the Show* he employs a good half of his gifts – the more savage half.

The curtain-raiser describes the arrival of the fat lady at the box-office and the emergence of Charlie from behind a heroic plaster nude in the courtyard of the vaudeville show. Charlie is dressed like a toff, with an insolent sneer on his face and an air of jaded indifference to the world around him. There is no swagger in him. He is eaten up with contempt for the human race; he will, if he can, make everyone suffer. In all this he is the complete opposite of Rowdy, a guttersnipe in the gallery who wears baggy trousers and a walrus moustache. Both parts are played by Chaplin. The honours go to Mr Rowdy, who has only to appear on the screen, deliriously impatient with the performers on the stage, to evoke a sense of warm human-heartedness. But Mr Pest, in the orchestra stalls, is the cold precision machine of destruction. Unfortunately we see comparatively little of Rowdy, and far too much of Pest.

Pest, sitting in the second row, turns to look at the lady sitting by his side. She is offensively ugly, he smiles weakly and begins to clap his hands. This infuriates her and everyone else, whereupon Charlie rises, bows to the audience and takes a seat in the front row, where a short-sighted conductor mistakes his head for a music-rest and taps it impatiently at the rise of the curtain. There is a great deal of unhappiness between Charlie and the orchestra, but his real hate is directed towards the audience. He wanders about trying to find a place where he can be most offensive. Eventually, he is gently removed by the bouncer. He wanders into the courtyard, takes one look at the fat lady, and promptly dunks her in the fountain. When he slips into the theatre again Edna Purviance, wearing pearls and looking like a Renaissance princess, smiles politely at him. He imagines she is overcome by his charm. Her husband is sitting beside her, and at the precise moment when Charlie's hand steals out to touch hers, her husband's hand does the same. There is a meeting of hands – Charlie's and the husband's. Meanwhile the rowdy in the gallery has been observing what is happening below, and he opens a bottle of beer and allows it to spill down on the pest. The pest retires in confusion.

When we see him again he is sitting behind a woman with an enormous hat decorated with towering ostrich feathers. Charlie removes them one by one. A fat woman is singing on the stage. Charlie is infuriated by her, runs up on the stage and picks a quarrel with the stage manager. When the fat lady curtsies,

Charlie assumes that the applause is for him, and bows to the audience. Shortly afterwards we find him sitting with a fat boy, who is eating tarts. Tootsy Frutti, the celebrated snake-charmer, dances across the stage, pipes on her trumpet and awakens the king cobras from their sleep. Charlie is snoring. He has had enough of the vaudeville. He never wants to see a vaudeville show again. The snakes crawl into the trumpet, trombones and bassoon, the orchestra takes to flight and when Charlie awakes, the king cobra is handsomely coiling all round him. His expression of polite astonishment is wonderfully convincing. The snake-charmer is followed by Dot and Dash, a fat man and a bearded dwarf who sing sentimental songs in an endless duet. The rowdy in the gallery takes one look at them, jumps out of his chair, runs down to the edge of the gallery and is so impatient of the sentimental ballad-singers that he has one foot over the balcony before he has thrown his tomato. Later he will throw ice-cream cones. Dot and Dash continue singing. They are used to this kind of thing. The whole gallery is busy throwing things at them, but they continue undaunted, troupers that they are. The fat boy begins to throw tarts. The pest throws tarts. Everyone is throwing something. The stage manager is bowled over by a barrage of tarts, and Dot and Dash are still singing, blinded by ice-creams.

Finally, there is Professor Nix, the fire-eater. The stage darkens. The mysterious spells are woven, the fires are lit and Professor Nix swallows hard. The stage looks like hell's flames, and the pest hides behind the fat boy. The rowdy upstairs is not in the least put out by the darkened stage and the mysterious mumbo-jumbo of fire-eating. He simply runs back to the top of the gallery, unhooks the hose and turns the water on the stage, and anyone in the gallery who dares to interfere with him receives a blast of water in the face. Soon the stage is drowned, and half the audience are wet through. In the final passage of the film the rowdy takes an intense dislike to the pest and directs the hose on him alone.

One cannot unreservedly admire *A Night at the Show*. The tempo is furious, the comic clichés run fast upon one another, the uproar is calculated to a mounting vertigo, but except for the occasional appearances of the rowdy in the gallery, mischievous as the devil, there is no warmth, and the pest's icy contempt for the world is only too evident. One knows exactly what he would do if someone came upon the stage and sang well. He would poke out his tongue, squirm, cough, and utter catcalls. Only the rowdy, for ever in his eagerness throwing himself down the gallery steps and getting one leg hooked over the gallery rail, would applaud.

That too-fast tempo, that tempestuous cold chill also occurs in many of the opening passages of *Carmen*, those cavortings which seem endless only because they had passed out of Chaplin's hands before he could edit the film. He was deliberately wasteful with film, turning 100,000 feet to achieve 2,000, and the repetitions of *Carmen* are dreadfully wearisome, for it was stretched out by the Essanay editors to make a four-reeler, when Chaplin had intended only to make a two-reeler. Yet the duelling scenes are superb, and in the realm of wit they belong to the greatest things he has done. The duel begins fiercely. The antagonists are at one another's throats. They have a world to gain. They will hack their way to victory. And then quite suddenly both tire of the game, and they fight in order to demonstrate the infinite swashbuckling possibilities of the dance. So they dance and wield their curved swords like feathers or like billiard cues and gently cut one another down and as gently rise, and all the time their expressions are ferocious. In the end, of course, Darn Hosiery must kill his Carmen when she refuses him. With the same suddenness with which the duel turned into comedy, the comedy now turns into tragedy. Charlie, in his fireman's helmet and monumental epaulettes, throws the props out of the window. Mocked by Carmen, he will stab her, and make her tragedy as real before our eyes as the death of Desdemona. His face drained of blood, while gazing at her with the utmost tenderness, he stabs her, and then gently lowers her to the ground, and she turns her head a little, as though she wanted to say something to him, but there is no time, all the life is flowing out of her, and then he kisses her and gazes at her once more for the last time, for he slowly stabs himself, and falls dead over her. All this is done to the leaping music of tragedy. The toreador enters, and he too has the look of tragedy on him. Slowly Charlie's backside comes lifting up from the floor, and a beautifully aimed foot throws the toreador out of the scene. The lovers jump up, smile, embrace one another and Charlie removes the fake dagger from her back with a backward glance of supreme mockery and triumph. What is wonderful is the way the woodenness of death, its stark rigidity, is so suddenly become a laughing thing. 'There is no death,' he is saying. 'See, all swords have hollow handles, and the blade instead of piercing flesh——' The last brief scene has the quality of one of those Elizabethan lyrics where death is visualised as a gay dance of black plumage.

Carmen was the last of the films Chaplin produced for Essanay with the exception of *Police*, which employs too many of the old tricks and is too repetitive to be accounted among the major films. There once again, as in *The Bank*, he makes play with the complicated opening of things: he regards an oven with the same circumspection as he regarded the bank-vault, and cunningly ensures himself that he has the correct combination. *Police* is the product of weariness. *Triple Trouble* is the product of no one's fancy. Its chief virtue is that it contains a long passage from the uncompleted *Life*, which Chaplin never completed. *Life* was to be the real story of Charlie. The greater part of it would take place in a doss-house among thugs and ruffians. It would be the story of the ashcan world, where no one danced in tinkling epaulettes and no one wore immense plumed helmets. In its odd and terrible way *Life* would be funny; it would not be amusing. All that remains of *Life* is a single sustained passage inserted half-way through *Triple Trouble*, where Charlie appears in the doss-house late at night when all the other inmates are asleep, or trying to sleep, for a madman is there, bawling away. Charlie goes to bed, but the bawling goes on. The man is old and toothless, with a cavernous black wobbling mouth. He raves on the edge of his bed. Charlie can stand it no longer, gets a bottle, knocks the man on the head, tenderly kisses him good-night and puts him to bed. Then the thief comes in. He is the wildest looking thief who ever appeared in any of Chaplin's comedies. He steals a purse. Charlie, wide awake and frightened, wonders how to preserve his few remaining coins. He takes off his coat, slips it under the shoddy mattress and for greater security puts his money in his mouth. Quietly he goes to sleep.

Awakened by a noise, he wonders what has happened to the coins, pats himself all over – no sign of them. The thief is counting his money. Charlie decides to frighten him out of his wits, but how do you frighten a bold thief? Charlie burrows under the coverlet, takes off his shoes, puts his hands in them, and having reversed himself completely on the bed, one finger peering out through a hole in his shoe, he resembles some strange sea-monster. The thief looks up to find two broken shoes and one finger facing him———

It was out of such simple things that Chaplin made his comedies in those early years. The brightness of eternal suns shone on him, he seemed to move in a world where every mortal thing became his toy, and this is as it had to be. He was to say afterwards that he was lonely and miserable during those years, uncertain of everything except the mastery of his craft. It was only very slowly that he came to realise fully that the vast popularity he enjoyed was due to a strange marriage between his own misery and the misery of the world about him. They knew why they laughed. Chaplin knew, but he could not put it successfully in words. By the spring of 1916 he knew that Charlie had come to stay, and he would have to spend the rest of his life with the clown.

CHAPTER XI

THE HERO

WITH the coming of the war Charlie's popularity could only increase. By some means which we shall never fully understand, he answered a deep human need. There was compassion in him, and a generous understanding of human foibles, and the wit which people cry out for in a mechanised age. Outside the little cinema houses with their collodion smells and tinkling pianos the *papier-maché* tramp, the size of a cigar-store Indian, waving his jaunty cane with his hat a little on one side, was like an invitation to licence. Someone – perhaps it was Chaplin – remembered the cry of Grimaldi in the ancient pantomimes, and the words: 'Here we are again!' or 'Here's that man again!' accompanied the portrait of the bewildered little tramp. He was never again to reach the popularity he received during the war, for he became the emblem of all men's hopes and all their bewildered fears for the future.

By 1915 the children were singing: 'The moon shines bright on Charlie Chaplin'. This strange little song with its obscure origins went through many versions. There was one version sung by the children and another sung by the soldiers in the trenches. The soldiers' version began:

> *The moon shines bright on Charlie Chaplin*
> *Whose boots are crackin'*
> *For the want of blackin',*
> *And his little baggy trousers*
> *They want mendin'*
> *Before we send 'im*
> *To the Dardanelles——*

In polite circles it was agreed that the song was a parody of a sentimental ballad on an Indian maid called *Redwing*, sung to the melody of Schumann's *Merry Peasant*. It is much more likely that the origin of the song was devoutly obscene, and went back to the eighteenth century street-song which T. S. Eliot has echoed in *The Waste Land*. This ancient and ribald song, which was also sung in the trenches, contained some surprising verses:

> *The moon shines bright on Mrs Porter*
> *And on her daughter:*
> *She washes out her —— in soda water,*
> *And so she oughta,*
> *To keep it clean.*

But there were a hundred other songs about Chaplin, who had captured the public imagination as it has rarely been captured before; and long before *Shoulder Arms* street-arabs, playing hopscotch, would sing:

> *One, two, three, four,*
> *Charlie Chaplin went to war.*
> *He taught the nurses how to dance,*
> *And this is what he taught them:*
> *Heel, toe, over we go,*
> *Heel, toe, over we go;*
> *Salute to the king,*
> *And bow to the queen,*
> *And turn your back*
> *On the Kaiserine.*

It was the time when Charlie was in his glory, before the world grew embittered with failure and war. People cried out for a hero, and now they had one, and there had never been a hero less demanding. There was nothing swashbuckling about him. He asked for nothing, only to be let alone, but if he was not let alone, he was pure defiance, the most savage of opponents. Consciously or unconsciously Chaplin had caught the mood of the Allies, a mood compounded of tenderness, defiance, a desperate desire to be finished with the war, and contempt for a swarthy spike-helmeted enemy. The Mutual and Essanay films could be, and were, read as veiled allegories. Those huge bearded or heavily-moustached 'heavies' were Germans, and Charlie ran rings round them. Even the Keystone Cops – for the Keystone films were revived again and again during the course of the war – those elephantine monsters with tattered epaulettes, oversize police badges and coats which resembled blankets too often slept in could be identified with the enemy, and Charlie had them at his mercy. In our day there has been no successful mockery of the enemy. The Soviets once produced a picture showing Hitler as a tormented lunatic, and in the end by means of adventures derived straight from *Shoulder Arms,* they showed him neatly bound up in a wicker cage which patrolled through the length and breadth of Russia. But what if some film director gifted with foresight had depicted during the war the vast and terrible comedy of Hitler's last days – the cheap bourgeois wedding to a mistress discarded long before, the sighs and the solemn parades and the last handshakes in the underground cellar, then the quiet murder on the love-seat. We shall see later that Monsieur Verdoux was a far keener portrait of the dictator than anything provided in the life of Adenoid Hynkel.

The mood of the First World War demanded comedy reduced to its essentials, and there is some significance in the fact that between May 1916 and October 1917 Chaplin produced his finest comedy two-reelers. Of the twelve films produced for Mutual five were masterpieces. Four of them derived by direct descent from *The Bank,* while the fifth, *One A.M.,* an example of the sheerest virtuosity, derived from nothing so much as all men's quarrel with the world.

Chaplin's stay with Mutual began with two false steps. *The Floorwalker* and *The Fireman* were excellent comedies. They said what needed to be said, but without *brio,* without depth and without that wild knowledge of the ways of the world which was Charlie's proper contribution to human happiness. As a floor-walker and as a fireman, Charlie was in receipt of a regular income. It is possible that the trouble lies there, for Charlie in receipt of a regular income or any income at all is a strange anomaly. We do not expect him to have a job. If he pretends to be a barber occasionally, no one will question him, for it is clear that barbering is not his vocation. He is at his best as a janitor or a poverty-stricken immigrant or as an underpaid drudge in a pawnshop serving his master for a few days until the inevitable dismissal, and he is best of all as a tramp or a vagabond: then he comes out of nowhere, trailing clouds of glory, beholden to no one, and wholly credible.

The Floorwalker is not Charlie, who merely walks the floor. The real floorwalker is a thief who vaguely resembles Charlie, and who tries to run away with the store's money. Some of the running takes place on the elevator. There are wonderful moments when Charlie and the floorwalker face one another, thinking they are watching themselves in mirrors – it is a foretaste of the scene in *The Circus* where Charlie is lost in the mirror maze and doffs his hat to the strange creature who keeps smiling at him out of glass. There is an exquisite moment when Charlie picks up a wax leg, dazzled by its perfections. But there is no film. Instead, there are some wonderful little strips of film, and some very boring pieces, and there is no bite in the camerawork, nor any sense of illusion. Everything is ambiguous in the film. We know from the beginning that there will be nothing but confusion, but there is no purpose in the confusion, no hint of any real drama, and he offers us no reason why we should care two hoots what happens to him.

In *The Fireman* we have even less reason to care. Charlie in a fireman's uniform is no more convincing than when he wore the uniform of a hussar in *His New Job*. He is out of character, simply by being a fireman. He is wonderful, of course, at putting out fires, climbing up the sheer walls of a house to rescue a maiden on the third floor of a burning house, and he is prodigiously competent with the hoses, but he is a ridiculously young man to be Charlie (he now resembles a boy of eighteen) and we care for him no more than we care for those presentable clever young men who hang around poolrooms. He is smart. He is very nearly funny. And he has no soul. And though for the first time since *The Bank* the photography is brilliantly clear and sharp, this in itself is a defect; on those early films a good lens was a disadvantage and coarse grained film sliced with running silver streaks only added to the illusion.

In *The Vagabond*, the third of the Mutual films, Charlie comes into his own. The story begins with a preliminary flourish which has nothing to do with the main plot – a scene in a bar room with Charlie playing on his fiddle, and no one paying the slightest attention. A German band is playing. Charlie shrugs his shoulders, removes his hat and passes it round. Then the *furor Germanicus* is awakened, and Charlie has to run for his life. When we next see him he is a thousand miles away, deep in the country, climbing over a fence, with a nail sticking to his trousers. He carefully removes the nail, makes a profoundly horrified face at the imbecility of nails, and then he sees Edna Purviance washing clothes beside a gypsy caravan, a wicked old crone belabouring her. The girl is frightened. Charlie believes it is his task to please her with his fiddle. He plays soulfully, smiles tenderly, assures her that the world is still beautiful, still worth living in, and after he has played *The Honeysuckle and the Bee*, he bows politely, applauds himself, bows again, roars with happiness over his own proficiency in ·fiddling, and then tumbles into the washtub. The old crone returns, and Charlie, horrified by the ugliness and brutality on her face, is about to run, but the girl pulls him back. When the threat has passed, Charlie plays for her again, puts one foot on her lap, smiles confidingly, embraces her, is all smiles and sweetness, till the leader of the gypsy band comes running with his whip, and Charlie in sheer fright falls into the tub again. All this is the purest poetry, the most delicate flattery of the mind. The tub, of course, takes the place of the trapdoor in the pantomime; and as he falls in and out, shaking himself like a dog, smiling with the most gentle effrontery at the girl, we are aware of a warmth and intimacy in their love-making, of secrets suddenly revealed: it is as though we were watching real lovers in a fairy-tale. But there must be an end to love, the gypsy caravan departs, Charlie is left alone, and without warning we are shown a grey-haired woman with chocolate-box sweetness gazing at the photograph of her long-lost child.

The long-lost child, like the likeness between twins, is the stuff of comedy, and Charlie has used them to the hilt. He is himself the long-lost child, and it is only by the most cunning use of sleight-of-hand that he convinces us that the girl is lost. The grey-haired woman, of course, is pure intrusion. If she adds nothing, she takes little away, though we regret the moments when Charlie is off the screen. That the gypsy girl is her lost daughter may be true. We are even prepared to believe it but we wish devoutly that it was not true. Significantly, the camera-work of all the scenes in which the mother appears has a faded dusty look, like the bloom on a peach.

The caravan has departed, but when we see it again, Charlie has caught up with it. The bully is still striking the girl with the whip. Charlie climbs a tree and lies like a snake on the limb. When the gypsies come out of the caravan, he knocks them out with a club, and when they are all sprawling like rotten fruit at the foot of the tree, Charlie loses his balance and falls among them. Then, with no more than a glance at the defeated, he takes her into the caravan and they drive off. The gypsies come running after, and the old crone, admirably played by Leo White, is bowled over with a sudden kick in the stomach from Charlie – it is one of the most extraordinary pieces of brutality ever committed by the clown, inevitable, effortless and terrifying, for the hag crumples like a doll stuffed with horse-hair, and almost you hear Charlie's wild demented laughter, the laughter of pure triumph and freedom as he rides off with his girl.

The idyllic scene which follows repeats the motifs of the first encounter. All is tenderness and light, and at the same time there is the threat of impermanence. The girl sleeps in the caravan. Charlie sleeps in the straw outside, his hands tenderly wrapped around his fiddle. He scratches. He discovers he is sleeping on a cactus, then remakes his bed and knocks discreetly on the caravan door. She too is scratching herself. Through the woodland comes an artist, the snake in the grass. Charlie sends the girl out with a bucket to fetch water, cracks eggs open with a hammer, prepares their breakfast. Meanwhile the girl is posing for the artist, and Charlie, when he learns of it, makes his own drawing of the girl. His drawing makes her look like a horse. He rapidly rubs it out. Here the themes of *The Face on the Bar Room Floor* are repeated at a slower pace and with a wonderful tenderness and a poignancy so unbearable that when the legend, 'His romance fades', appears on the screen, we feel the words as an affront.

In the peach-bloom atmosphere of a picture gallery the artist's painting is recognised by the girl's mother, who immediately faints. Later she asks the painter where he has seen her daughter. He talks of the caravan, and then the caravan appears in an iris, and we see a car approaching at the same time that Charlie comes into view, balancing some eggs. In the car are the girl's father and mother. They spill out, take the girl in their arms, and Charlie, of course, is delighted with the reconciliation, claps his hands, goes into a little dance, expects to be taken away with them, drops the eggs on the man's foot, smiles, then apologises for smiling, and suddenly the car is rushing away down the slope, and Charlie gazes after it, intense and miserable beyond all expectations of loneliness, and your heart is twisted as you watch him groping with his own miseries. With something of the same look he had paused outside Edna Purviance's office in *The Bank*, when he knew she had rejected his gift of roses; but there was hope then, now there is none. In the coda to the film as it was shown publicly, the car inexplicably returns and Charlie is joyfully carried away in it. In the more accurate version, which Chaplin has occasionally shown privately, Charlie commits a quiet suicide, having first been rescued by a harridan who brings him to shore, and then, seeing her face, he plunges into the water for the last time. Neither ending is satisfactory. The film ends, as it must, with Charlie's heartsick look down the long road, in panic fear and horror at the impermanence of love, and then the faintest of shrugs, the smallest of happy smiles.

The Vagabond possesses a perfection which was never quite reached by the other great Mutual films. Here the comedy was as swift and clean as a mountain stream. Charlie with his gypsy caravan is in his element. It is his world, as later on he finds a tolerable world in a circus. When he goes to Alaska, or trumpets from the dictator's throne, we are aware that he is not in the milieu he knows best. There was something tawdry in his assumption of a fireman's spurious dignity. Chaplin was himself aware that something was missing. When *The Fireman* was being shown, he received a letter from a correspondent in the Middle West complaining that he was becoming the servant of the public, performing the rôles that the public demanded, and there was a lack of spontaneity in his movements. He was still immensely funny, but the fun was cold. 'You are becoming the slave of the public, but truly you should let the public be your slave.' Chaplin decided that henceforward he would let the public go hang; he would perform as he pleased, and then he would be certain of touching the authentic comic nerve. *One A.M.*, *The Pawnshop*, *Easy Street* and *The Immigrant* were the fruit of the new resolve.

One A.M. is the most fastidious of Chaplin's comedies. It is comedy reduced to its brute essentials, and it has nothing whatsoever to do with the image of Charlie. Here, for the first and last time, Chaplin the clown was photographed, and it must be clearly understood that Chaplin the clown is only distantly related to Charlie. They share a few mannerisms, and that is all. Chaplin, who is perfectly capable of miming the part of an enraged bull, a matador and the woman with the mantilla who is hoping that the matador will be gored to death, miming all these simultaneously, with every inflection of movement in place, dragging the whole audience into the sunlit arena, imitating the yearning on the matador's face with a flicker of an eyelid and the onrush of the bull's horns with a jab of a finger, is a clown in his own right with a repertoire which extends far beyond the limits of Charlie's experience. This is as it must be. We can only regret that Chaplin has so rarely been seen on the screen. With *One A.M.* Chaplin entered the realm of pure poetry.

Theoretically the film is a study of a drunken man returning home in a taxi and going to bed. In practice, it is considerably more. In this extremely subversive film, which praises drunkenness and offers the most alarming reasons why no one should ever sleep alone in a Murphy bed, Chaplin's clowning takes on the aspect of a perpetual dance. He dances with everything, and because he dances with them they become animate. Arriving in a taxi, and faced with the fact that he must pay the fare, he dances a solo with his own hands which are wildly attempting to extract money from his own pockets. He dances with the door, that terrible motionless door which refuses to dance, refuses to open, refuses to understand his need to go to bed, and in despair of the door Charles Chaplin climbs through the window and opens it from inside. Finding himself on the porch he is at first surprised, then terrified, then delighted.

He must now pursue his perilous way upstairs, confronted by the obscene *bric-à-brac* which had once littered the hill-top mansion where Tillie enjoyed her punctured romance. He moves

delicately. The carpet slips. The stuffed lion roars. The stuffed
bear growls. The table leaps at him. He tries to pour himself a
drink to calm his fears, but the bottle is on the table, and the
table is drunk. Discouraged, he makes his way upstairs, trips,
falls over the banisters, shrugs, climbs the stairs again, falls flat
on his face, and the bear growls again and the stuffed tiger has a
look of the utmost contempt, and there is nothing to be done
except to flee from these ominous animals, this world of *bric-à-brac*.
The next time he climbs the stairs the stair-carpets enclose him
and wrap him up as if he was a parcel. The malevolence of
things only increases when he reaches the landing and has to face
an enormous sharp-pointed pendulum, which knocks him down
into the parlour, and the whole horrid business of climbing the
stairs has to begin again. In this celestial game of snakes and
ladders, the snakes have all the advantages. He sighs, adjusts
his top-hat, succeeds by the employment of the utmost caution
in reaching the landing again, and after climbing a teetering
rubber clothes-horse finds himself in his bedroom.

The bedroom is an offence to the eye, ancestor of Martha
Raye's bedroom in *Monsieur Verdoux* with its striped wallpaper
and tasteless reproductions of sentimental paintings torn from
ladies' magazines. He presses a button. The Murphy bed, more
malevolent, more cunning than any pendulum, springs out and
knocks him on the head. He decides to master it. He will deal
with it as a man must deal with a recalcitrant woman. He throws
one leg over it, forces it down, and is not particularly astonished
when it swings up and spins him into the closet, from which it
emerged, that closet which is like the lair of some ferocious
animal. Now he is at his wits' end. Ethereally drunk, happy and
delighted with the world, having long ago recovered from the
exhaustion following his combat with the stuffed animals
downstairs, he regards the state of being at the end of his wits
with magisteral calm. It is a state he is accustomed to. He refuses
to be conquered by the bed. He will fight it to the last drop of
his blood, the last flutter of an eyelid, and so once more, exerting
all his force, he grapples with the enemy, forces it to surrender,
grapples with it as a knight at the court of Charlemagne might
grapple with a Saracen paladin in full armour, and having accomplished his purpose, having settled himself very comfortably,

he leans over to pick up a cigarette and is instantaneously thrown overboard. One might have thought that the comedy would end there, that there was a limit to the number of things which could happen to Chaplin in the struggle with the Murphy bed. Happily, there is no limit. Defeated, he re-engages in the battle. Over the imperious face there flickers the shadow of cunning. He will wait. He will advance stealthily. He will surprise the bed with a sudden assault. He will retreat. He will pretend that going to bed is the last thing on his mind. He will allow the bed no advantages. He approaches it with a tracker's caution, and at the moment when he is about to make his first tentative explorations, the bed for no reason at all leaps out of the wall right side up. Charlie jumps into it. It collapses under his weight, and becomes a thing of twisted wires and grinning bestiality. He has had enough. With a look of supreme politeness at the bed – it is the look which Byron described in *Vision of Judgment:*

> *His Darkness and his Brightness*
> *Exchanged a greeting of supreme politeness——*

Charlie marches into the bathroom, and after an unfortunate encounter with the shower makes his bed in the bath.

One A.M. is more than an example of virtuosity. It exists on many levels. It can be regarded as pure clowning, as a remorseless study of the dithering of a drunk, as an exhibition of flamboyant acrobatics, as a bitter attack on beds which can be let out of the wall and as a perilous adventure through the forest of things. And on that level it is supreme. Never again was Chaplin to give himself so wholly to the examination of the malevolence of things.

The Count, which immediately followed *One A.M.*, was a mistake. It belongs to the category which produced *The Floorwalker* and *The Fireman*, and can be disregarded. *The Pawnshop*, which explores some of the things introduced in *One A.M.*, cannot be disregarded. It has none of the sharp outlines of *The Bank* and *The Vagabond*. There is no tenderness in it, no attempt to relate Charlie to the real world, and it succeeds only because Charlie emerges in all his glorious and unwavering idiocy as the creator of a whole dancing world of folly. The greatest scene, which is concerned with Charlie's awestruck examination of an alarm-clock, mimics at a distance and in another contex this fabulous encounter with the bed.

From the time of *The Face on the Bar Room Floor* and even before, it had become clear that Charlie felt secure only when he lived on the teetering edge of the world. He was the monkey who climbs to the highest branch of all, where the wind blows strongest. Inevitably, then, if he is to be shown as a janitor in a pawnbroker's shop, we must see him first innocently shoe-polishing the three golden balls which hang outside. The ladder teeters as he reaches over to polish the signboard, even the policeman on the corner teeters as he watches Charlie swaying; the ladder swinging backwards and forwards belongs to the stuff of legend. There never was such balancing on the edge of nothing. There are roads in the Alps marked: 'Only for those who never suffer from vertigo'. From the time of *The Pawnshop* Charlie showed that he suffered from vertigo, but delighted in it.

Like all of Charlie's films there are two beginnings. There is always a preliminary flourish as the musician warms up his instruments. So in *The Pawnshop* we see him tripping into the shop, comparing his watch with the calendar on the wall, erect and officious, wearing an Old Etonian tie, twiddling his cane which he absentmindedly inserts into a trumpet and then deftly cleans with a feather duster. He places his derby in the canary cage for safety, dusts his desk, turns on the electric fan and gently inserts the feather duster in the fan, till the whole room is a churning mass of feathers. All this surprises him faintly. As for the plucked butt of the duster, it may have its uses later – this, too, goes into the canary cage. Annoyed by the effrontery of the world, and determined not to show his annoyance, he dances a little jig, then stubs his toe. At once he begins to shadow-box with the invisible enemy; and with this furious shadow-boxing the curtain-raiser comes to an end.

The third scene describes Charlie's dismissal from the pawnbroker's shop. The bearded old ruffian who owns the shop has now come to the end of his rope. He can stand Charlie no more. He is gruff, impersonal, determined to put an end to the nonsense, and he does this in the manner of a heavy-handed Victorian 'old nobodaddy', with his hands behind his back and his watch-chain dangling. Charlie appeals for mercy. He has eleven children – so high, so high and so high, and with a wonderfully pathetic expression Charlie demonstrates their height. The height of the tallest is somewhere near the ceiling. The old proprietor remains ruthless. Charlie goes sorrowfully to the door, and there receives his reprieve, whereupon he dives at the old man, hugging him by the neck and twining his legs around the paunch, and kissing him. Then he wanders off to the kitchen, quarrels with the other clerk, passes dishes through a clothes-wringer to dry them, being especially solicitous of a cup, which passes through the wringer twice. Then in the same way he dries his hands. He is about to throw some dough at the other clerk when the old proprietor appears again. Charlie merely swings the dough in the direction of the wringer, passes it through, takes a pie plate, trims the dough over it and goes out to work, but not before he has accomplished several more miracles, including a beautiful Hawaiian *lei* made of dough which he wears perhaps in imitation of Joe Cook refusing to imitate four Hawaiians playing a ukelele, and indeed Charlie does play a ukelele, and he dances a little shimmy to it, though your eyes see only a soup-spoon with Charlie thrumming on it.

The prodigious verve of these scenes is frightening, but there is more to come. It is all spontaneous, quick and darting as a bird's wing. The drab world has become a dance. He throws aside all the advantages which come to him from his comic costume; we are no longer aware of the comic costume, only the dancing. The deft beauty of his clowning illuminates the space he dances in. We are in that perfect world described by Stephen Dedalus in *Ulysses*, that world where 'gesture, not music, not odours, would be a universal language, the gift of tongues rendering visible not the lay sense but the first entelechy, the structural rhythm'. It is the rhythm of these passages which is frightening: it is a rhythm near the edge of rhythm; beyond that rhythm itself would become something else, sharper, more destructive. It is not that Charlie dances so much as that he makes everything in the room dance. The clothes wringer becomes his accomplice, and even the pastries dance in his hands. Significantly, he finds other uses for pie-crusts than flinging them in someone's face.

The Gold Rush, 1925

The Circus, 1928

City Lights, 1931

The fourth scene continues the dance, which we have long suspected to be the dance of a hurled hand-grenade. Now we hear the first rumblings of the explosions; the explosion itself will also take the form of a dance. There comes into the scene an aged actor, whose coat-collar is formed of weary squirrel-fur. He comes in very haltingly, and Charlie knows why he has come. He is evidently a Shakespearean actor out of work, and what can one do with Shakespearean actors? Charlie prepares to use a hammer, strikes a Napoleonic pose, takes the photograph which the actor shows him – the photograph evidently reproduces the portrait of the actor playing King Richard III – and thereupon Charlie leans over the counter and auscultates the actor's heart. The actor shows Charlie his wedding ring. Charlie weeps, munching biscuits, which he coughs out when the weeping turns to sobbing. Charlie returns the ring, takes ten dollars out of the till, and is astonished when the actor pulls out an enormous wad of dollar bills, and offers Charlie his change. The scene fades out when Charlie strikes himself on the head with a hammer.

The fourth scene, with Charlie playing the part of the eager and agonised sympathiser of those who have suffered from the world's ills, leads us nowhere, and Charlie is quite aware that the dance must continue. He returns to the back room, which serves the office of a magic box. An invincible logic rules in the shop; no logic at all rules in the back room. He sees a piece of rope on the floor. He tries to sweep it up, but the rope defies all his efforts. Immediately he decides to walk along the rope as a trapeze artist will walk along a trapeze, and this he does with a magnificent swaying and balancing of his hands. At the end he applauds himself. There is another fight with the other clerk. Charlie is on the point of winning when the girl enters. He decides it would be better to play dead. The girl comes to console him. In the mood of a man who knows he will be consoled whenever he desires consolation, he returns to the shop.

The fifth scene is one of the great wonders of the cinema. It is a scene of flagrant violence, and eerie leaps of the imagination. The hurled hand-grenade explodes. A man who looks like a wharf thug enters the shop with an alarm-clock, evidently stolen from some law-abiding old lady with a passion for keeping

F

regular hours. Charlie suspects the wharf thug from the beginning. Charlie examines the clock with professional interest. Then he auscultates it, taps it with his forefinger, like a doctor examining a patient for tuberculosis, flicks his forefinger at the bell, stares at the clock, taps it again, starts drilling with an auger, but the auger does not penetrate into the solid fabric of the clock, and so he employs a can-opener instead, and opens the whole thing up, all the time giving reassuring glances to the wharf thug, who is hurt and astonished by the dance of Charlie's destructive hands. Meanwhile Charlie sniffs at the clock (the smell is clearly distasteful), and with a disparaging gesture allows the thug to smell it. He removes the mouthpiece of a telephone, inserts it in his eye – he has now become the professional examiner of a clock's entrails – and carefully oils the clock. But the oiling has no effect, and more constructive efforts are needed. A plumber's hammer is near by. He taps the clock, listens to its reverberations, decides that the plumbing is deficient. It is time now to use forceps. He now assaults the defenceless clock physically, with the purpose of laying it bare, perhaps in order to discover the secrets of time. He pulls out the spring, measures it off like a ribbon, snips six inches off, then shakes out the remaining pieces on the table. The sight of those squirming eel-like objects displeases him; to keep them quiet he squirts oil over them. He begins to collect the pieces together and to wind the empty clock, and then a sudden thought occurs to him. Why trouble? Why on earth should one trouble? He collects all the pieces, sweeps them into the thug's hat, and returns it with a sad shake of his head. In this scene the clock has become successively a human heart, a sardine tin, a defective lead pipe, a roll of ribbons and a mess of eels. It has also been perhaps twenty other things.

What is wonderful in the scene is not so much the pure and unexampled virtuosity of the actor as the casual way in which Charlie makes the clock dance. Wyndham Lewis wrote once that Charlie's popularity arose for the same reasons that brought Bergson's philosophy into prominence. This is nonsense. Bergson's theories of intuition and time never accepted the possibility that intuition could dance and that time could be broken up into its dancing elements. W. C. Fields said of

Chaplin: 'He is the greatest ballet dancer who ever lived.' Fields omitted to observe that Charlie has the power to make every mortal thing dance to his tune. We shall see him in *Sunnyside* parodying classical Greek dancing in a burlesque which is never far from appreciation of the original, and may very likely improve on the original, but once again we see Charlie as the puller of strings, the master of the marionettes, that god-like figure so brilliantly described by Kleist in his essay on the marionette theatre.

The Pawnshop does not end with the parting salute to the clock. There is one further scene in which a robber, disguised as a pearl-merchant, holds up the pawnshop. Charlie jumps into a trunk. When the pearl-merchant has gathered all the valuables from the safe and is about to flee, Charlie leaps out of the trunk like a jack-in-a-box, fells the robber, embraces the girl, swipes at the other clerk with a back-kick, applauds himself and winks with the fadeout.

Six more comedies were produced for Mutual. They are *Behind the Screen, The Rink, Easy Street, The Cure, The Immigrant* and *The Adventurer*.

The Rink and *The Cure* can be dismissed briefly, not because they fail to achieve the quality one expects, but because both of them introduce freaks and take place in a world which is largely constructed from props. Charlie's outrageous behaviour in the rink, his magnificent acrobatics, his dancing with the stout lady, the strangely beautiful pattern he makes on the ice, the insane way he tips his hat simply by pressing his head a little closer to the wall, the famous scene in which he mixes drinks while performing a hula dance, all these are as wonderful as we expect him to be, but the total effect is of a set piece circumscribed by the circle of the rink. It is true that he tries to break through the circle, assaults the shape of the ice, weaves impossible patterns over it, but there is no substance in the drama, no reason why we should identify ourselves with him or concern ourselves with his fate.

The Cure takes place at a shabby hotel where the patients are wheeled around in bath-chairs and a revolving door at the head of the stairs offers remarkable constraints to men with bandaged and gouty legs. Charlie arrives in a bath-chair,

wearing a straw hat, pushed by the most incompetent of all
bath-chair pushers. We wonder what he is doing in the chair,
and we are never told. He is out of his element. He dislikes the
freaks who haunt the place. Most of all he dislikes the little
dwarf of a bearded janitor who helps to take his luggage into
his room. The luggage consists of an immense chest which opens
up to show tier upon tier of bottles. Inevitably the janitor drinks
the bottles; inevitably, when the chest is closed, his beard is
caught in it. The fun is with the revolving doors, as mysterious
as mirrors, through which Charlie sails with the greatest of ease,
but so arranging his passage that gouty gentlemen are wedged in
them. The film is prodigiously fast, incident follows incident at a
merciless pace, Charlie is forever running around the massage
room and along the edge of the pool from which the curative
waters may be acquired and up and down the stairs and through the
revolving doors. There are long sequences of these chases, and
if you play them backwards through the projector, you are not
aware of any very great difference, and when the film is played
backwards and Charlie leaps up from the ground instead of
falling, this is as it should be. There are occasional magnificent ·
moments: when Charlie has demonstrated the strength of his
biceps to the nurse, he proceeds to test her muscles. When
Charlie's bottles are found and the whisky finds its way to the
curative waters, the following scene is played in quick motion,
and those excited freaks, running backwards and forwards at an
unearthly pace, perform a hideous ballet of their own. In the
end, having found Edna Purviance, Charlie makes love to her on
the edge of the pool. Finally he trips into the pool in one glorious
drunken splash.

   Behind the Screen and *The Adventurer* form another pair.
Each of them possesses moments of acute observation and
mimicry, but the mood is shrill, restless, even defiant. Slapstick
predominates, but the slapstick has an oddly uncertain quality.
In *Behind the Screen* no one is content with throwing a single
custard-pie; there must be a torrential flow of pies, with everyone
acting the part of Jupiter with doughy thunderbolts. Charlie is a
stagehand. He employs stage-props as he employed a mop in
The Bank: stage-props are useful for knocking people over with.
We believe in the mop. We never quite believe in the heavy

stage-props which Charlie carries with such jealous attention to extracting the last ounce of humour from them. There is a wonderful passage where he carefully combs a bear rug, parts the hair and wraps a hot towel over the face. The passage is inserted for no credible reason, and might have been inserted to greater advantage in *One A.M.* In the end everyone falls through a trapdoor.

The Adventurer, the last of the Mutual films, is a relapse into the style of the early Keystones. It begins with Charlie wearing the striped uniform of an escaped convict while running among the rocks by the seashore with the incompetent cops chasing him. He looks like one of the *koshare*, the 'Delight Makers' of the pueblo festivals, and indeed whenever he is in convict's uniform he gives the impression of reality. As he peers from behind the rocks, laughs at the cops who fall over themselves, or comes running down to the beach with a whole troop of cops behind him, he resembles the pure spirit of comedy. When later in his starched shirt, he attends a party somewhere in Beverly Hills, and with exquisite timing drops some ice-cream from a balcony down the dress of a matronly lady below, we are aware that intense calculation is now playing a part. The only moment during the party when Charlie springs to life is when, during a chase, he wears a lampshade and pretends to be a lamppost: that is, when he pretends to be invisible, remote, even dead.

With *Easy Street* and *The Immigrant* the comedy acquires amplitude and depth. The clown is always at his best when he clowns his own life, and both these films had sources in Chaplin's own life. In *Easy Street* he becomes a cop. For Charlie to become a cop is of course an outrageous simplification, but Charlie's intentions are plain. They are also dishonourable. He will subvert the whole organisation of the police, and he will make them the servants of the public, not their overlords. He will do this quietly, cunningly, methodically, and if necessary fiercely. The play begins with Charlie, the familiar tramp, wandering into the Mission, where he sings the mission hymns, makes eyes at Edna Purviance, steals the collection box and suffers from a change of heart. It is clear that the change of heart is a tribute to Edna's beauty. He will become a respectable citizen, but how?

The police are in despair. Gang war has broken out in Easy Street. In the police station wounded policemen are brought in on stretchers. Charlie watches the procession of bleeding police-men, uncertain of his own intentions, and then remembering the eyes of Edna he decides to demonstrate his bravery. Then, wearing an enormous helmet, we see him wandering up and down Easy Street, twirling his night-stick. The bully appears. The mood is the same mood which Chaplin recaptured later in *The Kid*, and indeed *Easy Street* may be regarded as a less complex version of the longer play. The bully has everyone in the street at his mercy. He can bend a lamp-post between two fingers. With his narrow waist, his enormous height, his heavy-jowled face, dressed like a boxer in training, the bully regards Charlie with contempt. Charlie runs to the call-box and attempts to telephone for reinforcements. He plays with the box, pretends that the mouthpiece is a spyglass, and demonstrates the uses of the magnificent machine to the bully, who looks on uncompre-hendingly, uncertain what game Charlie is playing. Charlie kicks him. The bully has the hide of an elephant, does not feel the kick, continues to look through the eyepiece, while Charlie deftly jumps on his shoulders, forces his head through the top of a lamp-post and turns on the gas. The bully is asphyxiated, but not quickly enough, for after taking the bully's pulse, Charlie decides to turn on more gas.

The bully is now defeated by an officer of the police and Charlie walks down Easy Street like a plumed cock. It is a temporary victory. We know the bully will return. Meanwhile, captivated by Edna, Charlie goes about improving the aspect of the street. He comes upon a woman stealing a ham. Caught in the act, she tearfully explains that she was hungry, and Charlie thrusts in her arms all the vegetables he can pick off a neighbour-ing stall. The path of virtue is a dangerous one: he receives a flowerpot on his head as the woman's only sign of gratitude. No matter: he will continue to dispense a proper charity. Ten wailing children are found in a tenement. Charlie pins a police-badge on the unemployed father, perhaps as a reward for having fathered · so many brats, and then distributes cornflakes to the children, very much as a farmer's wife will feed corn to her chickens. Afterwards the invention flags. The bully returns to life, and beneath a trapdoor anarchists are plotting destruction. We know they are anarchists because they leer and stuff bombs in their pockets, but they include dope fiends. Charlie accidentally receives an injection of dope, his courage returns, he performs amazing feats of valour and once again the dismal street is officered by a smart little policeman twirling his night-stick. We might reasonably expect the film to end there, but instead there is an announcement to be made and one final apotheosis. The announcement, based on a song sung by London street-arabs while playing hopskotch, reads:

> *Love backed by force,*
> *Forgiveness sweet,*
> *Bring Hope and Peace*
> *To Easy Street.*

They do indeed, and much more than we ever expected, for the curtain scene shows Easy Street already sprouting wings. Everyone is reformed, and even the bully and his wife, wearing their Sunday best, dance off to the mission to receive the blessings of divine peace. Charlie and Edna walk together. The pilgrim's progress is over; the trumpets sound on the other side.

The Immigrant is made of sterner stuff. The reckless gaiety of *Easy Street* is absent; there is no attempt to recapture emotion in tranquillity. Charlie is the perpetual D.P., wise beyond his years, a poor devil crowded among all the other poor devils on the immigrant ship, where the passengers are roped off like cattle and the gamblers steal from the poorest and the ship's officers are unyielding. We see Charlie leaning over the rail. It is obvious that he is being sick – terribly sick. His sufferings are atrocious. He stands on tiptoe, shuddering in every fibre of his being, and after his shoulders have shaken with terrible violence, he turns to face the camera with a fish on the end of his line. It is not a very large fish, but Charlie is content with the small things of life. Suddenly the comedy disappears. An old Jewish woman and her daughter have been robbed by gamblers. Charlie's face becomes taut with anger. He is all fire. He invites the gamblers to a crap game, cheats wonderfully and restores the money to the old woman and her daughter, while the ship's purser looks on, sure that Charlie is a thief. The Statue of

Liberty is seen, the immigration officers come abroad, and now the immigrants are herded behind ropes. Oddly enough, Charlie allows himself to be herded in, cocking an eyebrow on the statue.

Next we see him down and out in New York. He finds a coin in the street, picks it up and thrusts it into his pocket, that wide and capacious trouser pocket which is full of holes. In a restaurant he settles down to spend the coin, sees Edna, dances up to her, behaves with childish delight, brimming with joy. Suddenly the joy freezes, once more there is that look of helpless anger. Edna has a black-bordered handkerchief crushed between her fingers. He can do nothing. He can only delight and amuse her with the wealth of his comic invention. He will make her smile, and he will do this in spite of the world's malevolence, and the world, as he knows only too well, is excessively malevolent. His coin is lost. He cannot pay for the meal, and the waiters are adepts at manhandling impoverished diners. The desperate game is played with ruthless efficiency. Everything depends upon the toss of a coin. An old beggar found the coin which slipped through Charlie's pocket. The coin is then offered to the waiter, who drops it. Charlie with his eagle eyes sees it while he is attempting with all his means to please Edna. His foot darts out and covers it. The waiter stamps on his foot. There is no end to the adventures of the coin, or rather there is an end: the coin is discovered to be counterfeit when the waiter puts it between his teeth. An artist enters. He is delighted with Edna's beauty, strangely attracted to Charlie. He offers to pay for the meal. Charlie refuses, out of bravado, politeness and the pure pleasure of meeting the artist. The game of the coin is continued in the game for the check, as both grandiloquently thrust it at the other, and Charlie's face, so eager, so winning and fiery, assumes a thousand shapes of contentment and joy in the new friendship. An outcast, he now has two friends, an artist who understands him and a girl he will marry. 'Money?' he says. 'Good lord, why should one worry over a little thing like money?' The artist gently acquiesces, and Charlie is left with the check. As they leave, Charlie observes that the artist has mercifully left a tip which more than covers the expense of the meal. The rain falls in the empty street. The two waifs, Charlie and Edna, huddle outside the marriage bureau, and then, with a sudden swift turn up the stairway, they disappear into the anonymity of marriage.

The Immigrant is fashioned in two parts, but so deftly are they woven together that we are not aware of the break. The scene in New York follows logically on the scene in the ship; so much sympathy is created for Edna and her mother that the mother's death comes as a shock of the utmost poignancy. The desperate game with the coin is played out to the end, but it is a real game, a game to be played with unregenerate courage; the prize is Edna, a sense of security in the world. There were to be occasions later when Charlie's fate would hang in the balance: in *The Immigrant* this very balancing partook of splendour. He had never quite touched this nerve before; he very rarely touched it with such accuracy again. If the most accomplished single scene of the Mutual comedies was the alarm-clock scene in *The Pawnshop*, the scene of the lost coin in *The Immigrant* runs it close. The humour belonged to the comedy of the soul's and body's fortitudes; having its habitation in the place where urgent sorrows, ghostly catastrophes and all our useless striving meet. The coin was a coin, but just as the alarm-clock became anything Charlie pleased, so here the coin became everything that gave Charlie acute displeasure; and his mortal anguish and bewilderment, his wonderful and frenzied efforts to destroy each uprising of anguish as it appeared, belongs to the human situation and the 'tears of things'.

With the last of the Mutual comedies Chaplin had explored most of the territory Charlie ever came to know. In the five films that followed the influence of *The Immigrant* can be discerned, but now the music will no longer be played on a single instrument, it will be performed by a full orchestra.

CHAPTER XII

THE ANGEL IN A CLOUD

IN THE second act of Jean Giraudoux's *Mad Women of Chaillot* we are presented with the spectacle of three old hags discussing in an obscure cellar in Paris how they will put an end to all the evil in the world. They talk with wit and understanding. They are alarmed by the presence of evil, and they know exactly who the evil are. In a conspiratorial whisper, Aurélie, who calls herself a countess, announces:

> Everywhere men are giving themselves the air of construc-
> tors, but in fact they are all secretly resolved upon destruction.
> Everything they build as masons they destroy as freemasons.
> They construct the embankments to the ruin of the rivers, and
> houses to the ruin of quarries. They have built the Palais de
> Chaillot only by destroying the Trocadéro. They even use up
> space and the whole heavens with their telescopes, and they
> use up time with their watches. The primary occupation of
> humanity is the universal business of demolition. I speak, of
> course, of the males.

So they go on, these obscure and wonderful old women, in love with the past, concerned with the imaginary poodle which runs between their legs, remembering one another's titles, always talking wisely on the edge of hysteria and as though they had all time to talk in, dismissing the obvious ways of putting an end to evil, the hatchet and the sulphuric acid bath, for there must be other ways – but what ways? The Countess ponders.

It occurs to her that there is a very simple solution, and she cannot understand why she never thought of it before. All that is necessary is to invite the bankers, the presidents, the robbers and the thieves to meet her in her cellar. They will come: so much is certain. And what then? Why, nothing could be easier. Everyone is in love with wealth. She will point to the buried oil-wells beneath her bed, and they will come trooping down to examine this buried wealth; then very calmly, when they are looking the other way, she will move the bed over them, and prevent them from ever returning. And this is what happens. She has their addresses in her little notebook. She invites them into her web, and so they die, but when it is all over, she announces that something else has happened. No, they did not come, it was not even necessary for them to come, the proud and the evil had simply evaporated, for it is the characteristic of the proud and the evil that they should evaporate. 'They think they are eternal,' says the incomparable countess Aurélie, 'and men believe them, and they do everything they possibly can to be eternal – they avoid colds in the head and speeding motorcars. But they are not eternal: their pride, their cupidity, the evil in them makes them so hot that they simply evaporate. I remember reading about a millionaire who was killed when his airplane fell into the sea. It's all lies. The airplane simply took it into its head to fall in with some innocent sardines, and the financier evaporated.'

In the world of the Countess evil proliferates. She knows its signs. Like Alice in Wonderland, who lived in the same world and fought a very similar battle, she employs all the weapons of wit, cunning and hysteria to straighten out the entanglements of the world, and in all this she resembles those tightrope walkers who are not content merely to walk along the rope, but must simultaneously play a musical instrument, balance a billiard cue on their noses, juggle immense slave-rings round their legs and perform conjuring tricks with their free hands.

So it is with Charlie. He does not live in one world. He lives in all possible worlds, and plays with them all, and if he finds living in one world too dangerous, he will simply slip into another, as we do when we daydream, and always he is faced with the incontrovertible fact of evil, the financier who refuses to evaporate, the airplane which refuses to disappear in a shoal of sardines, the bully who refuses to don the wings of the angel. He is aware that his weapons are various, that he can step suddenly from one world to another or embrace two worlds at once, and like the Countess Aurélie he possesses the secret by which evil can be put to rout. What is the name of the secret? We can only guess at it. Partly, of course, it is his unbelievable heroism, for he will attack his enemies as the Countess Aurélie attacks hers, but it is also his dancing gaiety, his sense of the embattled holiness of life, his knowledge of the enemy's weaknesses. 'You do not need a battle-axe to kill your enemy,' wrote the Chinese philosopher. 'No, all that is necessary is to insert a knife-blade a little way into his flesh, and if you have found the right place, his flesh and his bones will come apart.' 'True enough,' says Charlie, 'but what if it is the enemy which first inserts the knife?'

During 1918 and 1919 Chaplin composed three films for First National which are more magical than any he composed before or afterwards. It is as though in a brief space towards the end of a war the figure of Charlie had suddenly sprung into its full maturity. They are the most poetic of his films, and he was never again to recapture the precise quality of that poetry. These films were *A Dog's Life, Shoulder Arms* and *Sunnyside*. One dealt with poverty, another with war and the third with paradise.

A Dog's Life is concerned with poverty so harsh that it is wholly without compensations. No daydreams can make it more palatable. Charlie is a derelict, a poor devil at his last gasp, asleep in a wasteland, protected from the wind only by a rotten fence. There are holes in the fence; he stuffs a handkerchief in the holes to keep out the draught. Not far away there is an ash-can, and the dog Scraps sleeps beside it. The ashcan is the centre of their world, just as the underground cellar is the centre of the world according to Countess Aurélie. Like the Countess, Charlie is compelled to put an end to the evils of his enemies. He has no desire to kill them; he will simply tie them into knots and so render them harmless. The smell of a hot-dog stand comes over the fence. Through a hole in the fence Charlie steals a hot-dog. Hungry, he is wholly absorbed in eating when he sees the cop gazing over the fence, whereupon with a show of innocence he returns the hot-dog to its stand. The cop, however, attempts to pursue him. Charlie first rolls under the fence when the cop climbs over it, then rolls back again when the cop comes out into the street. Finally, to keep the policeman from disturbing him, Charlie ties the cop's shoelaces together. It is a neat solution, and the Countess Aurélie might reasonably have attempted to do the same with the oil men and municipal councillors who were her declared enemies. Together with his dog, Charlie wanders away.

For Charlie the world consists of a straight line between the ashcan and the employment office. At the employment office he is at the mercy of the job-hunters. He rushes to the windows, but he is always edged out, Sad Sack contending with his doom. He runs madly from one window to another, and it is always the same. The tempo mounts. He runs around like a mad dog, and when at last he comes up to a window, it shuts in his face. There are no more jobs. There remains the ashcan.

Charlie, contemplating his own empty belly, looks up to see that Scraps has found some discarded bones, but Scraps has hardly fastened his teeth on them when all the other dogs of the neighbourhood come running at him. The theme of the scene at the employment office is repeated on another plane when Scraps has to fight with the other dogs for his bone. It is Charlie who saves Scraps, and that is as it should be: we recognise the justness of the vagabond who will save the dog even to the extent of being torn nearly to pieces by the dogs who are not content with their bone but must run howling after Charlie, jumping up at him, taking a great bite from his pants. All this is Charlie at his most tragic. 'Where do the dogs go at night?' Baudelaire asked once, and found himself bewildered by the thought of the immense and unknown tragedies of the lonely wanderers of the night. Charlie is just as bewildered, but he knows the tricks of his trade. When Scraps tries to get milk from a milk-bottle and cannot get his head in, Charlie thinks of the dog's tail, dips it in the milk and thereupon Scraps can have his lick. Sometimes he employs simpler tricks, as when he goes hunting after a string of sausages. Then, once again, we find ourselves on familiar territory: that audacious play with pies and sausages goes back to the Roman theatre, and both Deburau and Grimaldi had played those scenes to the uttermost. When the policeman is smacked across the face with a large sausage, it is as though the veils had been lifted and we were once more with Grimaldi at Drury Lane.

'Where *do* the dogs go at night?' The question has never been sufficiently answered. In tragedy and in comedy they find other lonely devils, and so comfort themselves by multiplying their loneliness. That night Charlie wanders off to a cabaret, hiding Scraps in his baggy pants. There, as one might have known, he meets Edna Purviance singing sentimental songs and making a bare living as a cabaret artist. She smiles at him. It is enough. His soaring spirit is at peace. He is brave enough now to invite her to a drink, and when he is thrown out by the bouncer he hardly cares: he has known felicity.

Charlie's felicity is always a tenuous thing, and when Scraps digs up a wallet hidden by some thieves, we know that he is tempting fate. The vision of a life lived with Edna and the dog in great wealth tempts him, but the classical sin of *hubris* has been committed: he must fight bitterly for that final contentment. In the concluding passages of the film Charlie virtually attacks the thieves like a one-man siege army. They find him; they know he has the wallet; and they are determined to regain it. In the finest western style they fire their six-shooters. Charlie has no respect for six-shooters. He knocks them off with a mallet. We see him wandering happily down the road with the girl and the dog by his side. An intolerable melancholy hangs over these concluding scenes. For how long will he keep the wallet, the girl and the dog?

He does not keep them for long. In *Shoulder Arms* he is once more alone in the world, friendless, far from any girl, in the muddy swamps of the trenches of France, embittered and silly and happy in his own way. We see him at drill: his immense boots are forever getting in his way. We see him in the trench staggering under the weight of a destiny which takes the form of trenching tools, knapsacks, a huge mouse-trap, a cheese-grater, whatever he could scrounge from the PX. He is Sad Sack with a glint of real madness in his eyes. In *A Dog's Life* he showed pity for the poor because he was poor. In *Shoulder Arms* he shows pity for the soldiers for the good reason that he is a soldier himself. Authority he regards as an ingenious addition to his burdens: he fights authority with an enviable carelessness, and when the sergeant dresses him down, he makes sure that the sergeant will catch his fingers in the mouse-trap. On guard duty, while the rain falls, he is in his element. The misery is so complete that he must set to dreaming of Third Avenue bars, but the dreams fade, there is only the rain falling, and there are no letters from home – where is his home? How eagerly he rushes to confront the postman, and how disconsolately he looks at the letters which are delivered to everyone else. He is alone in the world. He belongs to the wasteland of the spirit, to the world where all enjoyment is vicarious and all suffering is real. He peers over the shoulder of a soldier reading a letter from home, his face wreathed with joy when he learns that the soldier has become a father, and then crestfallen he returns to his mouse-trap and nibbles the cheese. When he does receive a parcel it is sent by one of those murderous pranksters; it is a parcel of dog-biscuits. No: he does not belong here. He belongs to the dugouts, the muddy roads, the leafless trees. He tries to sleep, but the water rises, and he is about to drown, as he drowned once before in *The Rounders*, but if he must drown, he is determined that he should accomplish his destiny in good style. Beneath the level of the water lies his soggy pillow. He reaches down for it, admires it, smooths it, fluffs it out, kisses it, and returns it to its watery grave; and when the water covers his face, he reaches over for a phonograph horn and breathes happily through it.

All this is but a prelude. Charlie's legitimate world is the eternally recurrent world of zero hour. He is forever being ordered over the top. Yet, in his charmed life, in his absence of counterfeit, in his strenuous incitement to good, he has the power to survive. The ladder is prepared for him. At an order he hurls himself up the ladder and runs to meet the enemy; but his foot is caught in the topmost rung of the ladder, and he sails down into the trench, into the mud, into the world where it is always zero hour. When we see him again he has captured a whole flock of Germans who wander within a lunar landscape with their hands above their heads. 'How did you capture them?' the sergeant asks with some surprise. 'I surrounded them,' Charlie answers; and when you see the film today, you shudder at the strange coincidences. In just such a miraculous way, Hitler announced his capture of some Scottish soldiers in 1917.

Charlie hates the trench, but it is the world he knows, and his accomplishments within that world are prodigious, accurate and always charming. Jean Cocteau once said of *Shoulder Arms* that it moved to the rhythm of kettledrums. It does nothing of the sort. It moves to the rhythm of Chinese crackers, and you never know when the next explosion will occur. Charlie in the trench never acquiesces to the disintegration of the world around him; he will use everything to his own advantage. The born scrounger, the born purloiner of discarded remnants, he employs a nutmeg-grater to scratch his back on, and enemy bullets sailing over the trench are employed to light his cigarettes by friction or to break open the necks of beer bottles. He will find enjoyment where he can. He chalks up his successes like a man chalking up his tally at billiards; when his helmet is shot away, he solves the problem of human justice by simply erasing the last tallymark; in that way justice will be satisfied.

Shoulder Arms is a comic film where there is almost no fooling; it is still the most serious and the most imaginative film produced on the subject of World War I. Its roots lay in the disasters of the time, disasters so terrible that they were only bearable when regarded as part of the pattern of an insane comedy. When Charlie emerges out of the trenches and performs a wonderful dance among the trees, he employs the traditional acrobatics of the *Commedia dell' Arte*. Charlie disguised as a tree, running away from the Germans, then advancing towards them, freezing into immobility when he is about to be discovered, is only the modern form of Pulcinella who, in the classic drama of *Pulcinella the Brigand Chief*, evaded his pursuers by becoming a weathercock, and then a milestone, and then a tortoise in a forest. But what Charlie did to the tree belongs to white magic. The hollow tree-trunk did not look like Charlie, did not walk like Charlie, possessed no moustache, no derby and no swagger-stick, but it was pure Charlie. If Charlie had been able to speak, then the tree would have been able to speak, and it would have spoken in Charlie's authentic voice. And when the tree jabbed a German who was bayonetting all the trees in sight, the jab was the appropriate jab as it would be performed by a wandering tree which had suddenly taken it in its head to be Charlie. Such moments of authentic mystery and wonder never occurred again in *Shoulder Arms*, and after these forest scenes the film gradually splutters out; but it is the virtue of Chinese crackers that their last splutters are more resounding than the first, and when

Charlie arrests the Kaiser and the Crown Prince while disguised in a German uniform, his fastidious pleasure in the victory as the car swings into the allied lines is itself as resounding as fire-crackers. It is a real victory, accomplished with a considerable amount of the inevitable casuistry which attends such victories: there are locked closets, huge processions of goose-stepping soldiers, bewildering escapes, a charming French girl who possesses some of Charlie's own *savoir-faire* and an oddly engaging German to help him. The allies toss their caps in the air. By the capture of the Kaiser and the Crown Prince Charlie has successfully brought the war to an end. This is as it should be, and when we see Charlie waking up from his dream in the camp we feel cheated.

The original ending was better. In this original version Charlie was honoured by the heads of the allied states for his single-handed capture of the Kaiser and the Crown Prince. An immense banquet is held for him in the Palace of Versailles. Poincaré and all the other dignitaries speak of Charlie's accomplishments; he smiles drowsily, drunk with champagne, and only rises to his feet to make a speech after the most illustrious of the guests have prompted him. While he is making his inebriated reply, the King of England snips a button from his uniform as a souvenir.

Shoulder Arms showed that Charlie possessed unsuspected powers. He had guyed the cops in Los Angeles, made havoc of pretensions as they showed themselves on Santa Monica Boulevard, destroyed with a single lift of his eyebrows all the esoteric charms of the well-fed, and now he was demonstrating that the same qualities could guy the German army and the treaty-makers. The concluding portion of the original version was in keeping with Charlie's thesis: that mockery is the happiest weapon of all. He had guyed the Kaiser. Why not guy the King of England? Abraham Lincoln said once: 'I laugh because I must not cry – that's all, that's all.' Chaplin could, and did reply: 'I laugh because I laugh, and to laugh is sufficient reason for existence, and there is no limit to our laughter.' There was always a hint of didacticism in him. He was not content to work miracles; he must find the reasons for the miracles, and explain them to his own satisfaction. 'Always preaching to himself, like an angel from a cloud, but in none ... here picturing a vice so as to make it ugly to those that practised it: and a virtue so as to make it beloved, even by those that loved it not; and all this with a most particular grace and an inexpressible addition of comeliness.' It is Donne delivering a sermon to His Majesty at Whitehall, but it might have been a description of Charlie; and the triumphant return through the enemy lines with the Kaiser in tow was among the most comely and gracious acts he ever accomplished. Nevertheless, it was ungracious of him not to permit the King of England to snip off his button as a souvenir. In the world of comedy, which does not obey the laws of the nations, such an action would have been perfectly appropriate; there is even a kind of impropriety in not allowing it to take place.

Charlie, the angel in the cloud, tumbling to earth whenever it pleased him, returning to the cloud whenever he desired, behaved with decorum even when he was living in the most improbable of worlds. One should therefore expect that among the true improbabilities of Versailles, the King of England should behave with the same disregard of protocol. In the history of the world there have been very few clowns, and their buttons, for all we know, may be precious.

In *Shoulder Arms* Charlie explored the enchanted world of war; in *Sunnyside* he explored the enchantments of summer. The film opens with the steeple of a small church dominating a quiet country village. Charlie is back from the wars. He is now a hired man on a farm, and this is exactly what he wants to be. He is happy there, though the owner of the farm operates a hotel and Charlie is hotel drudge as well as cowman, for ever at odds with his master. He works so hard that he has no time for sleep, and is the prey to all the enticements of labour-saving devices. He has accomplished miracles of labour-saving during the war, and he now finds no difficulty in milking cows into the coffee-pots. Edna Purviance will console him; and as he gazes dreamily into her young face, he knows the contentment of passion, and if he is pouring out sugar when he sets eyes on her, he will continue to pour out sugar until she has moved away, and if he is herding his cows and sees her at the crossroads, then he will allow the cows to go wherever they desire rather than forget to watch her. The pure tenderness of his enchanted gaze remains long after the cows have disappeared down a country lane, wandering to their hearts' content among the surrounding meadows. Charlie must bring them back into line. He is all hurry and perplexity; it was easier to deal with German prisoners. The sun is setting. If he cannot get them back into the lane, they will be lost for ever. He is half-blinded by the sun, mistakes a fat stranger for a cow, takes him by the shoulders and peers at him intently to see whether he is a lost cow. At last he herds the cows together, but when in his triumph he rides one of them bareback, he is unceremoniously thrown into a mountain stream, and the second reel of the three-reeler describes his dream.

. There never was a dream quite like the dream in *Sunnyside*. The French, who have great taste in these matters, called the whole film *L'Idylle aux champs*, as though it were nothing else but this dream, and indeed every incident in the dream is memorable and we can forget the rest without too much harm. Charlie awakes from the stream to see four girls dressed in transparent Greek tunics dancing in the meadowland where only a little while before the cows were wandering. He plucks a daisy and arranges his hair to represent two black horns. Now at last he is truly and admittedly Pan, with the flower as the badge of his authority; but since a flower can serve many purposes, he decides to play on it; and so piping Pan-like on the daisy he joins their dance. He dances superbly. He becomes the strange figure clothed in black and white who dominates the tragedy of *Les Sylphides*. There is no burlesque. The dance is performed as a holy rite. It is true that at a moment of Bacchanalian frenzy he steps on a cactus patch, but he keeps pace with the dance even when, with a disdainful glance at the cactuses, he removes them from his legs. When the dance is over the handmaidens tend him on a bed of flowers, and then he is in the utmost heaven, for all four of the maidens smile at him and demand his favours. But it is the dance one remembers most for its grace and agility, and the sudden opening of the lens into the wider perspectives of paradise. There were to be other dances later. When he dance-pantomimed the story of David and Goliath in *The Pilgrim*, and when he performed a table dance with rolls in *The Gold Rush*, and when he danced with a balloon in *The Great Dictator*, he showed that he could dance with a purpose; but in *Sunnyside* he pretended to no purpose. He was dancing because one dances in paradise, and there is no reason for it. The dance ends, and then it seems that there is no reason for the film to continue.

The last reel of *Sunnyside* is almost bathos. It could hardly be otherwise. The inevitable city slicker arrives, throwing Charlie into a state of anguish for fear that he will lose Edna. Charlie comes with a bouquet of flowers to her window, only to discover the city slicker in possession of Edna's heart. The flowers which are his perpetual emblem are now discarded; he will imitate the city slicker to the wretch's disadvantage, and this he does by the employment of all the artifices which his teeming brain can imagine. His waistcoat and cuffs are fashioned from paper, his spats from a pair of old socks, his elegant walking stick is topped, not with ivory, but with a carefully trimmed candle. So equipped, he advances towards his conquest, and once again he finds the masher in command. Charlie turns towards an oncoming automobile, determined to put an end to his sufferings and throw himself headlong. He awakes. Once more it is only a dream. The masher departs, and leaves him in sole possession of the beloved Edna.

In these three films the quality of tenderness was expressed with the most winning gestures and with a hint of weariness. The loneliness which characterised Charlie in the early films, and was to enshroud him again later, plays no part. We are not asked to sympathise with him: we are asked to rejoice with him, even in his moments of illimitable sadness, even in his greatest misery. It is the mood of Shakespeare's *Tempest* and the posthumous quartets of Beethoven, where the sharp and strident dissonances attempt, but never quite succeed, in mastering the simple aimless dance-tunes which form the ground-swell of the music. Caliban roars, but Ariel plucks at the sleeve and Miranda laughs gaily in her cavern adorned with seashells, knowing that the kingdom will be given back to her father. They are small films; they do not embrace a wide territory, nor do they go deeply into things. That pity for the poor, for soldiers and for dreamers was not pathos; it was pity, and nothing more. Afterwards, enlarging his canvas, the emotions became more complex, and the strident notes were more often heard. Never again was there to be that simple sweetness, nor should anyone have desired it.

CHAPTER XIII

THE KID

WITH *The Kid* for the first time Chaplin opened the shutter wide and said what he wanted to say in his own leisurely time. If we exclude *Tillie's Punctured Romance*, where he was neither the director nor the star performer, it was the longest of his films, the most obviously autobiographical and the most mature; and it was graced by the presence of Jackie Coogan who, on a smaller and gentler scale, was the spittin' image of Charlie, with the same air of furious refinement and casual indifference to the horrors of the mercenary world. Here, too, there appeared for the first time the full measure of the pathos which had been present in most of the earlier films, and nowhere more remarkably than in *The Bank*, but now the sense of pathos was explored, made credible, placed in a setting where there could be no doubt of its relevance.

In the past Charlie had always been in search of his *alter ego*. He found it in Mabel Normand, whose wonderful petulance imitated his own, and he was to find it again in Marilyn Nash when he came to portray Monsieur Verdoux. But Jackie Coogan was more than an *alter ego*; he was the young Charlie, bone of his bone and flesh of his flesh, the world's imp reduced to the size of a mocking child. Chaplin was able to do with Coogan what no other director has ever done or could do with a child star. He recreated him in his own image, with the result that the two together, the little ragamuffin and the tramp, were able to create an overwhelming tide of sympathy for both. And since Charlie, under one or another of his disguises, was continually present on the screen, there was never a moment when the attention flagged. In this sense the film was a *tour de force*. It was also an astonishing example of Chaplin's power to infuse poetry into the slightest gestures -- when he wipes his nose or picks out cigarette stubs from a sardine can, or sticks his big toe through the hole of a worn bed-cover, the artistry is now complete, rounded, perfected to a pitch which makes the best of the early films look as though they had been composed by amateurs.

Chaplin's progress had never been by leaps and bounds. It was always inch-meal, arrived at by the slow and careful examination of his own artistry. *Monsieur Verdoux* was to include a hundred touches which were employed before; they were more subtle, the manner of their arrangement had changed, but basically the touches were the same. So it was in *The Kid*. The doss-house scenes were not so comic as those in *Triple Trouble*, nor so ferocious, but they derived from them. The relationship between Charlie and the boy was very similar to the relationship between Charlie and the little mongrel dog in *A Dog's Life*. The dream sequence followed something of the same pattern as the wonderful dream sequence in *Sunnyside*. There were perhaps twenty other incidents which could be traced to their origins in earlier films, but there was also something prodigiously new. Previously Chaplin dealt in caricature, and there was hardly a film which did not contain its huge, grotesque and gesticulating giants, its mad pygmies, its fork-bearded dwarfs, its senile long-necked women. Quite suddenly the perspective changes. In *The Kid* everyone is reduced to a normal scale except the bruiser, and he becomes in time as normal as the others, to be accepted like the others as part of the lost world in the hideous little alleyway off the Kennington Road. Burlesque disappears; so do the freaks. And with the disappearance of the freaks, pathos comes into its own, for one does not pity the freaks, and it is only with difficulty that one can have tenderness for them.

In *The Kid* Chaplin bathes all his characters in the light of his tenderness, so that there are even moments when the tenderness becomes altogether too much, and he verges dangerously on the edge of being mawkish; but having reached that edge, he retires gracefully and just in time. The pity is real, intense, terrible. It is like the pity of the suicide at the last moment when he hangs on the window-ledge of his room on the fifty-ninth floor of a hotel and sees all the people crowding and milling in the streets below, and suddenly all his despairing love, all his tenderness for these people is expressed in a choking sob and with a little salute performed by the hand which a moment ago was clinging to the ledge. In *The Kid* Chaplin performs the salute without the need of climbing to the fifty-ninth floor and without the need of suicide; all that was necessary for him was to think back to his childhood on Kennington Road.

There are two kinds of pathos: the pathos of despair and the pathos of happiness. Both are present in *The Kid*. The pathos of happiness is seen at the very beginning when Charlie comes jauntily down the street, swinging his cane. Never has he been so jaunty. Rubbish is thrown out of windows on to his head. He not only does not care, but accepts the rain of garbage as though it were providential, delighted with it, delighted with these people who have nothing better to do than present him with the evidence of their good sense – what else can one do with garbage but throw it out of the window? There follows the famous scene in which he delicately extracts a cigarette butt from his shiny cigarette case, a doctored sardine tin, then tamps it to shake down the excess tobacco, and all the time holds it with the delicacy of a French aristocrat in a salon holding a cigar, but a still finer scene occurs immediately afterwards when he glances at his gloves where the fingers are worn through, and having gazed at them with a look of long-suffering acquaintance, as one might gaze at a maiden aunt, he negligently throws them into a refuse can. The negligence is superb; it is also pathetic, for though the gesture involves the whole of Charlie and underscores his courageous refusal to be discountenanced by slums and poverty, the slums and poverty remain: and one wonders why, having thrown his ragged gloves away, he does not also throw his ragged trousers into the refuse can.

It is a wonderful introduction to Charlie, and immediately there are more wonders to come, for soon we are introduced to a crone, sister of the wild gypsy woman in *The Vagabond*, who is trundling her worn-out baby carriage through the miserable streets, and Charlie's efforts to put the swaddled baby he has found into her baby-carriage are pure comedy, but they are also tragedy. There is a calculated ferocity in the woman which is astounding. She belabours him with an umbrella. She screams her curses at him. In *The Vagabond*, faced with a crone of such exemplary evil, Charlie simply kicked her into the dust, and the passage in which he kicks her has something of the impact of stark tragedy. This time the crone wins. A cop arrives. Charlie is compelled to assume his burden, and as he wanders disconsolately away, the baby in his arms, he very carefully removes his hand from the place which might reasonably be expected to get wet, and when he comes to a manhole he contemplates with the keenest imaginable relish the idea of simply dropping the baby into it.

There is a wonderful play on his features during these early scenes. The mood varies instantaneously. Shortly afterwards we see him living with the boy, and three or four years have passed, and by this time the tramp is tamed. No longer are there such quick changes of expression, such alarming visions, such terrible crones. Charlie is concerned with the boy to the exclusion of his own worldly joys, his own fastidious tastes, and from the moment when we first see him with the boy the pathos of despair hangs over him. We know, and Charlie knows, that the boy will be taken from him. Such pleasures do not last. But while he is with the boy he is determined to extract the maximum of sweetness from their relationship. The tragic overtones are everywhere. Consciously or unconsciously, Charlie has borrowed from the heroes of Greek drama the tradition of the actor's *apatheia*, his indifference to the world around him, his mockery which is so huge that it includes even himself, but though he can mock everything the boy is beyond the mocking ring which Charlie throws around the world. To the very end of the film the relationship between Charlie and the Kid sustains them, and for the first and last time Chaplin is immune from his loneliness, from the wilful rages that used to overcome him, and now there is nothing in the least wistful about him. When the boy is taken away from him, the blow falls as in high tragedy, suddenly, inevitably, with the force of a horrible catastrophe.

The presence of the Kid helps us to understand the workings of the clown's mind. The clown is a creator, like the poet or the great tragic actor. He lives in his own world, and defies the world we know by virtue of his illuminations, his secret knowledge, his power to weave spells, his protean capacity to assume what forms he pleases. To him whatever is accidental in the world belongs to logic; whatever is logical and expected is to be regarded with disdain. The world is suspect; therefore he moves in his own world, in perpetual conflict with our world. He moves with the terrible directness of a child, seeing no obstacles to his progress, and like a child he falls over every obstacle in his path and cannot understand why he did not see them, or why there should be any conflict. Partly, of course, the clown's world is that of a child, and therein lies the incongruity of Charlie setting up house with a child, for in those extraordinary sequences in which Charlie is seen living happily with the Kid, we are never certain whether we are seeing their adventures through the eyes of Charlie or through the eyes of the Kid. A transformation is continually occurring. As the film progresses we become aware that Charlie is assuming some of the expressions of the Kid, and the Kid in turn is coming more and more to resemble Charlie.

Chaplin had never used a child before for anything more than background, and he was now playing with fire. Eisenstein once suggested that the root of Chaplin's art lay in 'seeing things most terrible, most pitiful, most tragic through the eyes of a laughing child'. It was partly true. Many of Charlie's gestures can be traced to Chaplin's childhood, the little skip, the way he slides round corners with one leg sticking out in front, the look of abandoned glee whenever anything amusing happens, even the magnificent sense of mimicry, but all these were subtly compounded into the figure of the vagabond, who was more than child, because he had endured more than any child had ever endured. Chaplin had studied the joys of children, but he knew more of their griefs. He knew that children are never happy for long. He knew, too, that they are incapable of feeling sorry for grown-ups. The portrait of the Kid, eternally loving, eternally mischievous, eternally in a state of wild elation at the world around him was therefore an artificial portrait, and nearly every gesture performed by the Kid was the product of Chaplin's imagination. The Kid's performance was a triumph of art, but it was Chaplin's art. The Kid had to be taught to play the part of a child. The subtleties and complications were therefore endless, for at moments the Kid becomes Charlie, becomes more like

Charlie than Charlie has ever been, and it is as though the essence of Charlie has been extracted and placed within the soul of the Kid. At moments Charlie finds himself lost in a maze of mirrors.

Chaplin has told the story of how he first encountered the Kid. It happened in a hotel in Los Angeles. The boy's parents were acting in a neighbouring theatre, and when Chaplin appeared in the hotel they wanted Jackie Coogan to greet him in the proper manner. The boy was unruly, and decided to go to sleep. He was fast asleep when Chaplin came up to him. When he heard Chaplin's voice he woke, rubbed his eyes, greeted the actor with a polished imitation of one famous actor greeting another, and promptly went to sleep again. In a sense Jackie Coogan slept through the whole of the production of *The Kid*. Instead of the actor Jackie Coogan there was a charming sleepwalker who obeyed the magic impulses of his prompter.

The magic had never been exhibited before on such a scale. The spells, so intricately woven, were never repeated, for though Chaplin could charm actresses into acting as they had never acted before and would never act again, his power over them was never so complete as his power over the Kid. The child became more than child, more than an ideal image of childhood; he was the child that everyone dreams of possessing. Guillaume Apollinaire has a wonderful poem relating how some clowns spread out a carpet near the statue of Danton in the Boulevard St Germain in the cloudless days before July, 1914. They performed to the music of a barrel-organ, their livery falling to pieces, wearing rose-coloured tights, odd men who seemed to come from nowhere, faces covered with flour, lips painted like rosebuds. They parleyed with the audience, insisting that the performance could only begin when three whole francs were collected, but they were only able to gather two francs and fifty centimes. So they performed on that crowded little corner facing the church of St Germain-des-Près. They bowed to the four corners of the earth according to the practice of the ancient Egyptian priests, and suddenly they started to juggle and lift up immense weights. At this point the poem almost ceases, for there is little left to be said, and what remains is a kind of prayer:

Mais chaque spectateur cherchait en soi l'enfant miraculeux
Siècle ô siècle des nuages.

But each spectator looked in himself for the miraculous child
Century O century of clouds.

Something of that same wonder enters into those early paintings of Picasso where we see some pitiful little boy, wearing dancing shoes and a cast-off suit many sizes too large for him, standing beside a father who gazes out of the picture altogether, lost in the dreams of his own childhood, having forgotten the boy by his side; and on the pinched face of the clown's child there is such a look of dedication, such promise of miracles, that we pause, for we are ourselves that child. So it is in *The Kid*, where the magic of Charlie's love for the child has the effect of allowing us all to recapture our lost childhood, the centuries of clouds.

One should not enquire too closely into this magic, for like all magic it is dangerous. The lost child may be Charlie's youth, for he lives in the slums of London, and the terrible room where Charlie lives with the Kid is modelled on the room in Chester Street where Chaplin lived, and the little alleyway where the main action takes place seems to be Hamish Street, which Chaplin knew well. It is no more than a turning off the Lambeth Walk, a little side-alley which gives the impression of leading nowhere. The film echoes with recollections of London, and the famous scene at the end, where the feathered angels float over the street and paradise is miraculously brought forth in a dream may owe something to the fact that there is a pub called The Feathers at the corner of Old Paradise Street, and Chaplin must have known them both. Chester Street is called Chester Way nowadays, and most of the churches which Chaplin saw off Lambeth Walk suffered from German bombs. By an odd fate, the pubs survived. Even today the pub called The Feathers and the street called Old Paradise remain as they were when Chaplin was a boy. In *The Kid* he recreated his own childhood in the light of unearthly suns, his imagination running riot among his memories, his gifts at their greatest. It is Chaplin's *David Copperfield*, and his *Oliver Twist* as well, and just as Dickens was forever using the streets he knew well to create character, as though there was some power in a street which formed a mind,

so Chaplin's invention of the little alleyway with the ashcans at
the corners and the old tub outside the stables where the boy
washes in the morning belong to emotion recollected in tranquillity. In spite of the technical faults, the too-quick transitions,
the often senseless titles, he was now in full command of his
medium, and he was never again to produce a film so tender or
so close to the bone.

The Kid came at the end of a long process of discovery. In a
sense it was Chaplin's testament, a statement of his own youth
and a last look at his past. It included in the flop-house scenes
fragments borrowed from the uncompleted film *Life*, which also
had the qualities of a testament. *The Idle Class*, which followed
immediately afterwards, hinted at parody. The tramp appears
again, but he no longer trails clouds of glory. We see him on the
golf links, snoring away with a golf ball balanced on his mouth,
and sometimes the ball is propelled upwards by his lusty snores.
It is a moment a little like the moment when Hynkel dances with
the balloon. Then another tramp comes along, disguised like
Charlie, and this new tramp swings a club and strikes the golf
ball over the hill, then he wanders merrily on his way. In *The
Idle Class* he dreams of impossible adventures with women, takes
liberties with another man's wife at a masked ball, where he is
mistaken for her husband, and the film ends when the real
husband arrives in a suit of mediaeval armour which has to be
prized open with a can-opener. It is just possible that the suit of
armour provides a kind of pun for Chaplin's own name, which
comes from *capeline* and means 'a mailed hood'.

Pay Day was of more consequence. It is simpler, and follows
a precise logic of its own. Spare, beautifully constructed, it is the
best of the later shorts, the most luminous and the least manipulated. There is no story. It is simply an account of Charlie's
working day from the moment when he first arrives at the
building-lot with a flower behind his back in the hope of escaping
the wrath of his foreman to the moment when he goes to sleep
in the bath and in mortal fear of his wife. It is pay day, and
Charlie discovers that he has been overpaid. He is enormously
pleased with the discovery and tries to make out that even more
money is due to him. As a bricklayer's assistant he performs
feats of acrobatics on the staging, catches bricks faster than

anyone has caught them before, falls in love with the foreman's daughter and by evening he is happily drunk, singing drunken songs in the street. When it is time to catch a tram, he can hardly see. He stumbles against a hot-dog stand, thinking it is a tramcar, and strap-hangs from a sausage suspended on the ceiling, and then, like all the other late passengers in tramcars, he opens his newspaper and waits till he reaches his destination. The artificiality of *The Idle Class* is wholly absent; the fierce winds of comedy are allowed full play. He sways on the strap, smiles to himself, looks round to see whether there are any pretty girls and then shrugs: the tramcar is empty, but what can you expect when it is raining? When he returns home, his wife is waiting for him with a rolling-pin.

That sense of a real life in which the tramp can breathe his native air returns in *The Pilgrim*. Nothing is forced; the people and the incidents are real, tumultuous and a little silly. Charlie has escaped from prison, and is thinking of returning to the comforts of prison when he espies the clothes of a parson who is bathing. Charlie puts them on. Why not? The parson is blissfully swimming. Equally blissful, Charlie goes to the railway station, wearing the parson's clothes. He nearly gives himself away when he comes to a railway station and wraps his hands round the ticket-seller's grill, and when he gets into a train, he discovers that the fat policeman beside him is reading about the jail-break. He gets off at the next station, to find a welcome committee all ready to receive him. He is exquisitely polite to the welcome committee. He understands them. He can imitate precisely the smug gentility of their expressions. He leads them to church, carefully weighs the collection boxes, beams at the pretty women and gazes wistfully at the elderly ladies, as though he divined in them some remaining spark of life, and when the time comes to deliver a sermon he decides to amuse them by performing the parts of David, Goliath and all the armies looking down on the plain. We tend to regard this performance as pantomime; it is certainly pantomime, but it is also a gay dance, and Goliath dances as gracefully as Charlie – the enemy is given the honours of the house. David, the discerning marksman, has no animosity against Goliath, nor has Goliath any unfriendly feelings towards David. They spar as lovers spar. When Goliath falls at last, all one's sympathies are with him against the cunning street-arab who felled him. The congregation is puzzled, not only by the dance but by Charlie's repeated curtain-calls.

The first scene is over. As so often in Chaplin's films, the curtain-raiser is a little too long and the first scene a little too short. The design may be deliberate. What is clear is that the pantomiming of David and Goliath leaves us pleasantly expectant: there are another hundred Bible stories we would like him to pantomime. But no, he must return to the house of the church warden and partake of Sunday dinner in the company of Edna Purviance, who had smiled at him while sitting at the church-organ. The sweetness which attended him during the sermon continues throughout the Sunday dinner. Charlie makes himself useful. He is already deeply in love with Edna, and it delights him that he will stay at this house. He even endures with remarkable patience the showing of the family album. There is a terrible moment when the whiskey bottle in his pocket is smashed, but he has known worse events, and he puts it to good use. He had smoked a cigarette during the church service, and then explained that he was merely fumigating the air. But at this point an extraordinary thing happens: the Kid returns, this time as pure goat, pure principle of evil. Having experimented with the Kid as example of all that is most tender, joyful and divine in life, Charlie now experiments with the Kid as all that is most oafish, stupid and malevolent. This terrible child enters like a whirlwind, attaching flypaper to the ladies' dresses, throwing the goldfish on to the flower-beds, disconsolately determined upon evil. Recklessly, the child decides to demonstrate his power over Charlie. Charlie smiles benevolently, takes the boy by the hand, cajoles him, speaks sweetly to him, and all the while the boy's arrogance floods over the screen. Charlie waits till the others have left the room, then he administers condign punishment; he does what he always does when confronted with evil – he gives it a kick. It is a wonderful kick. All the *saeva indignatio* of which Charlie is capable enters the kick which is deftly directed into the pit of the boy's stomach.

This is not, however, the end of the child's malevolence, for when Charlie is helping to portion the Christmas pudding, he discovers that a derby has been substituted for the pudding, and

City Lights, 1931

Modern Times,
1936

over this derby sauce and whipped cream have been smeared. We know the Kid did this, because when the derby is finally abandoned, the Kid licks off the cream with his tongue. He is hugely delighted with himself. Charlie promises that still more condign punishment will be meted out, but the Sunday morning calm is interrupted by the appearance of a crook, who has known Charlie before and is perfectly capable of using his knowledge. Now, for the second time in his career, Charlie has to assume the guise of a defender of the law. The crook learns where the household money is kept. Charlie must keep it away from him. But how? Charlie himself is not sure. He eyes the crook warily. At night the battle is engaged. At the precise moment when the crook steals from his bedroom door to steal the money, Charlie also steals from his door. A fantastic battle occurs in an endless silence. Charlie must safeguard the money or lose his position in the church. When the crook opens the drawer, Charlie closes it, neatly catching the man's fingers, smiles apologetically, tries to reason with him, explains the dishonour attending upon all robbery, kneels at his feet, slips his hand up beside him to see whether the thief has purloined anything, threatens, begs and utters warning cries, and he does all this without moving his lips, in the most complete silence. Only the fight with Mack Swain in the Alaskan hut rivals this scene where the pantomime of robbery is expressed in the most lurid terms. Finally the crook, by setting a candle to Charlie's backside, succeeds in taking his enemy unawares; he skips to a saloon, and there Charlie catches up with him and gets the money back. His triumph is the triumph of innocence over adversity. He is 'the parfit, gentle knight' whose only thought is to return to the family which offered him his Sunday dinner, his only desire to attend the church for the rest of his days and pantomime all the heroic actions ot the Bible through a multitude of Sundays.

In the final scene the sheriff is on his track. Charlie, an escaped convict posing as a parson, is known to the police. Edna protests. She, more than anyone, knows the innocence of his heart. If he has been in jail, then it can only be because he has imitated someone who should have been sent to jail in his stead. The sheriff has pity on the parson. They are approaching the Mexican border, and so he tells Charlie to go and gather flowers

G

on the other side of the frontier. Charlie does as he is told. He gathers the flowers and comes running back to the sheriff, a magnificent creature on a black horse. The sheriff smiles weakly, and points beyond the border, Charlie following the direction of the pointing hand. 'No,' says Charlie, 'I understand perfectly well what you are doing, but you cannot fool me. I am your prisoner. Do what you must do.' The sheriff decides upon sterner measures: he boots Charlie over the frontier. In Mexico some bandits suddenly start shooting. Charlie is at his wits' end. He waves to the sheriff, who is gradually disappearing in a cloud of dust. He turns over in his mind the possibility of an arrangement with the bandits, but their shooting is dangerously accurate. The film ends with Charlie skipping and hopping along the boundary-line, prepared to jump into the country which offers the greatest prospect of safety, though he must know there is no safety anywhere. On the frontiers he hops and skips for an eternity.

The Pilgrim tells on another plane and with a sweet-tempered dramatic force the same story as The Kid, without any of the advantages of atmosphere and without the overwhelming sense of love. Once again Charlie is caught in the rat-trap and does his best to live with gallantry. He is on the side of the angels, but the devils afflict him, yet even the devils are kindly, and Charlie is exceptionally kindly. In The Pilgrim he is older and greyer, and knows more about the ways of the world, and the world in turn knows more about his peculiar proclivities. Even the sheriff respects his passion for flowers.

With The Kid, Pay Day and The Pilgrim Chaplin is at his ease. The sense of strain would enter The Gold Rush and The Circus until in The Great Dictator the fury and the tension overmastered the actor. This is not to say that the later films were better or worse than the happy trio; it is simply that in these three films we are aware of an innocence that vanished, a gaiety that never returned. As parson, convict, bricklayer, father he showed his mettle, and in these rôles there was no need to caricature or to go beyond the bounds of his experience. As gold-digger and trapeze artist he possesses a perfection of his own, but he is not naturally a gold-digger or a trapeze artist: these are things he has to force himself to do. He is best when force is absent, when he simply follows the delights of the moment.

Of the many poems which have been written about Chaplin the best is a short poem by Hart Crane written shortly after he had seen *The Kid*, which contains the following lines:

> *And yet these fine collapses are not lies*
> *More than the pirouettes of any pliant cane;*
> *Our obsequies are, in a way, no enterprise.*
> *We can evade you, and all else but the heart:*
> *What blame to us if the heart live on?*

What blame, indeed? It is the singular glory of these films that they were concerned with the heart, and had no other aim except to emphasise the heart's adventures. All are parables, but they have the advantage that they may be read to children, who understand them instantly: yet the complexities are everywhere. That slender figure with the look of a happy defiance in his eyes was well-named 'the pilgrim'; his progress leads only from the heart to the heart, and this is enough.

CHAPTER XIV

THE FROZEN HILLS

WHEN *The Gold Rush* was completed after fourteen months of work, Chaplin declared: 'This is the film I want to be remembered by.' There is no reason why we should take this statement too seriously, for he had said the same about *The Kid* and he was to say it again when he completed *Monsieur Verdoux;* and less than any other producer is he in danger of being forgotten.

The Gold Rush is mis-titled, perhaps deliberately. There is very little about rushing after gold. The gold-diggers in their long weary march through the snows, the heavy clouds brushing low over the earth, the eternal wastes, all these are things which belong to the natural habitat of the clown. He must go where danger is. On the edge of a precipice he is in his element. Before he had fought cops; now he must set himself against the elements, and in the frozen hills of an imaginary Alaska he creates his own setting. And where *The Circus* is cold, shining like the cold fire which is employed to cut through steel below the surface of the sea, *The Gold Rush* is all warmth, blazing like the hearth-logs of our remembered winters. So we see him first in the freezing wastes, appearing belatedly after a long line of prospectors has passed before the camera, a small defiant ink-stain among the hills, twirling his cane a little to keep his spirits up.

An announcement says the scene is the snowy Chilkoot Pass in the Klondike gold rush of 1898, but we know better. He has entered the mysterious world of snows, which children know: it is his own home, one of his many homes, and he is perfectly at ease there. He wanders along a narrow ledge. An enormous black bear follows him. He is not in the least discountenanced, pays no attention to the bear, smiles happily, whistles a tune, and twirls his cane. When the bear disappears in a cave and is no longer dangerous, Charlie hears a noise of stones falling somewhere – then he jumps with fear, and falls the whole way down the mountain. At the bottom he leans on his cane, and he is a little surprised when it sinks to the handle. Thereupon, like any child journeying in any fairyland, he takes out a map and follows the arrow pointing North.

We shall not understand the clown unless we remember that he is an adventurer. Unhappily, no one has yet been able to draw that absolute map of the mind where the real adventures take place. There are places on the map marked 'Here are tigers' and other places marked 'icy wastes'. 'The mind has mountains, cliffs of fall,' as Gerard Manley Hopkins has reminded us; it also has pleasant cottages and meadows flowing with milk and honey and odd-shaped rabbit-holes, and Mount Olympus has its place there, and somewhere in the east upon the sunset is Kafka's gilded castle. It is the function of the clown to hurl himself at the most dangerous places, if only to show that there is no danger there. So he will dither on the highest trapezes and cock snooks at the most muscular cops. As for his method of journeying, Giles Earle has expressed it well enough in an Elizabethan song called *Tom o' Bedlam:*

> *With a heart of furious fancies*
> *Whereof I am commander,*
> *   With a burning spear*
> *   And a horse of air*
> *To the wilderness I wander.*

> *By a knight of ghosts and shadows*
> *I summoned am to tourney*
> *   Ten leagues beyond*
> *   The wild world's end:*
> *Methinks it is no journey.*

Charlie is of the same opinion. Having come 'ten leagues beyond the wild world's end', he is in territory he knows well, and clearly he thinks it is no journey. Why, then, should he fear such little things as bears?

The journey up the pass is the curtain-raiser. There follows the real terror, the terror at the heart of terror. Charlie makes no bones about it. It is ridiculous to fear bears; as for men – fear them always when they are freezing cold, when they are miserable, whenever they are not laughing. The scene in the hut, where Charlie, Big Jim McKay and Black Larsen huddle against the storm is terrifying. It is the world of delirium and nausea, the lurid dreams of men in doss-houses, the evil in the heart and the knife gleaming in the unsteady hand, exhaustion and near-murder on the edge of nowhere, storms and the creeping cold and no escape anywhere, and this world of pure delirium is transformed into one which is lit with a magical tenderness. The terror, however, remains. It is there in the background, always ready to spring out. The hut belongs to Black Larsen. Charlie is blown in, and then Big Jim is blown in, and Larsen wants nothing more than to be rid of the two interlopers, and since Larsen has a gun the two together must put an end to him. When Larsen is subdued, Big Jim goes mad. Charlie treats him gently, throws an arm round him, offers him a bone and gazes at him with all the sweetness of a child, or like a puppy prepared to play with the first stranger who comes along though its master lies dead.

Charlie's behaviour during the storm is something to wonder at. The worse the storm, the more terrible the consequences, the gayer he becomes. Charlie attempts to make them laugh, smiles eagerly, salts a candle and offers it to them as though it were a celery-stalk, and shrugs his shoulders against the storm. A dog has wandered in and taken up its place in the next room. They are all hungry, nervously eyeing one another, and when Big Jim goes to the room where the dog is and then returns picking his teeth, Charlie has good reasons for thinking the worst has happened. They decide to cut cards and decide who shall go out foraging. The choice falls on Larsen, who ambushes two mounted police and wanders out into the wilds on their sled. Larsen has no part in the story. He is a *deus ex machina*, and not a very convincing one. But Big Jim, a huge bear of a man, resembling a cross between a bear and Jupiter Tonans, is the perfect foil for Charlie, shaggy where Charlie is still the dandy, blustering where Charlie is rapier-sharp; one is an elemental force, and the other is the human comedy.

While the storm increases in violence, so does their hunger. They are so hungry that Charlie decides to cook one of his shoes, those enormous shoes which have always resembled sausages. He cooks it expertly, places it on a dish, pours some of the gravy over it, holds his finger to his nose, sharpens a knife, separates the uppers from the sole, and then with a fleeting smile of satisfaction offers Big Jim the sole, only to have his offer rejected. Big Jim settles for the uppers. Charlie is perfectly content with the sole, sucks the nails and the laces, and finding a nail shaped like a wishbone offers to break it with Big Jim. When we see Charlie again he is out on a foraging expedition and both his feet are wrapped in rags. Another shoe is cooking. Empty-handed, Charlie returns to the hut and prepares dinner. In the middle of the dinner Big Jim goes hideously mad, and imagines that Charlie is a plump chicken.

Then the nightmare begins. Nothing like this nightmare was ever to occur to Charlie again; nothing like it had ever happened before. Big Jim is out to murder. He will take the neck of the chicken, lay it on the table and cut off the protesting head, and Charlie looks at him with immense sadness and pity, almost prepared to offer himself as a sacrifice. They chase each other round the room, and suddenly Charlie becomes the chicken, and the frightened chicken is standing on the table: all Mack Swain has to do is to wring its neck. But Charlie escapes his fate by the use of a transformation scene: he changes from a chicken back to a man again, and Mack Swain is sufficiently aware of the change to pause for a moment – no more than a moment. When he looks for the chicken again, it is fluttering in panic round the room. Mack Swain chases it round the room and out into the snowfields, seizes a gun, fires at it, and we see the flapping wings, but suddenly they are Charlie's arms. The scene is played with an unrelenting effect of tragedy, Mack Swain becoming Mephistopheles with a spurt of powder and a column of blue flame. The sense of real panic emerges, and it is still there the next morning when we see them in bed, shuddering against the storm. Charlie has taken the inevitable precaution: his hands, not his feet, are inside his shoes – a trick he had played successfully in *Triple Trouble*. He hopes Mack Swain will not see that he is prepared to run. Unfortunately Mack Swain resembles nothing so much as Dickens' Mr Bunsby who appeared over the bulkhead of the cabin 'with one stationary eye on the mahogany face, and one revolving one, on the principle of some light-houses'. Mack Swain sees everything. There is another fight, as tense and malevolent as the fights the previous night, and Charlie would have been smothered under blankets if a bear had not taken it into its head to enter the cabin at that moment. The bear is not altogether convincing. It has an extra-ordinary resemblance to Mack Swain, just as the plump chicken bore an extraordinary resemblance to Charlie in his padded clothes. But Charlie is not plucked and dressed for a giant's dinner. Mack Swain shoots the bear, and we see Charlie sharpening the knives.

The subplot concerns Larsen, and it is wholly mismanaged and unconvincing. We have odd glimpses of Larsen working his claim, and Big Jim goes to join him. They fight together, and we are not quite sure what has happened to them, for they are left casually in the snow. It does not matter. We are concerned with Charlie, who wanders off to the boom town and falls in love with Georgia Hale, a cabaret singer who has only to smile for Charlie to be lifted up to the highest heaven, but in fact she is not smiling at Charlie, she is smiling at someone behind him, and though this trick has been used before, notably in *The Cure*, the use of it in *The Gold Rush* has a sharpness which was not apparent before; and Charlie's pain when he discovers she is not smiling at him is unbearably painful to watch. Charlie wanders off to the bar and drinks disconsolately by himself, and never had he appeared so lonely as in the obscure shack in Alaska. The loneliness vanishes only when, gazing out from his little cabin, he sees Georgia playing with snowballs, and by good fortune one of her snowballs hits him smack in the face. He invites her into his cabin with her companions, two other girls of a weird dowdiness. While Charlie goes in search of firewood, Georgia sees that a discarded photograph lies under Charlie's pillow. It is her own photograph, one that had been torn and later patched together after a bar room brawl. For the first time she becomes aware of Charlie as a person, and when he invites her to enjoy a New Year's dinner with her companions in his own shack, she smiles winningly, and Charlie is convinced that she will come.

The preparations for her coming are among those handsome gifts which Charlie has given to the world. There is not a moment of those delighted preparations which is not memorable. He tears a newspaper cunningly into a resemblance of a lace table-cloth. He carefully arranges the knives and forks, touching them gently and with love as he places them on the table which is for ever in danger of collapsing. He writes out place-cards, sweeps the dust from the chairs, studies with mounting excitement the cooking of the chicken on the stove, but once more the chicken is himself, and there are no guests except a nanny goat which comes to munch the paper favours. What then? He will pretend they are late or unavoidably detained elsewhere. He is sure they will come. Have they not promised to come? He smiles wearily, heartbroken, but breaks out into smiles as he imagines them actually present, and suddenly to his intense joy they are present, and Charlie is bowing to them, and they sit beside the table as they would sit at the table of a king. To amuse them Charlie dances his wonderful bread roll dance, which is no more than the cavortings of two bread rolls on a pair of forks; but just as the chicken represented only too clearly Charlie himself, so the bread rolls exactly resemble two bleeding hearts dancing to keep their courage up. The bread rolls dance the cancan, hop sideways, pause magnificently before continuing the dance to the applause of the girls, and at the end they take their bows. It was the first time that bleeding hearts had ever bowed to an audience, and Charlie celebrated the occasion by performing with astonishing verve and brilliance. But at last the hearts lie dead upon the table, and Charlie wanders away, leaving the uninhabited room where the girls were present only in his dreams. He wanders among the dark huts, sick with loss and misery, and very timidly he approaches the lighted window where the girls are dancing and there is a furious air of festivity.

As he gazes through the window, Charlie is like someone looking at an unattainable paradise in a dream. Inside the dance-hall an unearthly mystery is being performed. He is like a child watching a gas-illuminated pantomime. There are shadowy grottoes and mermaids' crowns, and strange distorted shapes like fishes, and everywhere there is the sound of joy. The mysteriously diffused light in which he sees the celebrants, the sudden appearance of Georgia dancing there, the memory of the dancing bread rolls, all these fuse together to make a picture of misery seen in the light of an unbearable tenderness. His misery now is a child's misery, the misery of rejection. He wanders abroad in the dark, and while he is wandering Georgia remembers her promise to come to him, and when she comes to his shack, he is gone. This is the end for the time being of Charlie's hopeless love for Georgia. The bloody hearts had been torn out of the living flesh, and in the abandonment of sorrow he goes on his way – to the shack where he had fought so menacingly with Big Jim.

That shack on the world's edge takes the place of the ashcan; it is Charlie's natural habitation. Big Jim has amassed some gold; there is no longer a haunting terror of starvation, but there are things worse than starvation. A storm comes and hurls the shack half over an abyss, and as they sleep there, they are wholly unaware of danger. Frost covers the windows, the stove still burns, only they are appalled to discover that they have lost their sense of balance. When Charlie gets out of bed, the whole shack tilts. Why? There is no explanation except the hopeful one which Charlie brings forward. Perhaps it is their stomachs tilting; it is impossible that the shack should tilt. The icicles grow down from the ceiling. Charlie melts them for his breakfast. Still the shack tilts, and we see from a camera mysteriously placed outside that it is hanging to the cliff by a single thread, a single rope. Charlie makes light of the matter. 'So you think the floor is tipping? Well, perhaps it is, and what about it? Floors do tip, don't they?' Mack Swain agrees that they tip, but it is not reasonable that they should tip so much. Charlie goes blithely to the door. From the door all he can see is the eternal plain of virgin snow below; in front of them there is only air.

At this point Chaplin revives some of the tricks which were employed by D. W. Griffith. The shack is supported on a rope which is about to break, and they must escape before it breaks. Everything now happens in slow motion. Impossible that they should survive. We see the shack leaning tipsily over the abyss, we see the rope breaking, we see Charlie and Mack Swain, their faces agonised, their eyebrows white with snow, not daring to cough for fear the cough will rock them off their moorings, not daring to speak, trying to make their way through the door which swings back against them, and all the time they are only half-aware of their danger, because they refuse to believe they could ever have entered such a predicament. The excitement is breathless and continual; and if it smacks of corn, this is perhaps because all excitement smacks of corn. It is a race against time, like the race to free the innocent man from the gallows in *Intolerance*. In the end they crawl up a slope on their bellies at an angle of sixty degrees, and this perhaps is where the film should end. The concluding scene, as it was shown, lacks verisimilitude. Charlie and Mack Swain have discovered Larsen's gold, and now they are returning to America as fur-coated millionaires. On the same ship is Georgia, but she is in the steerage. A sudden lurch and Charlie finds himself tumbling off the promenade deck into the coils of rope in the steerage, and there is Georgia beside him. It is a pity. One wishes devoutly she was a million miles away. The film ends with a wholly irrational Charlie embracing a wholly incredible Georgia. Evidently, the orphans of the storm have found one another at last.

The Gold Rush has only one imperfection, and that is its ending. For the rest the world which Chaplin conjured out of the snows is terrifyingly real. The very simplicity of the snow scenes gives dimension to Charlie. Charlie, that thin black isosceles triangle hopping across the snows, partakes of geometry; the pattern he forms against the snow has the inevitability of Euclidian theory. There is the round face of Georgia, the square of the shack, the immense black V-shaped wedge of Mack Swain – out of these simplicities the film is constructed. It is comedy reduced to its geometric essentials, and the bread rolls can be interpreted as bleeding hearts or zeros as we please. To have placed the wildest comedy against the snowfields was a mark of genius, for in the field of the cinema this was the equivalent of playing out a comedy on the stage without props, and with only a single white sheet as a backcloth. This is comedy naked, and set in the white fields of eternity.

That there is a geometry to comedy Chaplin proved in *The*

Gold Rush. It is not so certain that there is a corresponding algebra, though one day in Paris Chaplin attempted to explain the algebra of comedy to his friend Cami. At the time they were trapped in an elevator, and Cami's account of the algebra may have been subtly affected by the experience of being trapped with Chaplin. As Cami explained Chaplin's theory, it went like this:

Let X be the laughter you are attempting to raise, and Y be the means at your disposal. Then:

$$100 = X + Y$$
$$20 = X - Y$$

By addition we obtain:

$$100 + 20 = X + Y + X - Y$$

Now represent the derby by D
the moustache by M
the boots by B
the facial expression by F

Then it follows immediately:

$$D + M = B + F + Y$$

But:

$$a + b = 2X$$

Also:

$$a + Y = a + D + M + B + Y$$

But:

$$X = 40$$

Therefore:

$$a + b = 80. \qquad Q.E.D.[1]$$

Such were the conclusions of Chaplin's algebra. They are no worse than the conclusions which Karl Marx reached in his study of the differential calculus,[2] and the magnificent irrelevance of $a + b = 2X$ should commend itself to mathematicians.

The miracle of *The Gold Rush* lay in Charlie's power to extract the last ounce of comedy from the endless spaces of the earth. It is related of Deburau that he preferred a dark back-

[1] *La Passion de Charlie Chaplin,* by Edouard Raymond, Paris, 1929, p. 107.

[2] On Karl Marx's knowledge of the differential calculus, see Edmund Wilson, *To the Finland Station,* Appendix B.

ground to set off his white clothes. Charlie, the aimless and happy black ink-spot, was performing against the same odds, but at a greater disadvantage, for the dark backcloth of the Funambules Theatre could be peopled with imaginary houses, streets, taverns, anything one pleased. In the snows there was no life, only the bleak horrors of endless space. It was as though Charlie had dared to perform on the heights where space and time vanish, in the loneliness of the highest trapeze of all.

CHAPTER XV

TRAPEZE ACT

Sooner or later it was inevitable that Charlie should join a circus. Those pale-faced clowns who wander round the ring with putty noses and disconsolate expressions, dressed in a jester's panoply or in rags, their noses lighting up as they try to distract the attention of the audience from the daring acrobats on the high trapeze, were after all his brothers. Chaplin in his youth had been something of a trapeze artist, until a fall cured him of a desire to join the circus. Charlie must therefore accomplish what Chaplin had failed to accomplish; and leaving the frozen hills of Alaska, he would warm himself in the glow of the sawdust ring. *The Circus*, which appeared in January 1928, two and a half years after the showing of *The Gold Rush*, belongs to the long list of Chaplin's classical films which includes *Shoulder Arms*, *The Kid*, *The Pilgrim*, *The Gold Rush*, *City Lights* and *Monsieur Verdoux*. It is one of the great seven, and the coldest of them all.

Why the film should be so coldly calculated, so elaborately chilling, is not difficult to explain. The story was built around Charlie as a trapeze artist or tightrope walker, substituting for the real acrobat. The climax was to be Charlie's dauntless behaviour when faced with an impossible feat of daring. But it is after all the clown who performs the most impossible feats in the circus ring. Simply by daring to exist the clown shows more daring than any trapeze artist. He is the immortal who comes to us out of death, bearing a burden of ghostly memories, the possessor of a mechanical neon-lit heart and a nose on which the graveyard earth still clings. He is all we have left in the modern world of the deathless delight-makers, and as he seeks to turn our attention from the bare legs of the girls and the silken horses, he is merely insisting on his right to proclaim his own immortality. So it was with Charlie from the beginning, and when he appears as a clown, with Deburau's nonchalance, we can believe him, but as a trapeze artist in a morning coat he is past belief.

The Circus, in spite of the chill running through it, is the most homogeneous and the most deftly constructed of all Chaplin's films. It obeys the classic unities. It tells a single story in a single place at a single time. All that happens is that Charlie joins a circus by the purest accident, stays long enough to turn it upside down and to ensure the happy marriage of the little dancer, and then the circus moves on, with Charlie left behind in the bleak glare of a spring morning. There is no plot, for there never has been a plot. There is only a succession of fast-moving incidents and a number of themes subtly interwoven, compounded, torn apart, held up for our enjoyment or our mockery, and then forgotten, for other, more urgent themes immediately take their place. It is a trapeze act as a conjuror might play it. The rabbits disappear, the monkeys and the lions come from nowhere, the conjuror's patter continually misleads, his sharp baleful eye watching every movement we make. 'No, gentlemen, the silk handkerchiefs are not in the top-hat. They are in your nose.' So he milks the nose of its handkerchiefs, and the next moment he is performing another trick altogether. But all the time, more magical than any of his tricks, is the conjuror's baleful glare, his studied insolence, his look of unabashed triumph when the trick succeeds beyond his expectations.

The Circus is the only Chaplin film where the setting is wholly credible. We never quite believe in the little alleyway where the Kid lives under a leaking roof. Adenoid Hynkel's palace exists in defiance of reason, and against all the evidence. Monsieur Verdoux lives incomprehensibly on a studio set. As for the frozen hills of *The Gold Rush*, we know exactly when Charlie is wandering in the icy wastes of Nevada and when he is comporting himself at the studio in La Brea Avenue. In *City Lights* the Embankment is real enough, but the courtyard where the blind flower-seller lives is evidently a stage property and so is the street where Charlie sees the adorable nude in the window.

The boxing ring is real, but the dressing room belongs to fiction. The millionaire's house is real enough, but what shall we say of the courtyard where Charlie is pursued by the wolfhounds, that courtyard where you can almost see the electricians at work. The strange and beautiful thing is that this weaving of fantastically unreal settings with settings we are only too likely to regard as real, made of the stuff of the world we know, is exactly right. We do not demand naturalistic drama from Charlie. We demand an imaginative coherence between the world of reality and fantasy, and the oddly designed backdrops of all the Chaplin films only add to the necessary illusion. In that insubstantial world we are bewildered and excited and delighted beyond measure, as Charlie is, by the strange oncoming forms of things. In something of the same way a man will watch with horror and trepidation and delight the face of a girl coming across a room, while the room vanishes.

The setting of *The Circus* is a completely valid setting. But a circus in a film has its own dangers. In a circus anything may happen. We expect the unusual. We would be astonished if anything so simple as an ordinary trapeze act took place. We must have a mounting excitement, with the unexpected hurrying in from all directions. Charlie, the genius of the unexpected response, is therefore at a disadvantage. When he hurries after a hen and gathers the egg for his breakfast, we are not particularly surprised; if a living dinosaur came round the edge of the tent and dropped an egg in his lap, we would be delighted. We might ponder a little if an elephant dropped an egg, but we could adjust ourselves to the elephant's egg without too much difficulty. All through *The Circus* Charlie is faced with the possibility that his own magical powers are likely to be equalled by the powers of the animals in the menagerie or even by the circus artists. Indeed, when Charlie is faced with the tightrope walker, Rex, the incarnation of all successful lovers and adventurers, immaculate in evening dress, Charlie must split himself in two, and one self rises to throw Rex to the floor while the other broods in the corner. In the old days Charlie would have cocked a snook at him, tricked him into revealing his inadequacies, shown him that he was not the King, only an incompetent performer like the rest of us. To create a balance between the magical forces controlled by Charlie and the magical forces of the circus, Chaplin is forced to compromise. So the lion is a sleepy lion with no taste for human flesh, the clowns are incompetent and the ringmaster is a character out of stock, a bully who thinks nothing of whipping the beautiful dancer.

Yet the film is a masterpiece, chock-full of grotesque ingenuities, happy inventions and clear, sharp images. There is no lull. The pathos has become conscious and deliberate, the actor is sometimes lost in his mannerisms, and sometimes Charlie looks as though he was tired of the whole weary weight of the world – only when he stumbles on to the forbidden button and lets loose the birds, rabbits, pigs, geese and balloons does the face light up with supreme pleasure. For the rest there is all the pain of clowning, the long shadows, the knowledge that even when he has performed admirably, the circus will leave him behind. Then, instead of the little leap up to happiness, the sudden blowing on the flame, the tip of a hat, the waving of a cane, there will be only a doll-like fixedness of expression while the shadows lengthen. It is the sadness of Deburau, the sadness which springs from the knowledge of the world's impermanence, and the bitter relish that it should be so.

The Circus begins with a star, a great silver star which adorns a circus hoop, and this is as it should be, since the stars have a peculiarly beneficent influence on circuses and cinema actors alike. We shall see the star again at the very end of the film, when a dejected Charlie on a discarded box crumples up a star on a piece of tissue paper and kicks it away with his heel. This, too, is as it should be. We expect that a comedy should be rounded off, and Charlie's comedies are only too rarely rounded off. We tolerate these improvisations along a nerve because there never was such a crackle of fireworks to hold our attention, but we are not often allowed the grace of a beginning, a middle and an end. And as we sit down to enjoy *The Circus*, the very shape of the star on the hoop gives us a hint that the drama will follow an orderly path, obedient to the heavenly dictates of dramatic law. And this is what happens. From the moment when the bareback rider plunges through the hoop to the moment when Charlie is left behind in the morning dust, we

are aware as in music of an endless delicate weaving of emotions
and images, and if there is a glint of frost in them, so it is
sometimes in the fugues of Bach, and we have no reason to
complain.

As always, there is the curtain-raiser. It is a little scene, very
taut and sharp, and half of it is caricature. Merna Kennedy is a
little equestrienne who fails to dive through the hoop. The ringmaster flicks his whip and curses her. The circus is half failing.
The acts are failing. He will see to it that she has no food tonight.
The threat of the whip hangs over all the scenes which follow.

When we first see Charlie, he is the old familiar bewildered
tramp who has come from nowhere. He is wandering through
the galleries of the fun-fair. He mooches along, hungry and
poverty-stricken as always. A pickpocket drops a watch and a
billfold in Charlie's pocket, intending to retrieve it later. Charlie
walks on. He knows nothing about the sudden wealth which has
fallen to him. He goes to a hot-dog stand, hoping against hope
he will be able to steal a frankfurter, and when he sees a child on
its father's shoulder happily munching a hot-dog, a gleam comes
to his eyes. He tickles the child. He crows at it. Surreptitiously,
he leans over the counter and ladles mustard on the hot-dog and
takes a bite. The child laughs with pleasure.

A little later the owner of the watch sees the chain dangling
from Charlie's pocket. The chase is on. The tramp plunges into
a mirror maze, where he is blissfully in his element: a hundred
Charlies converge upon him, and he tips his hat to them all. The
police are in full pursuit. The 'rally' of the Keystone cops is on.
Charlie escapes from the maze and freezes into immobility,
disguised as one of the specimens of Noah's Ark: a hint, though
we have received many hints, that Charlie is at home in the
world before the Flood. Recognised, he is chased into a circus,
and at this point the film is at once wildly improbable, beautifully
constructed and inevitable, for having found himself in the
circus while the magician is attempting to make the lady vanish,
Charlie, like a jack-in-the-box, pops up in the place where the
lady should have been. The police see him and give chase. They
are all over the ring, and Charlie is in and out of the trapdoor.
When at last the Vanishing Lady appears, Charlie is nowhere
to be seen.

All this is played with a kind of breathless prodigality, close to farce. It is Charlie's scene, and he is wonderfully excited to be in the circus, where the risks are infinitely less than in Alaska. He knows he can make people laugh. He knows, too, that he is better than the clowns in the ring. He is therefore not unduly surprised when the audience roars for him, and he accepts with good grace the ringmaster's offer that he should perform in a tryout the next morning.

The tryout is an exercise in skill. Everything that Charlie has ever learnt is put to the service of the exhibition of skill which occurs during the next scene. The comedy is boisterous and English; it is the kind of thing that Grimaldi performed to perfection. It is grotesquely silly rather than funny, but the silliness acquires such extraordinary resonance that the scene escapes from farce. The tryout takes the form of two different acts, neither amusing in itself; the amusement arises from the fact that Charlie is there, imitating bad clowns so perfectly that his mimicry endows the scene with unexpected passion. The first act consists of repeated efforts to shoot an apple off the head of one of the clowns. Charlie bites the apple until almost none is left. All that we see is a little stump of an apple riddled with worms – Charlie has indicated the existence of the worms by wriggling his little finger – and when the apple has reached vanishing-point, Charlie substitutes a banana. That is all. There is nothing to it. Anyone could do it, and no doubt many have done it. But, like Beckmann, Charlie performs with the wildest of impromptu gestures, and no Paris gazing at the apple of his choice has ever done with an apple what Charlie does in this scene. Every bite is excruciating delight and agony to the onlooker. He bites the apple with malevolence. The apple is alive. He must bite, but he can never explain the overriding necessity. The poor apple vanishes, and we are sorry, as we are sorry when we hear of a disaster in some remote part of the world, and when he substitutes the banana there is such a gleam of innocent triumph in his eyes that we are compelled to cheer him, as though he had won a great victory over the enemy. Perhaps the secret of this fabulous exhibition of skill lies in the vast significance he somehow attaches to his smallest acts: he bites an apple with the deliberation of an Alexander carving up the Persian Empire. The William Tell scene is followed by a barber-shop scene. Charlie is in his element. The barber-shop has been since Roman times the scene of razor-edge comedy, and Charlie was always happy with a lather-brush. He succeeds in lathering everything in sight, including the ring-master, and for this act of effrontery he is thrown out of the circus.

In revenge, he decides to take over the circus as his own. He does this cautiously, and only after he has first experimented with the comic possibilities of a circus. He examines the goldfish, wipes them, throws them back, and concludes that the comic possibilities latent in goldfish are negligible. He goes on to examine all the animals which the magician possesses – the rabbits and the squeaking pigs which vanish under the magician's hat. He examines them so carefully that they escape all over the circus grounds. He is now theoretically the prop man's assistant. Told by the ringmaster to give a pill to a horse, he puts the tube in the horse's mouth and is about to blow, when the horse blows first. There are satisfactions in this slow approach to greatness. From goldfish he comes to lions. An unfriendly donkey which has been the bane of his life throughout his brief stay in the circus – the same donkey penetrated his shack in *The Gold Rush* – takes an intense dislike to him and chases him into the lion's cage. The lock snaps shut. The beautiful bareback rider sees him and faints. Charlie casually tosses the lion's drinking water through the bars to revive her. The lion is still asleep, but it is no less dangerous because it is sleeping. Charlie is panic-stricken. He dare not make a sound. He gazes fondly at the girl and bids her farewell, and then at the lion – but the lion is yawning now, and soon it goes up to Charlie and sniffs him. At this moment the girl revives sufficiently to unlatch the gate of the cage. Charlie saunters out, disposed to play the part of the conqueror, smiling down from the heights of his self-satisfaction, whereupon the lion roars and rushes at Charlie, who goes running up a high pole. His ascent of the pole, so quick and yet so rhythmical, so effortless and at the same time so preposterously well-timed, provides a warning of acrobatic feats to come. Gazing down from his high perch, absurd, fearful, utterly ashamed of himself, he sees the girl, and suddenly there appears on his face the familiar mask of a love which is beyond love, so tender and child-like it is.

Charlie's love for Merna Kennedy is hopeless from the beginning. It is the tradition that the equestrienne must be loved, though she will never give her love in return. In a sense, Merna Kennedy is playing the part of Miss Louisa Woolford, who was born in the year before Waterloo and survived long into the Boer War. Miss Woolford – there were few who dared mention her Christian name – was formed from an assembly of stalactites. She was part of the English scene, and regarded with awe and delight, the same kind of awe and delight with which we regard stalactites. She possessed the most delicate milk-white hands in Christendom, and her appearance as she rode round the circus ring at Astley's was greeted with an immense sigh of recognition followed by a prolonged sigh of misery, for everyone knew she was impermanent and would never be possessed by mortal man. Both Dickens and Thackeray drooled when they saw her, for had she not been Columbine in the pantomime? and had anyone more beautiful ever existed? Standing on her white horse, her yellow hair streaming in the wind, she looked as though she had only to whisper an order for the whole tent to be transported to paradise. She lived to be eighty-six, and it was only after her death that men came to know that she hated circus-riding and wanted nothing so much as a respectable suburban existence in Bayswater.

In Merna Kennedy, Charlie has another Miss Woolford to contend with. She is ethereal, sweet-tempered, possessing a melting smile, with shapely legs and small feet, but her heart is not for Charlie. She has been to the fortune-teller, and in the crystal ball there has been revealed to her the dark, handsome man of her dreams. Charlie is dark; he is not handsome. When Rex, the tightrope walker, appears as a new attraction in the circus, Charlie is crestfallen. He, too, knows about the visit to the fortune-teller. He can only rage with himself, or, imagining himself a knight in armour capable of destroying Rex with a single blow, launch out on his endless dreams. He hopes Rex will die an excruciating death in a fall from the tightrope, and then his mind runs on to the inevitable time when he will be the tightrope walker, and Merna will be his wife. He practices tightrope walking in secret. One day Rex is absent. Charlie's opportunity has arrived. Wearing Rex's immaculate uniform he decides to show his utmost daring. The tightrope is stretched high up near the roof of the tent. Invisible to the audience is the rope round his waist. He therefore feels sure of himself, too sure, for the invisible rope on which he had depended inexplicably leaves him, and he is left alone with the long bamboo cane teetering on the edge of nothingness, and suddenly a plague of monkeys comes to torment him further, biting his nose, crawling all over his face and tearing at his clothes. Trouserless, he sways from side to side with monkeys on each shoulder; trouserless, he falls. By some miracle he survives, though he has fallen clean through the tent into the street outside. He comes running into the tent to take his bows.

In the end he is left alone with his misery and his heartache. Merna marries Rex, and Charlie himself superintends their wedding. They are no more than *dei ex machina*, godlike creatures who feed his appetite for glory, and he knows their marriage will be as miserable as the marriage between Miss Woolford and Alexander Ducrow, that strange and impenitent genius of the theatre who enlarged on glory and stretched it to its widest bounds with his immense phantasmagorias, his dewy curtains and fiery backdrops on which the hanging gardens of Babylon were painted and panoramas of all the Americas. Ducrow is forgotten now, but in his time he set a style for glory. Poverty-stricken as a child, he made out of his wildest dreams a living pantomime of the utmost splendour, for he would parade across the stage on horseback in the armour of Achilles, and then by some trick of the light he would emerge a second later in the guise of Genghiz Khan, and having paraded again across the stage he would appear as Antony in Egypt, and again as Pizarro in the Temple of the Sun, and still later as Henry pacing the Cloth of Gold. He had only to be on the stage for maidens to vow perpetual virginity, since no hero so beautiful as Ducrow was ever likely to rest in their arms. No man before or since has ever shone with such peacock feathers; he wore the raiment of Emperors as though born to it. He burned himself out by the age of fifty, a foul-mouthed bully and a charlatan who possessed the gift of pantomiming heroes. He knew how Alexander would raise a little finger and silence all the soldiers of the Macedonian Army. He was Napoleon on the Bellerophon, Caesar raging across Gaul, Washington at Valley Forge, and perhaps it was inevitable that he should have been a drunkard and a fool. Miss Woolford married a shopkeeper when he died.

Ducrow posing as the conqueror who never lived in mortal danger belongs to all men's dreams. Charlie was of sterner stuff; even in the circus he saw the world as it is.

CHAPTER XVI

THE DARK CITY, THIRTY YEARS LATER

W H E N Chaplin composed the scenario for *City Lights* he was faced with problems which had never entered his mind before. With the coming of sound the art of pantomime, which he had explored at length, in public and in private, received its greatest challenge. Everything in the early films had conspired to give depth and reality to the portrait of Charlie: the very jerkiness of the film, the outrageous simplifications of the cardboard settings, even the bad lighting and the inexpert lenses and the only too visible chalk marks which showed the actors how far they must stay away from the camera helped to make the illusion of a real, living and breathing character moving through a real, living and breathing world of exuberant and harassed people. Out of the imperfections of the cinema he built perfection.

'That light which brings a Garbo alive, in which a Chaplin cannot survive' was not yet invented. It was the time before the veils of mist and the silken spotlights and the absurd love scenes played against hazy photographs of the Bay of Naples. It was the time when we sat on hard chairs and the local music-teacher thumped on an out-of-tune piano, too short-sighted to see the film, so that she played a waltz during the battle-scenes and scraps from the Fifth Symphony when the lovers were in each other's arms, but no one listened to the music and no one cared, for there, hugely in command of himself, was the insolent tramp walking down the empty roads, swinging his cane in the shadow of the eucalyptus trees. He looked a little like a bottle to be uncorked, a necromancer's box of magic tricks, a clown on holiday. He was all things, but he was never a fool. He was dumb, but he spoke often. There was a roughness about him which we recognised in our own lives. He was full of character, and he had only to lift his eyebrows for us to detect a wealth of meaning in his eyes. He was as silent as a dream, and of all the myriad things which conspired to give depth, dimension and beauty to this strange interloper silence was the greatest, for since he was silent we could read anything we pleased in his gestures and in his voiceless words, and we heard every word he ever uttered.

With the coming of sound Chaplin was faced with a dilemma which he has not yet completely mastered. The mime is silent, and he is most expressive when he is silent. The dancer echoes the music, and is created out of the music, but music can only echo the mime. The mime creates his own rhythms; the dancer is created out of the rhythms of others. The mime demands silence, because silence connives at the mystery, because silence contains the most delicate sounds, whole octaves of sound. When Charlie turns to gaze with wonderful nonchalance at the cop he has tripped up and who lies sprawling in the gutter, we hear his mocking laughter without benefit of sound-track, and we hear it more accurately, more distinctly than if it had been carefully recorded. We heard his weeping and his laboured breathing as he went in search of the Kid, when the boy was stolen from him. We knew exactly the tone of his love-making, and all the tones of his enraged fury. Now that the public demanded sound, what was to be done? He hardly knew. Slowly, step by step, actors had developed a recognised form of art, as limited and precise as the artificial arts of the stage. 'Film players,' said Chaplin, 'have learned that the camera can reproduce ideas, though not words. Ideas and feelings are the things we play with, and they are richer than words. Film actors have grasped an alphabet of gesture, the poetry of movement. They know that gesture begins where words leave off.' With sound the infinitely rich world of gesture was to be abandoned; henceforward there was to be the limited little world of meaningless conversations, of I-love-you's and I-hate-you's, the poor emotion fixed in the tone of a voice like a photograph fixed in acid.

Since there was no escape, since the public demanded noise, Chaplin was compelled to develop a compromise. Through *City*

Lights, *Modern Times* and *The Great Dictator* he held fast to his
compromise. He would introduce sound, but on his own terms.
He would not play to the music; he would allow music the
privilege of entering on his own terms, as an echo of his own
miming, a sardonic commentary. It was a happy solution, but a
limited one, for there are only a limited number of brays, whistles,
rude noises, catcalls, and most of them are best imagined. The
delicious sound which a fat lady makes when she falls on a
heaped basket of fruit is not adequately reproduced by the blare
of a trombone, and Charlie's desperate little whistles when he
swallowed a policeman's whistle were not adequately reproduced
on the sound-track of *City Lights*. It is not only that we can
imagine these things better, but we are sometimes certain that
the sound-track fails to convey the richness of the sound that
first came to our ears. When Charlie eats spaghetti at the
restaurant, and then by imperceptible degrees finds himself
eating paper streamers, we are allowed to imagine most of the
subtle sounds which accompany his chewing of these things. We
hear the goose-gabbling orators, but we never hear the sighs of
the flower-girl, and this is proper. But there are occasions when
we miss sounds we had expected to hear. When the Rolls Royce
drives up to the corner of Hyde Park where the blind girl is
sitting, the car makes no sound at all and the door opens in a
mysterious silence, and these are sounds we had expected to
hear, as one expects to hear in any street-scene the vague background music of people passing. These were minute faults in a
film preposterously filled with good things.

   City Lights was long in the making. Whole scenes were
composed before the coming of sound. The most wonderfully
successful of all the scenes was already in existence in 1926, five
years before the first showing of *City Lights*. In those days it
was called *The Suicide*, a short fragment of film which he had
thought of employing in one of his earlier films and then
abandoned, because he could see no place for it. It opens with
Charlie on Christmas Eve sitting on a stone bench of the
Embankment facing the Thames. He shivers, gazes for a
moment at the lamps whose light shining upon the black river
provide the ironic title for the later film, then chews on a morsel
of crust, one of those crusts which the inexorable tramp had

stolen from the birds. He looks at the river, then turns away, then looks at the river again.

A great giant of a man in evening dress comes drunkenly down the steps. Charlie glances at him, and pays no more attention to him until he sees that the drunken giant is preparing to tie a rope round his neck and at the end of the rope is a huge stone. Charlie decides to reason with him. He explains that life is, after all, worth living. Are there not birds in the air? He smiles, and his fingers twitter. Are there not women? He smiles again, and draws the exuberant outlines of a woman on the dark air. Is there not wine? Once more he smiles, and makes the happy gestures of a drunk. The giant however is plainly determined upon suicide. Birds, women and wine – he has known them all, and he finds no comfort in them, and there is no comfort in Charlie, that little mouse of a shivering man who had come down to the river to contemplate his inevitable end. Engrossed in his task of suicide, the giant throws Charlie out of the way, and Charlie, resigned to his fate, can only shrug his shoulders miserably. He makes one last effort to intervene, and approaches the man who is in the act of bending down to lift the stone. As he bends the rope slips from his neck and falls over Charlie. Then the man straightens himself and with a huge, laboured straining of his muscles he lifts the stone and throws it in the water. Charlie is thrown with it. Seeing Charlie threshing his arms, sucked down by the weight of the stone, the giant teeters on the edge of the river, overwhelmed with laughter. When the river is quiet, he walks back jauntily up the Embankment stairs.

This incident was expanded when Chaplin came to work on *City Lights*, and the small changes he made were significant changes. Instead of a crust of bread, Charlie is seen to be holding the white rose which he has bought from his beloved flower-girl. It is no longer Christmas Eve, but one of those melancholy evenings in early spring. Charlie is no longer oppressed by the world's misery, but by the misery of love, and he has no desire to drown himself. On the contrary he has the most abundant reasons for living. He is no longer a down-at-heels vagabond, but a small clerk in the city who has just been thrown out of his job, with a clean shirt, a bow tie and an impeccable bowler hat. Finally, instead of the drowning scene, there is the hilarious comedy as each in turn throws the other into the river, yet the memory of the former version remains in the starkness of some of those scenes where they fall into the water, grapple, vanish and rise to the surface only when we thought they must have perished. Comparing the two versions, we can watch Chaplin's mind at work as he softens the contours of tragedy and gives them the shape of pathos, yet never quite succeeds in eluding the sense of tragedy which snaps at his heels, the mask of Cerberus. We see the dog-face when they dance in the water, a dance as savage and light-hearted as that later dance which is performed in a ring with Charlie at the mercy of a towering, hard-fisted pugilist, avoiding blows by miracles of toework and sleight of hand.

City Lights begins with an advantage lacking in all his other longer films: there is no narration, and almost no story. It is made up of odds and ends intricately woven together. The story of the manic-depressive millionaire has nothing to do with the story of the blind flower-girl, and the scenes in the boxing ring are almost entirely irrelevant, while Charlie's excursion as a road-sweeper who thinks he has finished his job for the day only to discover that a passing elephant has perceptibly added to his labours, is an affront to the delighted intelligence. Inexplicably, Charlie wears a sun-helmet and white ducks for his sweeping job; no explanation is offered, nor is any explanation desired; we assume that it is perfectly natural that Charlie should wear a sun-helmet in the course of his duties. Charlie goes to jail only because an ineluctable destiny has decreed that Charlie should go to jail if there is a jail handy. The scene in which he ogles a nude in a store window from his uncertain point of vantage on a sidewalk elevator could have been placed anywhere. The long scene which begins with the millionaire in a mood of blissful drunkenness, then passes through all the phases of manic-depression as the millionaire determines once again to commit suicide, then explodes into gunfire as the gangsters reveal themselves from behind curtains – this interminable scene with its grotesque pauses, its breathless gropings after revolvers, its air of real menace which was to return many years later when Chaplin came to outline the portrait of Monsieur Verdoux – all this is wholly wrong and wholly right, every detail admirably in place, every rhythm, as the Cheap Jack says in Dickens'

Dr Marigold, 'wonderfully like the real thing, of course a little refined and humoured'.

It is pure magic, this gentle coaxing of four or five separate stories together, the same kind of magic which was performed by Coleridge in *Kubla Khan*, which is hardly at all about Kubla Khan, for it brings together an Abyssinian maiden, an Emperor of China and a nameless magician who has drunk the milk of paradise, and places them incomprehensibly in a landscape where incense-bearing trees flower among domes of ice, and somehow near by the rivers are in full flood, a flood strong enough to destroy the maiden and the Emperor and all the incense-bearing trees of China and Abyssinia. 'Gentlemen,' Chaplin says, 'I shall tell you the story of a blind flower-girl, of gangsters and boxers and millionaires and road-sweepers and jail-birds and suicides and cops. I shall take you to the most delightful restaurant where I shall demonstrate how an apache dance should be danced and how a man may eat spaghetti to his greatest enjoyment. I shall show you the misery of a man with a whistle in his belly. At the end I shall show you a face so terrible and beautiful that you will almost wish you never set eyes upon him.' It is hardly possible to imagine that the most voracious schoolboy would ask for more. Humour is inseparable from charity, and in *City Lights* charity brims over. And since the Catholic theologians, who have studied laughter more resourcefully than the academic philosophers, are of the opinion that charity is one of the three chief virtues, we are entitled to believe in the moral goodness of the play. Fortunately or unfortunately such belief would be ill-founded. There is no moral to the story, and the heart-breaking stare which concludes the story is simply the face of Pan as he goes on his way, for ever in despair and for ever in enjoyment of the world.

The despair in *City Lights* reaches depths which are visible in no other film composed by Chaplin; the humour reaches heights soaring above anything he composed later; yet the violence of the humour, the way it takes wing and flashes and burns at the most dangerous moments of the drama, derives its strength from a despair so great that Chaplin nearly broke under the strain. The death of his mother occurred in October 1928, when the final form which the picture would take was still undecided:

there existed already, in his mind or in film, sequences with the blind flower-girl and the drunk on the Embankment, but as always the pattern grew slowly, gradually emerging as a pearl emerges, changing with every gust of experience, every new instrument he attached to his service, while grief shook him and the challenge to produce a film which would make use of music excited him. From childhood he had been a fair musician; now he taught himself to be a good one, and learned to compose music and then later went on to master the art of conducting – whatever happened he would place his seal on the film as the chief actor, director, producer, designer and composer, determined that it should not become the composite which was the fate of nearly all Hollywood films. Everything depended upon the success of the film. It was rumoured that he was 'played out', that he could never adapt himself to the new world of sound. He had no gift for seeming. He was incapable of hiding the hurts he received, and he still lamented the coming of sound. 'They're trying to force me to speak,' he told Sam Goldwyn. 'But I will not! I will not! If *City Lights* is a failure, I believe it will strike a deeper blow than anything else that has ever happened to me in this life.'

It was not quite true: the death of his mother had struck him with the deepest blow he had ever received, or was ever likely to receive. But the turmoil, the months and years spent on *City Lights*, left their mark. The portrait of the tramp assumed new dimensions. In *The Circus* he was already tense, fastidious, strangely remote, with more of Deburau in him than Grimaldi, white-faced with fear and shock at the world around him but still capable of an honest shrug of the shoulders, a sudden lunge at a pair of healthy ankles. In *City Lights* the blind flower-seller is an image of loss, just as the manic-depressive millionaire is an image of the powers of finance, which reward and punish with purely arbitrary favours. He does not insist upon them as images, but they are more than life-size, painted in heraldic dimensions, and both of them, like the roaring King and the woman rocking the cradle in *Intolerance*, have the aspect of a *deus ex machina*. Like the murderous boxer they represent vast powers almost beyond his strength to propitiate. Once again he returns to the tradition of the *Commedia dell' Arte*, for the flower-girl has become pure Columbine, the millionaire is pure Harlequin, the type of all worldly wisdom and the fickleness of its favour, and Charlie is Pierrot at last, the eternal poet and outcast, the possessor of a secret wisdom, the lover of the moon.

But it is in the portrait of Charlie that the greatest changes can be observed. He is still fickle, still fastidious, still strangely remote, but other elements have entered into him. It is not only that he has achieved new and unsuspected dimensions, but he has achieved dimensions one would have thought to be impossible: sharpness of grief and closeness to death have sent the wit rocketing – the wit of Villon while composing an ode on all hanged men as he stands at the foot of the gibbet, delighting in the images of death and savouring them, but only because he knows he has one chance in a million of escaping the noose. There is something of the supreme vanity of the suicide in the tramp as Charlie depicts him. If life, the world and the universe will not go his way, then so much the worse for the world. He will not forsake the stage. He will wait till the very last moment. He will neither beg nor complain. He will help the suffering and take the last ounce of amusement from a situation. The last privilege of cowards, which is to whistle in the dark, he will cheerfully surrender; he has better things to do in the dark. The perpetual misery of the world he believes to be unredeemed and unredeemable; but in the brief interval while he remains alive and can demonstrate his human courage, he will flaunt his bravado. His enthusiasm is terrible. He is all a dangling nerve. He is a spiritual dandy, a knight of the faith on a mission to save what can be saved: the blind girl, himself, whatever decency is left to the world. He does not care whether he wins or loses. In the peculiar world which obeys its own laws, he disregards the inessentials; the girl must be saved, money must be acquired to save her, she must never know the rent has not been paid. Almost he loves disaster, because in disaster all the inessentials fall away; and when disaster, so long expected, falls upon him, when he is taken to prison and he has no means of knowing whether the girl will ever recover her sight, he still waves his ridiculous cane in a defeat so jaunty it amounts to a triumph.

In *City Lights* Chaplin was saying things he had never said before, and would never say again. They were not things which

The Great Dictator, 1940

Monsieur Verdoux, 1947

can be easily translated into words. The enigmatic lonely figure of the tramp had set so many questions and answered none – a gesture, the raising of an eyebrow, some subtle twist of the body, the shoulders, the posture of his head, these were his answers, and since the movements of the human body are universally understood, this was enough, and we must make what we can of the fire and ice which contended in his nature during the progress of this film. It is part of the strength of an imagination like Chaplin's that he states the problem and leaves the predicament bare. There are no easy solutions. We can only guess sometimes at the emotions he expresses. Some things we know: we know that the clown's distress is permanent, we know that he walks in the landscape of irony like someone born to it, while there is always a strangeness in the way he walks upon the earth. We know that some of the characters are deliberate projections of his own mood: there is a sense in which the flower-girl is himself, as resigned and helpless as he is, with no hope except in the fortuitous workings of chance. The millionaire is also in a sense a projection of Charlie, for Charlie also suffers in himself those same rages, those same inconsequential changes of mood. It is as though, having called upon music to offer echoes to the mime, the characters themselves are also no more than echoes. The millionaire and the blind flower-girl are only the extremes of himself; his misadventures are those of a man in a hall of mirrors, continually confronting his selves, amused but otherwise unperturbed at each succeeding confrontation. Out of those simple confrontations with himself, those sly glances in the mirror, those delicate gestures of recognition, he creates a whole world where nothing is as anyone expected it to be, where giants loom suddenly out of sidewalk escalators, elephants parade out of nowhere and wander into nowhere, and boxers as fierce as Goliath are determined to batter him out of the ring.

The world of *City Lights* is a terrible world where the little tramp can hardly breathe. With unchanging *sang-froid* Charlie moves through one terrifying complexity into another, never sure of himself but always giving the appearance of assurance, never at rest, living in stark fear and terror of what may happen next, in that milieu where mad millionaires and shady boxers

H

prosper and the poor tremble at every knock on the door, where it is never possible to relax and wits are sharpened beyond any imaginable refinement, so that Charlie himself is continually being cut on the sharpness of his own wit. Yet – and this is the most wonderful thing about the film – Charlie never insists on the terror, greets it calmly, is never surprised. He even pretends to reassure the spectator. He says in that frail, piping, unheard voice: 'Keep your seats, please. That whiskered minotaur which suddenly came out of the grating – it is not very dangerous. No, no, not at all, it's perfectly natural – really a most charming beast.' And when the minotaur, in the shape of a homicidal millionaire or a boxer or a young tough, comes roaring after him, he will always tip his hat to it before running as fast as his legs can carry him.

But though Charlie exudes an air of friendly tolerance of terror, there are many moments when he is hopelessly cast down. He can face dragons, he will cheerfully beard the lions in their dens, he will dance his way out of almost any extremity, but there are some extremities which leave him witless and appalled, some cruelties which leave him blinded with tears. There is a scene in *City Lights* where he finds himself gently manoeuvring his fingers out of a glove. How lovingly he watches the emergence of his fingers! How delightful to recognise them again! With what *élan* he performs his fastidious gesture! A clown may be understood by the behaviour of his knees, but a gentleman is understood by the behaviour of his gloves, and so he attaches to the ritual of removing his gloves the most charming subtleties of recognition, and the fingers, freed of their protective prison, dance happily into freedom. The gloves, however, are threadbare. They are held together by minute threads, little pieces of string, perhaps a safety-pin or two. A young tough nips off one of the carefully husbanded fingers and dangles it mockingly before Charlie's eyes. Charlie snatches it back, horror-stricken; and on that face, so delighted before, there appears a look, not of anger or of hurt vanity, but of simple incomprehension before the inequalities of life, and all the enigmas of human cruelty.

So it is throughout the film. The hurt, appealing look when the dogs come bounding after him, larger than life-size, simply because he swallowed a whistle, and this whistle stuck in his throat continually summons the dogs; the look of pained perplexity when he tries repeatedly to light his own cigar but only succeeds in lighting the cigar the millionaire is waving in front of his face; the misery and joy with which he greets the flower-girl when he comes to her room; all these spring from the simplicities of life, from a knowledge of the world as it is. There is no longer any effort to caricature: no caricatures from Dickens, nothing approximating to farce. The world is so real that one must not play with it. Even in *The Circus*, where the mastery was assured, there are moments approaching farce – the sequences of the clowns shaving one another, the whole episode of William Tell, the mad monkeys on the tightrope – there are those moments of staccato farce, an attempt towards easy solutions, a playing to the gallery. But in *City Lights* these charming solutions are abandoned, and there is no effort to escape from a world whose careful limitations are only too well known. Even the boxing scenes, where Charlie manoeuvres himself into dancing an incredible ballet with his adversary, are of the stuff of life. We laugh ourselves sick. The ballet goes on beyond all expectations of time. Impossible to believe that Charlie could remain alive for more than a few seconds against that brute, yet he survives because he dances and because he possesses a magic talisman. It is a strangely powerful talisman. It is – a flower.

From the earliest days Charlie had put a flower in his buttonhole or simply twirled it in his hand as a badge of his authority. He was gazing at the flower in the beginning of *City Lights*, as though he hoped to divine its secrets, and at the very end he is still twirling the flower desperately as he gazes at Virginia Cherrill. What secrets does the flower possess? We may never know. Some clue, perhaps, is provided by Coleridge who wrote in his notebook:

> If a man could pass through Paradise in a dream, and have a flower presented to him as a pledge that his soul had really been there, and if he found that flower in his hand when he awoke – Ay! and what then?

Coleridge did not answer the question, nor does Charlie. It is enough that the flower should be there.

CHAPTER XVII

MODERN TIMES

RECENTLY Chaplin gave a private showing of a film. Before the lights went out he cleared his throat and announced: 'By courtesy of the greatest genius of our time, Mr Cecil B. de Mille, we are now about to show you *The Sign of the Cross.*' Soon there appeared on the screen the opening reels of *Modern Times.*

Chaplin's introductory remarks were not, of course, blasphemous. There is a sense in which *The Sign of the Cross* is blasphemous, and *Modern Times* is devout. De Mille produced a chocolate-box version of the Gospels arranged with considerable finesse, though the tortured Christ became a sentimental character in a well-worn charade. When de Mille was attacked for having produced the film, he answered that he had aimed simply to tell a familiar story with all the devotion he could muster. Unfortunately, it was precisely the devotion which was lacking. Christ was made to assume the behaviour of an enthusiastic Rotarian. There is one scene where He stands with His skirts billowing about Him as He faces a mob: the scene is on the verge of high drama. For the rest he proved that he was no better at telling the story of Christ than the writers in the Sunday magazine supplements; it was not only that reverence and devotion were absent, but they were never allowed to appear. Hollywood was a machine, and Christ was caught up in the machine. And though there are brief occasions when de Mille's sense of a theatrical gesture is superb, as when the dwarf in *Samson and Delilah* jabs at Samson's legs with the jawbone of an ass, he lacked the imagination to make drama from the Gospel story, and failed to see it in terms of agony.

Modern Times is an essay in the agony of our time. Though it is fantastically funny, it is intended to relate to a real world.

In this world devotion has a place, and though Chaplin clowned through *Modern Times* he was also expressing his pity for the poor devils who must race against the conveyor belts. In the foreword to the film he stated: '*Modern Times* is the story of industry, of individual enterprise – humanity crusading in the pursuit of happiness.' The foreword was not to be taken seriously any more than the programme note to *Monsieur Verdoux*: 'Von Clausewitz said that war is the logical extension of diplomacy; Monsieur Verdoux feels that murder is the logical extension of business.' But Monsieur Verdoux is not exercising the business of murder in the manner of a man running a business, or if he is, he is appallingly incompetent. As for the Charlie who appears in *Modern Times*, he has one good look at industry and flees in terror. Life in a dog-kennel, he suggests, is infinitely superior to life in a cogwheel. Once again comedy has become the decoration for desperate truths, for the agony of our time is precisely that we are caught up in the wheels of machines which have never known where they are going and will never know. Slowly, ineluctably, the machine is beginning to master us. As so often in Chaplin's films, the comedy is pure terror; and when Charlie is caught in the wheels and sent spinning from one cog to another and is fed with an automatic feeder which is insanely out of temper, so that it feeds him with nuts and bolts with the same careless effrontery as it flings pies at his face, we are aware that the monstrous invention is hardly more than a slight exaggeration. We laugh not because of Charlie's predicament, but because we are suddenly confronted with the world's predicament, and surely there is a touch of hysteria in our laughter.

Charlie, the cogwheel who is tired of being a cogwheel, escapes by going insane, but for a brief period before madness descends on him, he remembers his ancient royal dignity as the great god Pan. Picking up two wrenches at random and then holding them to his head like horns, he dances a ferocious little jig and leers at everyone, rolling his eyes. He is Pan incarnate, emerging from industry with a devilish gleam in his eyes, an unbridled desire to live the full life, and suddenly with the light of the gods in his face he begins to pull the switches, dancing and hopping from one switch to another – there never was such joy on his face as when he brings that whole grinding mess of machinery to a stop. Then, with a wrench in his hands, the memory of his former misfortunes merging into the memory of past desires, he runs after every mortal thing which resembles a nut, and proceeds to tighten it. He tightens the foreman's nose, the fire-plugs, and finally, as he rushes out into the streets, he proceeds to tighten women's buttons, and all the while there is the look of supreme, blissful abandon on his face.

According to the script and according to the film madness now descends upon him and he peers out at us from a psychiatric ward. This is subterfuge, no better and no worse than the train-wheels which join the various episodes together in *Monsieur Verdoux*. When we see him again he is still the old familiar tramp walking disconsolately down an empty street where there are not enough cigarette butts to make him happy. The first part of the film with the glowering manager on the huge television screen, its mad machines and their crazed attendants is over, as it must be, since all the long films are divided sharply into episodes, usually four separate episodes, each one amounting to the length of two reels, and now Charlie must go out and seek his adventures elsewhere. From this point onwards the film goes merrily to pieces.

The long opening scene in the factory is one of the most astonishingly successful that Chaplin ever produced, comparable with the dream sequence in *The Kid* and the final hundred feet of *City Lights*. It was comedy with a bite, and Chaplin was perfectly aware he was biting hard. 'The things I tried to say in this film are very close to everyone,' he explained. 'I know of a factory where the workers were fired if they went to the urinals too often. Everyone knows there are salesmen who have to maintain an incredible pace of salesmanship, continually driven by their bosses, and the ones with the lowest sales are automatically discharged, with no excuses accepted. You know about these things. Then you mustn't object if I put them on the screen and satirise them.' Yet there was considerably less effective satire in *Modern Times* than in *The Great Dictator* or *Monsieur Verdoux*. There was no message, only a statement of the merciless idiocy of machines once they get out of hand. Such a message must be equally distasteful to industrialists and Communists. Charlie simply wanders into a factory, ties himself into knots among the machines and jauntily wanders out of the factory again, glad to be in a world where he can breathe freely. Once again Charlie makes a monkey out of the harsh world of authority. 'Nonsense,' said Chaplin, when he was accused of propaganda. 'I was only poking fun at the general confusion from which we are all suffering.'

The film, which was released in 1936 at a time when general confusion was fast approaching chaos, was only incidentally concerned with modern times. Except for his appearance in the gigantic factory, Charlie still lives in the timeless world before 1914, a world of slapstick. There are fat policemen waiting around every corner. When Charlie presents himself for a job as waiter in a cabaret there are the inevitable two kitchen doors marked 'In' and 'Out'. It is still the world of *Tillie's Punctured Romance*. There is a football game with a roast duck, and for one miraculous moment Charlie finds himself launching a ship – the ship sinks – but the truth is that Buster Keaton did this kind of thing better by going down with his ship, straight-faced as ever. Charlie as a night watchman is an excellent and desirable invention, and he is wholly delightful when he shows off the furniture and fur-coats in the store to Paulette Goddard, and puts her to sleep in the softest of all the store beds. He is equally wonderful when he tries to sing, having lost the words written on his cuff, or when he dives across a road on skates and plunges recklessly towards destruction. The final scene, where he wanders off jauntily accompanied by Paulette who wriggles her hips while he does a little dance, is a further exploration of the inevitable ending. Paulette, of course, is Charlie in skirts. She is like the Kid, one of those images which he creates by a kind of parthenogenesis: a similar who will help him to fill out his loneliness. But all these scenes lack the verve, the abandon and the stark gaiety of the scenes where Charlie is caught up in the roaring webs of machinery, fences with long-stemmed oilcans and goes happily berserk.

Charlie shares with James Thurber an unusual attitude toward machines. In his study of the annals of Freudian criticism Thurber came upon the commentaries of Dr Bisch, who disagreed with Dr Freud. Dr Bisch studied the case of a man who saw a car bearing down on him, and then began to teeter back-

wards and forwards until he ran smack into the car; and while
not fully supporting the Freudian diagnosis that sex starvation
was at the root of the trouble, Dr Bisch does remark that an
automobile bearing down on you may be a sex symbol at that,
especially if you dream it. Austerely Thurber replied that in his
view, even if you dream it, it is probably not a sex symbol; it is
more likely to be an automobile bearing down on you, and
should the event occur in real life and in the open air, it is
reasonably certain that it is an automobile. It is an odd commentary on our times that we laughed when we saw Charlie
among the machines, and still odder that it should need Charlie
to remind us that the world of the machine is infinitely more
dangerous to the human being than anything invented by
Dr Freud. Marianne Moore talks somewhere of real toads in
imaginary gardens. What happened in *Modern Times* was the
spectacle of a real man caught in the real cogs; and one day we
may have to do with them what he did with them.

It is all too easy to imagine that Charlie in the film is merely a
depressed and neurotic man who cannot keep pace with the
world of machinery. Who can? We pretend we can. We even
pretend that the time will never come when the television screen
is set up in the workmen's urinals. Can we be certain they are
not there already? We know that in some factories hidden
microphones are installed in urinals; it is only a short step
from a microphone to a television screen. And what happens
after the television screen? What unknown monsters lurk there?
Or will everything be rainbow-coloured like the atom bomb?
When Pan shrieked in the engine-room, it may have been – it
probably was – the equivalent of the first little whimper of panic.
What happens when he really screams?

Conceivably (for one must expect the worst) the subtle
commentators who describe a hundred years hence the age
we are living in will forget to consult the works of Chaplin and
Thurber. They are kindred spirits, resigned to the world's ills
and devoted to the earthly joys, and they know the ground
swells on which we walk. Consider Thurber's academic essay
called *Preface to Life*, which should be regarded as an essential
textbook in any biology class. In that nightmarish story he tells
of a Person hopelessly and for ever displaced while never

moving a yard from his native land. He is the supreme D.P., the
forgotten man of the century, who makes his living the hardest
way by writing light pieces of one thousand to two thousand
words for the *New Yorker*. It is not, of course, he asks you to
understand, that he would not prefer to be doing something else;
it is simply that when an angel stuck a pin into the lists, this is
what he got. His life is a constant misery; he would kill himself
with a razor blade if he had not nicked himself too often. But he
is lonely for his own company. Three or four times a day he will
telephone to his own house, ask for himself in a low tone and,
on hearing that he is out, sigh in hard-breathing relief. The fear,
however, remains. Nothing is solved by the telephone conversation with the housekeeper, who may be his wife but is probably
someone entirely unknown to him, someone who lives three
streets away. No, the important thing, the matter which weighs
on his mind, is that one day he may find himself in, and then he
will discover that all his expensive training has been wasted: he
has developed no technique to deal with that hideous possibility.
How in God's name does one address oneself on a telephone?
And then – what would happen if one failed to recognise one's
own voice? Worst of all, what of the astonished silence at the
other end if one made some casual and completely inappropriate
remark, like saying cheerfully: 'Fine day, isn't it?' – when it is
raining. There are no answers to these problems, and the
theologians have only just begun to deal with them. One does
not hope for solutions from theologians, but it is always comfortable to know that they are facing *our* problems, not the ones
they invented to amuse themselves with on holidays, at church
synods and at festivals. There are times when Thurber raises
problems which Charlie would not recognise as problems, for he
has never met them. What, asks Thurber, is the correct behaviour
of a man walking along a darkening street when he looks quickly
behind him and sees that he is being softly followed by little
men padding along in single file, about a foot and a half high,
large-eyed and whiskered?

Charlie, of course, has never met these gentlemen, and would
be tongue-tied in their presence. He is more accustomed to
living in a world where the cops are nine foot high and correspond-
ingly broad, and where the manager's accusing face is the size

of a wall-map. Charlie can deal with the earth's immensity. He can, as he demonstrated to perfection in *His Prehistoric Past*, deal with the small trivial things of life: witness the way in which he bludgeoned a flea to death with a single throw of a club. Goblins are outside his range, and so is fantasy. He lives in a real world. One's own voice at the other end of the telephone is something we may have to reckon with before long, but there is considerable evidence that the whiskered little men eighteen inches high have departed. In that faith Charlie continues to contend only with visible authority, having already enough trouble, and with no desire to further his burdens with an exploration of the creeping things that come out of the earth at night.

Modern Times is not faultless, as *The Kid* is faultless. It has the fault, unusual in Chaplin's films, of beginning with a bang and never banging so loud again. Partly it was a fault of arrangement, the too-logical sequence of events from factory to psychiatric ward, and then to prison and shipyard and dog-house and then to prison again. There can be very little excuse for sending him to prison twice, for we know already that he passes a few days every winter in prison, to keep warm, and do not need to have it rubbed in. There are faults which arise from conscious attempts by Chaplin to impose his will on Charlie. Chaplin had read of prisons where the prisoners had everything their own way, with stag parties in the cells and free beer for the warders. He decided to put the scene in the film, and so we see Charlie, after preventing a jail-break, rewarded with a private cell with all the modern conveniences. Inevitably he is pardoned at the moment when he is most enjoying himself. This is not, however, the inevitability proper to Charlie, who can step out of prison whenever he wants to, and therefore may be assumed to have the power of staying in prison as long as he wants to. He misbehaves in prison. He makes gargling noises and deliberately offends old ladies. At such moments he is acting out of character, and Chaplin has confused him with a monkey in a cage. What is surprising is that such moments are extremely rare at all times after the Keystone comedies, and still more surprising that he should go out of his way to offend old ladies, for he is a bit of an old lady himself. As for the incident where Charlie takes 'joy powder' and so acquires the strength of Popeye the Sailor – the strength enables him to hold back the tide of escaping prisoners – it must be accepted that this is a scene of crass ineptitude, the one major fault in the Charlie opus, and one that cries to heaven. Up to this point Charlie has always exerted his native wits, relied on his wits, seen no reason to employ anything but his wits. To have recourse to 'joy powder' is like having recourse to opium when one cannot face the realities of the world, and this film was the one most deliberately concerned with the world's realities.

It is interesting to enquire why *Modern Times* contains so much of the best and so much of the worst of Chaplin. Composed in an unusually short time, at the end of a leisurely tour round the world, with the usual vast expenditure of film – he exposed 215,000 feet and used only a little more than 8,000 feet in the final film – it never found a central *point d'appui*. It could have been written wholly around a factory, but the prospect was hardly inviting. It could conceivably have progressed from a small handcraft factory to a nightmare of an elephantine machine-shop. It could have progressed from any direction he pleased except the one direction it took – the direction of the pure vision of the opening scenes to the gags which attended its gradual decline. It is impossible to avoid the conclusion that Chaplin was so overwhelmed with the horror of the opening of the film that the rest became a deliberate escape from horror; when we see Charlie in the dog-house, or watch him diving into what he thinks is the sea, though it is only a small puddle, we are at the opposite remove from Charlie in the factory. The rest is light relief, and if it is excellent of its kind, it failed to show the measure of Chaplin's genius.

One cannot ask an actor always to show his best. There are bad paintings by Cézanne, atrocious paintings by Rubens and at least one terrible painting by Leonardo. Unfortunately, the character of Charlie is such that he is no longer Charlie when he is not perfectly in character. Since he is a trapeze artist walking on the points of his toes, we are surprised when we find him slogging manfully down a road. We do not expect a pianist also to be a boxer. The Charlie who immersed himself in the factory is not the same as the Charlie who quietly accepts life in a dog-house. Some clue to the failure lies in Chaplin's use of sub-titles. There seemed to be thousands of them. Voices spoke in *Modern*

Times, but they were never direct and human voices; they came through television, phonograph and radio; and when Charlie sang, it was wonderful gibberish, but not wonderful enough.

Yet one should be grateful for the greater mercies: the scenes in the factory and the subsequent scene where Charlie falls off a truck with the danger flag in his hand and waves it frantically to attract the attention of the truck-driver, only to be arrested by the police as though he was inciting the workers with a red flag. We should be grateful too for the scenes when the night-watchman carefully displays the store's wealth to the little working girl. Above all we have every reason to be grateful for the dance of the cogwheels and the dance of Pan which brings it to a shattering end.

In the year 1906 the poet Christian Morgenstern entered a disturbing note in his diary. He spoke of a time when a new kind of story would be invented far more potent and hallucinating than any existing hitherto. He wrote:

> A time will come when stories will be written 'from beyond'. I mean stories about much the same things as those of today, but whose peculiar fascination will be that the people portrayed will be made transparent – held up against the mystery. They will be characterised with entire belief in their reality, yet they will have the effect of hallucinations, they will hold us spellbound like some of the themes of poetry as we have known it hitherto, but the awe experienced by him for whom the old world has collapsed will be communicated in their portrayal too, so that they will at once entertain and excite a profound, uncanny wonderment.

There is a sense in which Charlie had been composing such stories from the very beginning. In the opening reel of *Modern Times* we hear the authentic shudder of a world on the edge of doom. This was his art at its best; beyond this it was not possible to go.

CHAPTER XVIII

THE GREAT DICTATOR

The Great Dictator was the fruit of long pondering, of many mysterious coincidences and of a fierce intolerance of dictatorship in all its forms. It was not merely directed against the Fascist states; it was directed quite openly at forces which existed within the non-fascist states. Confused, brilliant, wonderfully constructed, with passages of comedy as exquisite as any that came before, it was unlike anything he had created before, for it could not be called a comedy simply, and it was not in any real sense a satire. There was no name for this kind of desperate knife-edge adventure into territory never penetrated before – the territory of the darkest shadows, the most incontrovertible evil, the most tragic dilemmas; and under the strain of these evils the old character of Charlie broke down, and an entirely new character was brought into being, with only a faint passing resemblance to the Charlie who appeared on the streets of Venice. Beginning with the real Charlie, who appears in a kind of curtain-raiser, we watch the gradual emergence of a host of Charlies until at last, when we have penetrated through all the veils, when we think we are about to see the final apotheosis of the Tramp and the Vagabond, we see – the despairing face of Chaplin himself.

American art has failed to grapple with the forces of evil. Alone of the great creators Melville saw evil plain, the huge brute force of it wallowing in the Pacific. In the plays of Eugene O'Neill the stage is littered with notices saying: 'Here is incest' or 'Here is evil', or sometimes there are larger notices saying: 'Here are Tigers', just as the Elizabethan stage showed notices saying: 'Here is the field of battle'. But the real evil, the sullen unmoving ponderous and quick-witted thing, the evil which is like the eternity described by Dostoyevsky, 'and which resembles an old lavatory in Siberia where the spiders crawl', this evil had escaped him, as it has escaped Robinson Jeffers. The terror at the heart of terror appears momentarily in the early gangster films, where the gangster becomes the tragic hero, destined for death not for the crimes he committed but for those he would have been incapable of committing, shot down by accident when he was thought to be someone else, obtaining to dignity only because the death of the hero was as accidental as the death of a fly, and by his very anonymity, his extraordinary resemblance to everyone else, the hero assumes a genuine tragic character. In something of the same way the little Jewish barber by a series of accidents becomes the Great Dictator Adenoid Hynkel, the Napoleonic invader of Austerlich and convinced Emperor of the World.

We are accustomed to see the emblem of evil in Melville's portrait of the White Whale, but what if the whale had been a mackerel? Or better still, what if the whale had been a sprat? Clearly, the fact of size has little enough to do with the fact of evil, and when Blake, in one of his most powerful designs, showed 'the ghost of a flea', a design which emphasised only that the flea was supernaturally evil, he was not trying to be funny. On the contrary, he was saying that evil may be every-where, even in microscopic things close to the skin. As Chaplin designed *The Great Dictator* he seems to have been faced with a perpetual dilemma: should the dictator have the size of a whale or the size of a sprat? In the end he avoided the problem. To the dictator was granted the dignity of comedy, and he becomes far more comic, far more resourceful in his comedy than the little Jewish barber can ever be. We can believe in the barber. We never quite believe in the dictator, for his mad capers, even the maddest of all, are close to the bone. How, he must have asked himself, does one caricature a caricature? How to use one mythology – the mythology of Charlie – to counter the mask of evil with its own mythological origins? When Adenoid Hynkel runs up the curtains with the agility of a mouse, or when he dances with a huge inflated globe of the world and hugs it to his breast in a wild longing to possess the whole, he is not being in any real sense comic, for Hitler had done exactly these things, or things very like them. A man who gnawed at carpets and regarded himself as the predestined inheritor of the Holy Roman Empire and most of Asia defies caricature because he is himself a caricature, the caricature of a mythology. But the two mythologies, the one expressed by Charlie with incomparable gentleness and tenderness towards all suffering creatures and the other expressed by Hitler with his brute force and rasping voice, have no point of contact. Hitler, the witch-doctor in a world of armed force, living in a madhouse surrounded by the mad servants of his will, was very much Melville's whale doomed to drown in one last explosion of terror, attempting to the very last to take the whole world with him. Without natural dignity, Hitler possessed the dignity of the powers he controlled. Hynkel possesses no dignity whatsoever of his own. What dignity he possesses he receives only by the grace of Chaplin, and even this dignity is often withdrawn. It is all dangerous ground. One false move, and the whole thing will topple to the ground. The genius of Chaplin kept it alive, but we are conscious of the sense of strain, while Chaplin blows on the embers and somehow keeps the dictator alive.

It is not, of course, that Chaplin had any desire to keep him alive. His horror of Hitler was real, swift, direct and personal, and horror was continually getting in the way. The imitations of Hitler at a party rally, ranting and grimacing, screaming gibberish, the face streaked with sweat and the eyes set in an asinine glare, were wonderfully contrived, but it would be absurd to deny that there was something wonderfully effective in Hitler's bestial roar, and Chaplin's imitation was a tribute from one genius to another. To those who have heard Hitler and felt the hot animal rage blowing on their faces, Chaplin's parody was no longer amusing; it was far too close to the real thing. Worse still, it was precisely in those moments when Hynkel ranted that he achieved a vicarious dignity, for there entered into that absurd screeching with its meaningless and insane travesties of the German language the healthy roar of a trapped animal. So perhaps had Pan roared in the forest glades when he was deprived of the sceptre by Apollo. The most successful, the most amusing and the most artistically conceived piece of mimicry in *The Great Dictator* was also the most dangerously accurate reproduction of the real thing. Chaplin was quite aware that the ranting was inadequate, however brilliant, and long after the film was completed, he discovered that by breaking the voice into shorter explosions and by substituting more real words, he could achieve a parody which did greater violence to the original. By this time it was too late, and new enemies had arisen to take the place of a ranting ghost.

The story of *The Great Dictator* went through many changes. Originally conceived around 1935, when the full impact of Hitler was being felt upon the world, it received nourishment during the Axis war against Spain. Chaplin's sympathies, like those of President Roosevelt, were supremely on the side of the Republican forces, and he made no effort to disguise them. The result was that the portrait of Hitler became inextricably confused with the portrait of Franco, and though the little Jewish barber belongs to the German ghettos, he is also at times any Spanish peasant caught up in the struggle to survive. The little fleshy Franco, posturing in the Escorial, so small that he seems to be all boots, stomach and moustache, can be seen at intervals – one more of the many clowns who disguise themselves as Hynkel throughout the desperate comedy.

Originally, according to newspaper reports, the story was simpler. It was to begin with a concentration camp, the long parades of shuffling Jews and outcasts from the Hitler regime, and a bullying camp commandant, who demanded instant obedience of his savage and meaningless orders. Charlie attempts to carry them out, fails, is thrown into a prison, escapes and runs away with a Jewish girl, only to find himself in the hands of conspirators who have arrested Hynkel and do not know what to do with him. They find that Charlie is prepared to do anything rather than enter the concentration camp. He will even assume the disguise of Hynkel, while Hynkel himself is forced to enter the camp, where he barks orders, insists he is Hynkel, and is kicked for his pains. Charlie becomes dictator. The stormtroopers prostrate themselves to the ground before him. Extraordinary ceremonies take place, and Charlie, who cannot in the least fathom what is happening, grows more and more miserable until he desires nothing so much as to return to the concentration camp, where he at least enjoyed greater freedom than in his palace. Finally, there is an assassination attempt, but the woman who is sent to assassinate him finds him weeping and he reveals his misery to her. She helps him to escape into Switzerland, and we see them for the last time when they have avoided the frontier guards and are making their way down a Swiss lane.

The original story, so much closer to the Charlie mythology, was abandoned for many reasons. In the first place it could be interpreted as pure comedy, and Chaplin had no intention or returning to pure comedy. Determined to say things which needed to be said, and still retain the elements of slapstick, he decided to widen the story of mistaken identity, and by the end of 1938 there was already a version in existence called *The Dictator*, which was described as a dramatic composition in five acts and an epilogue and bore the sub-title: 'The story of a little fish in a shark-infested sea'.

In this provisional story most of the elements which later went to make up *The Great Dictator* appeared, but they were curiously out of focus. Put together in another form, with a slightly different background and with a sharper emphasis, they might have contributed to the comic drama which Chaplin had always hoped to make – a film which would have the kind or impact which the comedies of Aristophanes had on their Athenian audiences. He wanted to shake people, and at the same time he wanted to be funny in a desperately serious way. Confronted with the image of Hitler, how could it be done? He did not know. He made his way forward by a series of preliminary skirmishes, and though the second version has a greater profundity than the first, it is also strangely unsatisfactory, and we can see now why Chaplin was forced to more complicated solutions.

The second version begins, characteristically, in 1919: which is to say that it begins outside of time altogether, in the world before history began, the world of the kids' auto races and the custard pies. On some unknown battlefront in Europe Charlie is seen shouldering arms for Ptomania (Bacteria) against the 'Alliars', and after a series of trench experiences deriving from *Shoulder Arms* Charlie returns to Ptom, the capital of Ptomania, only to discover that though the war has been won, a little cock of the walk called Hinkle has entrenched himself in authority; the war won by the Ptomanians has been the means of Hinkle's rise to power. 'Furor' Hinkle is, of course, a parody of Hitler. All arms are raised when he appears, and even the dachshunds must raise their legs. There follows a scene where Hinkle meets Dictator Mussemup of Ostrich, and they swear eternal loyalty to óne another. Meanwhile Charlie is arrested, shipped to a concentration camp and escapes in a storm-trooper's uniform, and soon he is mistaken for the Furor, while the real Furor is arrested as an impostor. Meanwhile Herring, the Air Minister, has decided upon an aggressive campaign against the state of Vanilla, and there come the great day when the Furor must dedicate his armies for the war against the insolent state of Vanilla, but instead of declaring war Charlie makes an appeal for peace. In this big speech, which follows with important differences the same rhythms and the same mood as the speech of *The Great Dictator*, Charlie calls upon all nations to put down their arms. 'I don't want to conquer anybody,' he says. 'I want to do good by everybody. Because – because this is a big world, and there's plenty of room for all of us in it. Yes. Even for dictators. Even for Hinkle. He wants to do right. He's just full of hate and bitterness – that's all.' Having made his speech, Charlie stumbles away, the lights fade and he wakes up in a concentration camp with a storm-trooper glaring down at him – the image of all the bruisers and cops he has fought in the past. Charlie smiles, with that smile which is his perpetual weapon against adversity. The storm-trooper also begins to smile, but immediately afterwards the smile freezes on his lips. Then he says: 'Get up, Jew, where the hell do you think you are?'

The final version of *The Great Dictator* was very different, or rather it included the second version as it included (at a great remove) the first version, but Hinkle changes to Hynkel, Mussemup to Napaloni, Ptomania becomes Tomania, and Vanilla becomes Austerlich. Something more than a change of names has occurred. The emphasis is no longer simple or ironic. Hinkle might be endearing in an odd, idiot way, and so might Mussemup, but there is nothing endearing in Hynkel, who begins from this time onward to assume the violent eccentricities of a modern Napoleon; for if Franco enters the portrait, so does the deathless Napoleon Chaplin had once dreamed of playing, a man who returns from St Helena to find himself unrecognised and unknown, without power or armies, forgotten by the French and content in his weariness to lose himself in obscurity until he sees how gullible the French are, and then he determines to put himself at the head of a conspiracy. The insurrection is just about to begin when news comes from St Helena that Napoleon is dead. Thereupon Napoleon cries out in remorse and frustration and agony: 'The news of my death has killed me!'

It is interesting to watch in Chaplin's mind the gradual development of the portrait of Hynkel, to see Chaplin stripping away the sentimentality layer by layer, coming at last to form a portrait which has clear outlines, though the outlines themselves are extraordinarily complex. Chaplin said once that he regarded Hitler merely as 'a small, mean, nervous and neurotic man'. True enough; but just as there is more to the devil than plain badness, so Chaplin, fascinated by the comic possibilities of a modern devil, found himself perplexed by the continually obtruding Napoleonic overtones, the sense that he was dealing with something larger than life and must make his enemy credible. In the end he only half succeeded. The final portrait of Hynkel has something of the grace of a hyena, and a hyena's blind will to kill. Hynkel is at turns ferocious, stupid, boorish, determined upon power and jealous of power, strident, nervous, delicate, sweet-tempered, bewildered and insane. He is all these, and more, as he must be, for how else could one represent Franco, Napoleon and Hitler in a single character? There never was such a medley of opposing charactertistics in a single comic character, and where the film fails, the failure arises from the extraordinary incoherence of the portrait of the dictator, who is no longer simply the dictator, but the Great Dictator, another kind of animal altogether, more than Napoleon and only a little less than God. The pity, which was present in the earlier versions, now disappears, if only because the time for pity had passed. Originally conceived as a play in defence of the Jews, the film was begun when a tragedy even greater than the tragedy of the concentration camps was occurring – Hitler had begun the conquest of Europe. So the small details of the war in *Shoulder Arms* are exchanged for the larger details of Big Berthas and aircraft, and the loaded last lines of the second version have to be abandoned. Perhaps it is a pity. To emphasise even on the comic stage Hynkel's grotesque madness may have been a fault, for it is inconceivable that the armies of Tomania would ever have attacked Austerlich at his command. They might – they probably would – have attacked Vanilla, which has no overtones of Austerlitz. Yet, though there are abundant imperfections in the play, the imperfections which connect the author to his play also connect him with the audience. He was drawing the picture of a very real Hitler, and *The Great Dictator*, when it was first performed publicly on 15 October 1940, did mirror in a surprisingly accurate way the popular imaginative portrait of Hitler. It was also prophetic. Hynkel was an experiment in Napoleonic grandeur, bourgeois simplicity and madness, and these were precisely the qualities which Hitler showed during the last months of the war.

The Dictator was an attempt to write a tragi-comedy on the plight of the Jews; *The Great Dictator* attempted to describe the plight of men everywhere, and particularly of the soldiers, and to do this seriously and with the utmost comedy. All would have been well enough if the little Jewish barber had been half as credible as the dictator. Unfortunately, he is not. Only one magnificent and irrelevant comic scene is given to him: his performance as he shaves a customer to the tune of a Brahms Hungarian dance. For the rest he is the foil for Hynkel, and he never acquires the stature which would permit him to make the final curtain speech. The authority of the speech stems directly from Chaplin, not from the little barber, who has neither suffered enough nor known enough to be the vehicle of a speech of such magnitude.

The third version of the play begins with a recapitulation of some of the themes already announced in *Shoulder Arms*. Charlie is about to fire an enormous gun, but he has no conception of what the gun is about, and regards it very much as primitive man might have regarded a dinosaur. He fires it. The first shell hits an outhouse, the second dribbles out of the muzzle like a huge spluttering Chinese firework, turns on him and begins to follow him all over the gun and all over the neighbouring landscape. The mad destructive shell, like the destructive wheels of *Modern Times*, caricatures the malevolence of machines, the horror of war and the blank face of Hynkel, but in *Modern Times* Charlie was able to put a term to the destructive wheels by pulling the switches. On the battlefield he can only put a term to himself. The comic possibilities of the shell are soon exhausted, yet they announce the theme: the senselessness of destruction. Long before Hynkel enters the scene we are aware of him: he is the shell with legs. It should be observed that in these preliminary scenes Charlie is not the only comic character; the shell also possesses, in its amazingly contrived efforts to outwit Charlie, a dancing gait and a desperate comic character of its own. 'Everything that touches upon death is of an astounding gaiety.'

Unfortunately the statement is only too true: the best moments of *The Great Dictator* are those which come close to death, Charlie with a loose hand-grenade wandering in his sleeve, Charlie suddenly turning and running back during a charge, saying 'Excuse me' politely to the soldiers who are still advancing, Charlie in the aeroplane flying upside down and doomed, it would seem, to a certain death. This mad flight in a mad aeroplane was very close to Chaplin's heart. Asked once which of the adventures of Charlie gave him the most amusement, he said he would cheerfully put this at the top of the list. The scene is completely incoherent. Seeing the sun shining below him, he takes out his watch which immediately sweeps past his face and stands vertically above him. The water from the canteen spills straight up into his face. Everything is going the wrong way; and as he gazes entranced upon an inverted world Charlie has an expression of consummate happiness. His companion in the aeroplane launches into a dithyrambic poem on Spring, which oddly announces one of the themes of *Monsieur Verdoux*, for the pilot speaks gently of his girl who never wanted to cut daffodils, but preferred to see them untouched and virgin. At that moment the aeroplane crashes. After the blaze, the pilot emerges, gently continuing with his rhapsody, speaking about the beautiful spring-like soul of his beloved and how she loved children and animals. All this is the purest nonsense, for we know that it is not the pilot but Charlie who is dithyrambic and possesses that ingenuous soul. Nothing in this scene has very much to do with plot or story. This is as it should be. If there was plot or story we should feel defrauded. All we have is a few threads joining the incidents together, and even these are perhaps unnecessary.

There follows our first introduction to Hynkel gabbling like all the wild geese of the world. It is masterly gabble, but as we have already observed, there is danger in that mastery. 'Democratia shtunk!' Hynkel yells. 'Libertad shtunk! Frei sprachen shtunk!' He has a furious fit of coughing, and begins again. Hynkel is on the rostrum, addressing the mob, and Herring is beside him. Herring jumps up, and inevitably splits his trousers. Hynkel addresses the world, brother of the mayor in *City Lights* who made his wordless speech to the sound of a trombone. The trombone had the effect of depriving the mayor of his dignity; the terrible macaronics of Hynkel have a completely opposite effect. He is almost credible. The voice, in its daemonic fury, has a beauty of its own, and when later Hynkel kisses a baby and gets his hands wet from holding her, and when he raises his arm in a fascist salute towards Venus and the Thinker, whose arms are also raised, we are aware of no incongruity: in this way it happened, and Chaplin has only parodied what is above parody.

The thin threads which hold the film together are sharply visible when Garbitsch (Goebbels) turns to Hynkel and complains that the Jews are not being punished enough. 'Yes, things have been too quiet in the ghetto recently,' Hynkel answers, and then we fade into the ghetto where Charlie is suffering from amnesia as a result of the aeroplane crash. There follows a scene which possesses all the rowdy overtones of the Keystone comedies. Charlie, the barber, enters his shop after months of absence. The cats come running out, there is dust everywhere, cobwebs cling to the ceiling. Some Storm Troopers are painting the word 'Jew' on the window. Charlie immediately wipes the sign off, to be clubbed for his pains. In a hilarious scene, which derives from his rope-walking experience in *The Pawnshop* and the drunken orgies of *One A.M.* Charlie teeters up and down the road, having been hit during the subsequent brawl with a frying pan accurately aimed by Hannah, the girl whose presence in the play is never sufficiently explained. Then the pilot, now a big-shot Storm Trooper, enters the scene, releases Charlie from the attacks of the other Storm Troopers and says wistfully: 'I thought you were an Aryan.' 'No,' says Charlie, 'I'm a vegetarian.' It is as though Charlie was determined to wear his Keystone disguise to the very end.

Some of the obscurities of *The Great Dictator* arise from the different forms of comedy employed. Slapstick is followed by cunning passages at arms, Deburau by Grimaldi, remembered fragments of *The Kid* by fragments of *Laughing Gas.* The little Jewish barber is mostly slapstick, Hynkel alone is allowed the privilege of entering the world of the tightrope dancers, though at odd moments he will show that he is perfectly capable of slapstick. The trouble is that he is altogether too delightful. When an inventor enters with a new kind of parachute and falls to his death after springing out of the window, Hynkel turns to Herring and remarks: 'I wish you wouldn't waste my time like this.' The remark is excessively appropriate. When Garbitsch says the prisoners are complaining about the sawdust in their bread, Hynkel says sweetly: 'It's from the finest lumber our mills can supply.' We shrug: we are not in the world where these things happen, but in a world where fear is removed by virtue of the mind's licence to say what it pleases in defiance of the consequences, for the mind knows there will be no consequences. So the philosopher David Hume could say, quite deliberately and without archness: 'It is not contrary to reason to prefer the destruction of the whole world to the scratching of my finger.' When Hynkel discovers that three thousand strikers are keeping back production he orders them all to be shot, explaining: 'I don't want any of my workers dissatisfied.' Once again parody hugs the original too close.

For the rest of the film the parody and the original are almost inseparable. When Hynkel is told by Garbitsch that he will soon be dictator of all the world, and will be worshipped as a God, Hynkel simpers: 'You mustn't say that. You make me afraid of myself.' Then, shaken by a paroxysm of fear, Hynkel darts across the room and runs up the window curtains like a mouse. It is a magnificent moment, and one of the greatest in all Chaplin's work, but it is not comedy. It is at once truth and tragic farce, an exploration of the character of Hitler leading to the pure mimicry of the dictator. This mimicry is perfect, but it is not funny, for the fearful little animal who runs up the curtain and the juggler who subsequently dances to the tune of the *Lohengrin Prelude* are magnificent recreations of the real horror. This is no longer Hynkel, but the insane mask of Hitler. Even when Hynkel, juggling with his balloon on which the map of the world is painted, breaks down in sobs when the balloon bursts, we are in the real, tangible world of the Berlin Kanzlerei.

The dance of Hynkel gives place to the dance of the little Jewish barber, who shaves his customer to the tune of a Brahms Hungarian dance. The scene has the perfection of great comedy, but since it comes immediately after Hynkel's dance it is wholly misplaced. It is as though Chaplin were saying: 'Well, I have shown the dictator dancing, now I must show the barber dancing.' Yet the sheer brilliance of the two dances has the effect of suspending disbelief. Both dances are pantomimes, both make use of stylised sound and stylised movement without speech. They are music-hall turns, as artificial as classical ballet, and to have dared to introduce them so nakedly into the play shows incredible boldness. It is in these passages that Chaplin for the first time showed his mastery of the use of sound in pantomime; in *Monsieur Verdoux* he never reached these heights.

Slapstick follows when the Storm Troopers attack the ghetto, and Charlie is forced to flee. He dives into a barrel head first, hides in a cellar and takes part in an extraordinary scene of conspiracy where it is decided to blow up Hynkel's palace – all that is left of the earlier version in which the conspirators played a far larger part. The conspiracy is parodied. A coin has been buried in a cake. The man who finds the coin must blow up the palace. The barber eats his cake slowly, masticating carefully, and we hear three tinkles – three coins. The girl Hannah has deliberately sabotaged the conspiracy, saying it is wrong to blow up the palace – she has filled the cake with coins. Afterwards the conspirators go on their way, Hannah to Austerlich and the little barber to a concentration camp.

Into Hynkel's palace comes news that Napaloni is massing his armies on the Austerlich frontier. Hynkel falls into a rage, strips Herring of his medals, declares immediate war, tears up the declaration of war and invites Napaloni to a conference. Napaloni arrives. There is some wonderful fooling as his train refuses to stop in a way which will allow him to step directly on the red carpet. With difficulty the two dictators greet one another while edging each other out of camera range – a trick which derives straight from *Kid Auto Races in Venice*. Hynkel plans that while they are at conference, Napaloni shall sit in a low chair facing the light, under the steady gaze of a massive statue of Hynkel. Things do not work out like that. Hynkel is waiting for Napaloni when he observes that the Italian has entered by another door and has no intention of sitting in a low chair. They discuss the war they will wage against Austerlich and go out to take the salute at a mass parade of troops. Aircraft fall out of the air, and Napaloni comments: 'They're yours all right.' The atmosphere is strained. It grows even more strained during the ball in which Hynkel dances with the fat Signora Napaloni. The dictators ·decide to celebrate by some duck-shooting, but it so happens that the little barber has escaped from the camp and comes wandering near the duck pond. Mistaken for Hynkel, he is carried in triumph by some Storm Troopers to the grandstand where Hynkel is expected to deliver his orders to invade Auster-lich. The little barber climbs ponderously up the immense stairway to the dais, and begins his speech. He speaks simply, straightforwardly, with all the passion in his soul. He says: 'Hope,' and then pauses, as though the word was so beautiful that he could only pause. 'I'm sorry,' he says apologetically, 'but I don't want to be an emperor. That's not my business. I don't want to rule or conquer anyone——'

The curtain speech of *The Great Dictator* aroused controversy; today it would probably arouse less. The very simplicity of Chaplin's impassioned text, which falls at times into loose pentameters, gave it peculiar depth and resonance; such simple words are not often heard on the screen. The long speech, which covers two pages of text, said what Chaplin wanted to say, and he saw no reason why he should be deprived of saying these things. He said:

Fight for liberty! In the 17th chapter of St Luke, it is written: 'The Kingdom of God is within man' – not in one man nor a group of men, but in all men! In you! You, the people, have the power – the power to create machines. The power to create happiness! You, the people, have the power to make this life free and beautiful – to make this life a wonderful adventure. Then in the name of democracy – let us use that power, let us all unite. Let us fight for a new world – a decent world that will give men a chance to work – that will give youth a future and old age a security. By the promise of these things, brutes have risen to power. But they lied! They did not fulfil that promise. They never will! Dictators freed themselves, but they enslaved the people! Now let us fight to free the world!

What Chaplin was saying was precisely what millions of people in occupied Europe desired to say over the radio. Such words had been employed before; there was nothing new in them, except the manner of the speaking of them. He had painted the Great Dictator as the supreme Lord of Misrule; now it was time to come to earth; and if he said things which were corny, it can be argued that the Beatitudes were already corny at the time they were delivered. Understandably, the film was never released in the Soviet Union.

Chaplin was faced with no alternative. He could only end the film with the vision of blessedness, for no other vision was possible. The folly of the dictators was his theme, and he dared not suggest even by implication that their folly was enduring, for it was precisely their mad folly which he found unendurable. 'It would be much easier,' he said, 'to have the barber and Hannah disappear over the horizon, off to the promised land against the growing sunset. But there is no promised land for the oppressed people of the world. There is no place over the horizon to which they can go for sanctuary. They must stand, and we must.' It was as simple as that then, and as simple as that now.

CHAPTER XIX

THE SWEET WORM TURNS

''IT IS only the artist, and maybe the criminal, who can make his own life,' wrote Somerset Maugham in his autobiography, and though the first effect of the words is more startling than the second, they are worth pondering. One day, when he was talking to Clare Sheridan, Chaplin found himself pondering the same problem, and said: 'Criminals, you know, and artists are psychologically akin. Both have a burning flame of impulse, a vision, a deep sense of lawlessness.' It was a passing remark, thrown off in a casual moment. Is it true?

Perhaps we shall never know the answer, because we shall never be able to isolate the mind of the artist or the criminal. The artist's devotion to his craft involves a sense of law, a hard and tortured mastery of his material. He deals with uncertainties, and must make them certain, and he lives at such a pitch of emotion that he is in perpetual danger of becoming inhuman, a world in himself at odds with the world he is living in. But to live in such a world is not to be a criminal, and in spite of Wainwright the poisoner and Oscar Wilde very few artists have been criminals. Yet throughout history they have been fascinated by the minds of criminals, seeing in the criminal something they lack, some explosive power denied to them.

Monsieur Verdoux is many things – there never was such a complex film – but it includes the study of a murderer. By definition, since the film is sub-titled 'A Comedy of Murder', he is a comic murderer, and in fact he never murders; we are conscious only of the perpetual threat of murder seen in its most comic aspects. The burning flame of impulse, the deep sense of unlawfulness which characterised Raskolnikov in *Crime and Punishment*, are wholly absent. But the vision remains, and it is the quality of Chaplin's vision, as he examines the figure of *Monsieur Verdoux* through four improbable murders which take place offstage, that repays our study, for what he says in the film is very close to the bone. In this film, which is pure comedy and one of the three greatest that Chaplin has produced, there is also pure pity, and this pity is deliberate. 'I intended,' said Chaplin at the time when the film was first being shown, 'to create a pity for all humanity under certain drastic conditions.'

The staggering importance of *Monsieur Verdoux* lies in the fact that in an age of murder it is the only film which deals honestly with murder, holds it to the light and shows it to be the contemptible thing it is. Hollywood and the Soviet cinema in their different ways had attached a glamour to murder. They had shown how exciting, delightful and breathtaking it was to shoot down defenceless men, how delicious it is to torture, how enviable are the men with guns. The death of a man by shooting him down provides an appropriate solution for bringing a film to an end, so that even in a film like *Crossfire*, which claimed to have a high moral purpose, the curtain falls on a defenceless man running down a deserted street while the windows open and invisible guns fire down on him. In the Soviet films the murders are on a larger scale. They show battles unlike battles which have ever taken place. In *Alexander Nevsky* the Teutonic Knights are caricatured, made to resemble heraldic beasts, with iron chimneys on their heads, and deprived of any grandeur; the cadets in *The End of St Petersburg* become fat young women bursting through their military clothes; in *Chapayev* the enemy is composed of ridiculous tailor's dummies, pompous and effete beyond credibility. No pity is shown for the enemy, nor for their own dead who are, by the fact of dying for a cause, translated into that world of cloud-lit sunrises and trumpets with which Mr Cecil de Mille has painted so many of his conclusions; and indeed there exists a terrible similarity between the films of Mr de Mille and the Soviet producers.

Outside of *Monsieur Verdoux* and other Chaplin films I can think of only two moments of real pity in American and Soviet films. One occurs in Fritz Lang's *Fury* where the camera hovers over the prisoner in his cell, his face glowing with flames and shadowed by prison bars. He is waiting for the time when the prison doors will be burst open and the mob will enter, and somehow, but only for a moment, Fritz Lang was able to identify the prisoner in his cell with all the suffering of trapped humanity, all its hopes, its fears and its nobility. The other occurs in *Ten Days That Shook the World*. A dead girl lies on the edge of a bridge, and as the bridge is raised her hair is swept upward, and this black slowly moving wave of hair showers its beauty like a blessing on the dead girl. There are moments which approach to pity in *Intolerance*, where the woman rocking her cradle was a symbol for the pity which was felt by D. W. Griffith, but there are not many such moments in film.

The triumph of *Monsieur Verdoux* lies in its pity, the poignancy of the tramp invading the whole of the world in which Monsieur Verdoux lives. Inevitably, Chaplin was faced with the problem: what happens when my tramp is tired of gathering crumbs? He has always hankered after respectability. Let him gather diamonds. Let him murder. He has always been the most humble and the most ordinary of persons, and now that we are living in an age of murder, and all of us are most humbly taking part in wars, where shall we begin? Shall I have him wearing his tramp's uniform walking down a street, and suddenly committing a murder for no reason at all? No, there must be a reason for it. Then let him murder as we all murder, gently, indirectly, giving assent to the words inscribed on the political documents, and at the same time (since he is after all a tramp and a clown) let him take his fun in murdering, and let us see what amusement can be extracted from it. It was only later that the air of menace entered the scene. It came perhaps with the music, that haunting music which he invented for the purpose, those lighthearted little tunes which had in them all the menace of the organ-music playing in London streets at twilight.

But murder, as Monsieur Verdoux observes, is a serious business and must be regarded seriously, even in a comedy. It may be – there are no certainties, and no final conclusions are ever possible in discussing a film which outraged so many sensibilities – that it was precisely because Chaplin discussed murder seriously in this film that he was so bitterly attacked. Somewhere in the shadows of this film there was a savage indignation and a hint of mockery, Pan roaring in the shrubbery, even a flash of hate and horror of the men who murder. For most people when they attend films murder is seen as a form of light relief, a pleasant titillation of the senses, the emergence of drama where there was only the required posturing of actors before. This time there was real murder, or rather there was the image of a man who looked in every way as though he was disposed to murder for the fun of it, far more murderous than Edward G. Robinson whose hideous mask announces 'I am a murderer' in nearly all his films, but the announcement is not wholly convincing.

Monsieur Verdoux was convincing. From the moment when he stepped out from behind the garden incinerator with its little black dribble of smoke announcing the death of one more rich woman to the moment when his trial begins, he assumes an air of authenticity. He says: 'Here I am! I present the first real murderer who has ever appeared on the stage! Look closely! See, I am not so very different from the man who keeps the tobacco-shop at the corner of the street and who disappears every Thursday evening. I am what happens on those Thursday evenings. I am also what happens in the headlines. I am every-where. I love little children. Like Hitler, I weep when my dog dies. I have a fund of amusing things to tell you. Listen and observe. If you are careful you will see yourselves stripped to the bone. I am the world's lack of conscience, all your collective wickedness and folly, and if you will only look in my mirror——' Whereupon it was assumed that Chaplin was 'guying' murder and amusing himself ghoulishly at the expense of people who are murdered, and if the irony passed unobserved, so did the savage indignation.

There were many reasons for the failure of *Monsieur Verdoux* to reach the large public it deserved, and not the least of them was Chaplin's success in making Monsieur Verdoux credible. The old-fashioned camera techniques, the way Chaplin would sometimes appear to be acting on one of those circular stages divided into four parts, the way he continually occupied the limelight and seemed to move among the audience, continually injecting ribald comments and pointing to himself, the character on the stage, saying: 'He is evil. Do something quickly, or better still search your own consciences,' the extraordinary way in which Chaplin's moral conscience is present even in the

most comical scenes, all these reinforced an illusion which
Chaplin had hardly counted upon – the illusion that now at last
the tramp and Chaplin himself had come together in the person
of Monsieur Verdoux, who was assumed to be Chaplin himself
subtly disguised. But to identify Monsieur Verdoux with
Chaplin is an error of the same magnitude as to identify Botticelli
with a Botticelli Venus. Traits of Botticelli's physical appearance
do in fact appear in all his Venuses. He could hardly avoid it, for
he placed himself wholly at the mercy of his art, completely
surrendering himself to it, and while he painted his model he
was absorbed in the process of creation to the extent that he
became himself a part of Venus. But the air which Venus breathes
is not the air of Florence, nor with her bone-structure would she
ever have been able to walk down a Florentine street, or any
street in this world. She was an ideal figure compounded from
the artist's imagination, living in the world the artist created for
her, independent of our world though reflecting its splendour.
Monsieur Verdoux only too successfully reflected the world's
horror, and at the same time he incriminated the whole human
race.

Monsieur Verdoux is a document which incriminates, but it is
also uproariously funny. How can these be reconciled? In fact
they were never completely reconciled, for though Monsieur
Verdoux incriminates he gives the utmost pleasure. He is the
judge condemning a man to death while at the same time blissfully inhaling a nosegay and talking so happily about the smell
of the roses in the intervals of giving sentence that we are first
amused, then appalled. The utmost tragedy we know; the utmost
comedy we can recognise; when they are combined we are at a
loss. It is not the world we are accustomed to. We have com-
partments in our minds which register tragedy and comedy
separately; tragi-comedy is a world which has never been
sufficiently explored, perhaps because it is too close to the world
we live in. When the Duke in *Rigoletto* sings his mocking and
triumphant paean of love to his new mistress while an older
mistress with her throat cut is taken past him in a sack, we do not
laugh, nor are we particularly sorry. We recognise the world as
it is. It is the way things happen. The murderer carefully smoothes
down his hair, the boy in the electric chair as carefully settles

I

himself comfortably, the dictator weeps over the death of his dog.
These things appal us because they are a part of our humanity,
and so, though we laughed at *Monsieur Verdoux*, we were
appalled by the bloodstains which were all the more monstrous
because they were invisible. Seeing Monsieur Verdoux we
recalled things like the wisp of human hair on Sikes's club, that
sizzled for a second when he threw it on the fire. For here at last,
disguised and at the same time stripped of disguise, we saw
murder as it is.

Chaplin was not the first to find laughter in murder, but he
was the first to let the laughter flow out of the screen and mock
the audience. The audience, shocked by the sound of that
laughter, was not pleased. What was astonishing was the fury
of denunciation which followed the first showing of the film,
the sense of imagined outrage (as though he had not been
deliberately outrageous), the belief that Chaplin was at last
revealing his true face, and it was the face of a murderer. A
leading Soviet producer denounced him as 'a traitor to the
working class'. The Catholic war veterans and the American
Legion denounced him as a traitor to America and to art.
Westbrook Pegler denounced him in a whole series of scurrilous
attacks, and suggested among other things that *Monsieur
Verdoux* was the product of a diseased imagination. He received
large quantities of anonymous abuse, mostly condemning him as
a 'damned Communist Jew'. On the occasions when he troubled
to reply, he denied heatedly that he was either a Communist or
a Jew, but he regarded our whole murderous age as damned and
therefore there was little point in insisting on damnation.
Ruefully, he realised that Chaplin had become what Charlie had
always been – a scapegoat. He had no desire to be a scapegoat.
He fought against the public sacrifice until in the end he lost
interest in the fight, and this only exasperated his accusers still
more. What happens when the sacrificial goat refuses to lay its
head on the altar and wait for the knife, but instead gallops out
of sight? With the same levity, with the same sense of impend-
ing doom, Voltaire had described a holocaust of murders in
Candide, and the same wild uproar of denunciation arose when it
was first published.

Since it is undeniable that we live in an age of mass-murder, and we are capable of allowing mass-murders to happen without protest, the accusation which lies at the heart of *Monsieur Verdoux* could hardly be treated with indifference; it could be accepted stoically, or it could be denounced. The accusation was not the hoary platitude: 'War is a business, and you are all contributing to it.' It said: 'Murder is a fine art, and you are all busily practising it. How outrageously clever you are!' The accusation in these terms was an affront to the intelligence, which preferred not to believe in its own cleverness and sought refuge in its own innocence, that protective innocence with which we all clothe ourselves as we wander among the screaming headlines of our time.

But if the film was prodigiously successful in revealing the sensitive places where we have all been wounded, it revealed, too, that Chaplin was a master at tightrope walking. Nothing is so difficult as to describe a tragic comedy, though the lives of all of us are tragic and comic at the same time. André Malraux, as previously said, tells the story of a small Chinese woman who slaps the face of her dead husband in bed, hoping to wake him, and while the old man's face wobbles from side to side, the children are overcome with ringing laughter. Why? What has happened? What is there about the dead which sometimes makes us laugh? When Raskolnikov in *Crime and Punishment* has a ghastly nightmare in which he sees his victim, after each stroke of the axe turning round and laughing in his face, we know that the nightmare is real and the laughter can be heard even by the reader living at a remote distance from Dostoyevsky's Petersburg. There is nothing comic or happy in this laughter. Our gentlest laughter and the raving laughter of the hysteric are very close to one another; and this untravelled world of laughter, which few have successfully penetrated and where we dimly suspect the existence of landscapes still unrevealed, is precisely the territory which Monsieur Verdoux has taken for his own. With what glee he advances on his victims! With what effrontery he destroys the evidence of his guilt! With what disgraceful contentment he regards his chosen trade! Behind him, reaching to infinity, are the shadows of the other murderers, whose glee was as great as his and whose contentment is expressed by the medals on their breasts and the banknotes in the pockets of executioners.

'The murderer hates himself,' wrote Otto Weiniger in one of his extraordinary essays in human psychology, 'and it is because he hates himself that he desires to kill. He desires his own nothingness to include others.' It may be true, but it is possible that there are other reasons. I suspect that the murderer desires to abase his victim, to abuse him, to make him feel an endless hurt, an endless punishment, and in so doing he generally fails to accomplish his purpose, for the victim once murdered is unconscious of punishment and the murderer is eternally pursued by the knowledge of his own guilt. There are murders of passion which resemble suicide, for inexorably the murderer is hounded by his victim, and for every inch that the knife goes into the victim's flesh, an invisible knife penetrates two inches into the flesh of the murderer. But what if the murderer murders simply for gain, casually, with the weary simplicity of a man looking up from the morning headlines and saying: 'Great Britain has behaved abominably. I think it is time those islands were sunk below the level of the sea.' Such casual hints of murder, without passion, belong to our time. 'The whole world can disappear,' says a character in Dostoyevsky's *Notes from Underground*, 'as long as I have my cup of tea.'

It is in this world that Monsieur Verdoux finds himself delightfully at home. He, too, will have his cup of tea. Indeed, he enjoys his tea even when Madame Grosnay, having encouraged his advances and asked him whether his intentions are honourable, allows him to pursue her with the cup of tea in his hand, which he balances carefully even when he falls off the sofa in his ardour. He is the most decorous and most modest of lovers, who hides the tailor's shapely dummies because they are an offence to the eyes. He chooses his victims for their vulgarity, just as Hitler, with all the beauty of adoring German womanhood to choose from, chose an Eva Braun. He never excuses himself. When he tries to put a rope with a huge stone at the end of it around Annabella Bonheur's neck, and assumes a pleased, innocent smile when she suddenly turns round, the smile puts her off the scent, but it is also a tribute to his own cleverness, his dexterous delight in himself. He observes the absurd and laughable shapes into which these hints of murder disguise themselves, but he is himself completely without dis-

guise, whether he goes by the name of Monsieur Verdoux, or
Floray, or Captain Bonheur, or Varnay, or Charlie, or Count
de Ha-Ha, or a nameless pawnbroker's drudge, or the great god
Pan leaping out of the shrubbery to mock the lovers in the
meadows.

What is monstrous in his cold bloodedness and laughing
gaiety, the tightrope walking on the edge of tenderness and
hysteria, the sudden realisation that Monsieur Verdoux is at
once judge, victim and executioner, and that we know him only
too well, though we have never set eyes on him before. We know
that when he comes to the platform and the rope coils round his
neck, he will carefully feel the weight of the platform and he will
adjust the rope as though he were adjusting a tie, smiling to
himself, even singing some desolate little tune; and when the
trapdoor opens he will fall gracefully, waving sweetly to the
onlookers, and perhaps on the way down making a little dive for
the hangman's feet, as in *The Kid* he dived after the feet of a
pretty girl. We know, too, that he is indestructible, and having
dropped through the trapdoor, he will leap out again, like any
Mephistopheles leaping up in a blaze of red sulphur from the
pantomime stage.

But all this is only one side of Monsieur Verdoux's many-
facetted existence. His charm, his quick wits, his instinctive
sense of decorum are misleading, perhaps deliberately so.
Though it is inconceivable that he really commits the murders
which are his pleasure and his method of obtaining a goodly
income, there appears at intervals the face of the casual murderer
of our time. More than *The Great Dictator, Monsieur Verdoux*
succeeds in describing the vanity of Hitler, the kind of mind
which Hitler possessed. Chaplin makes him die in 1937 and
gives as the reasons for acquiring money by illegitimate means
his losses during the depression of 1929; but all this is subterfuge, an effort to put us off the scent. It is even doubtful whether
he was ever bankrupt; it is certain that he has no compulsive
need to commit murder. With those quick wits, he could easily
acquire an income as an insurance agent, an army officer, or even
as a film producer. Henri Verdoux, merchant in *objects d'art*,
rings false, and Captain Bonheur has never commanded a ship.
He might be a flower-seller in some reputable neighbourhood,

or a dress designer: there are moments when he hints at these occupations. But his chosen occupation is the most terrible of all: it is to show by mimicry and defiance and by all the arts he can summon to his service the face of the casual murderer who hides in all of us. The moralist's intention is to denounce murder unequivocally and at the same time to coat the pill with comedy.

The difficulties arise when we realise that the murders of our time are themselves essentially comic. 'It was only possible to understand the concentration camps with all their hideous murders and genuinely arbitrary terrors,' wrote David Rousset after three years in a concentration camp, 'when you realised that the Nazis were playing an insane comedy. They were playing the parts of clowns – clowns with knives, and simply because they had the knives in their hands, they acted in the murderous way we all know. But what if they had been given coloured balls?' The answer, of course, is that we simply do not know, but we can assume that they would have been very nearly as murderous with their coloured balls as they were with their knives. What is important is Rousset's suggestion that the concentration camps formed a meaningless impromptu comedy, where the punishments were curiously unreal and passionless, and if they had any purpose it was to amuse the Storm Troopers, to keep them awake and prevent them from dying from boredom, so that, when a man was hanged, broomsticks would be inserted in his sleeves and trouser-legs in such a way that even when he was hanging he appeared to be dancing, for his legs and arms were made to fly in all directions. It is the kind of comedy which Grimaldi played when he put a cop through the mangle and was delighted when the cop came out completely flat and five times larger than life, an effect arrived at without great difficulty, because the cop who came out of the mangle was made of cardboard. What is comic derives from the sudden shock of delight when we see the policeman transformed into cardboard, and we know that when the mangle is turned in the opposite direction the cardboard will become a policeman. Grimaldi had not debased the policeman. We see him in a ridiculous posture, and we identify the cardboard with the cop by a leap of the imagination. If we had seen him really put through the mangle,

we would have screamed with horror. In comedy it is essential
that the dead be brought back to life. In the concentration camps
there was a travesty of comedy, for the living were brought back
to death, the world of death already inhabited by the guards in
the concentration camp.

What Grimaldi was doing in his gently murderous way is
exactly what Chaplin has been doing in his films. He cannot
murder. He cannot even hurt anyone. He can clamp a bully's
head in a lamp post, as he does in *Easy Street*, but the bully will
never show the mark of the agony he has gone through. He will
kick people to his heart's content, but those immense and savage
kicks have no effect except to send his enemies into graceful
flight. He has Deburau's privilege: he alone may give the kicks.
As for murder, this is beyond the clown's power; he could not
murder even if he tried. As for being killed, it can happen only
in his dreams. The only time that Charlie is ever shot dead
occurs in the superbly comic scene in *The Kid* when Charlie,
flying through the air amid a snowfall of feathers, makes a
sudden dive at the ankles of a pretty girl, only to be shot by the
policeman for his pains; when he wakes up, he is sitting slumped
over a doorstep, and the policeman is shaking him. In comedy
death can only take place off stage, for it is the purpose of
comedy to announce in the loudest tones that death is at all
times highly improbable.

Grimaldi's play with the policeman was repeated a century
later by Jean Cocteau and the composer Darius Milhaud in
Le Boeuf sur le Toit. Milhaud had composed some music based
on Brazilian folk themes, intending the music to accompany any
short Chaplin film. Cocteau, who heard the music, was entranced
with the possibilities of adapting the folk music to a ballet based
on Chaplin's films. Unable to acquire the services of Chaplin in
the principal rôle, the bartender, he did the next best thing: he
acquired the services of the great Fratellini. The setting, designed
by Raoul Dufy, was a speakeasy. The time was the early spring
of 1920. The characters wore masks three times larger than life,
so giving them something of the air of characters seen on a
screen. There is a long, involved introduction. We see the bartender drying glasses, and the music repeats the whistling sound
as each glass is cleaned with a twist of a rag. A Negro boxer

.

enters, flexes his muscles, dances as boxers dance in the ring, and suddenly wearying of all this nonsense he collapses in an easy chair and picks up an enormous cigar. The cigar is not clipped. He asks the bartender to clip it for him. The bartender whips out a revolver and shoots off the cigar-end. Shortly afterwards a whole crowd of patrons enter the speakeasy: a Negro dwarf with a billiard cue, a woman in a red dress, another with paper hair, a bustling bookie who knocks out the huge Negro in a quarrel over one of the women, and finally, inevitably, the policeman enters, his progress announced by a long blast of his whistle. The bartender simply puts up a notice reading: ONLY MILK SERVED HERE. The policeman smells the glasses, sips the 'milk', smells the breath of the patrons, sips the 'milk' again, and to his surprise discovers that he is performing a jig. The bartender has only one desire – to rid himself of the policeman. Logically, there is only one thing he can do. He pulls a lever, and the huge revolving fan descends upon him and cuts off his head. This event astonishes no one. They continue to dance and make love and sing sentimental songs to one another. The Negro dwarf throws the head on a silver platter and dances with it up to the lady in the red dress, who gazes at it with the air of someone completely bored by so inevitable a thing as a policeman's head on a silver platter. Then she decides to dance round the head on her hands, but she loses her direction and dances off the stage altogether, followed by all the other patrons except the bartender, who carefully picks up the head, puts it back on the policeman's shoulders, comforts him, pats him on the back, and then presents him with a check three or four yards long. In *Le Boeuf sur le Toit* Cocteau and Milhaud have produced the only imitation of Chaplin which bears a close imaginative resemblance to the original; and here, too, as one might have suspected, the death of the policeman is only an excuse for bringing him to life.

Monsieur Verdoux is concerned with death in exactly the same way that Grimaldi and Cocteau were concerned with death, but the mangle and the electric fan are absent. As we watch the film we never believe that Charlie is killing people, nor are we asked to believe it. There is no *danse macabre*, no savagery, no violence. We are invited to live on the borderland where murder is only hinted at, never openly committed. It is murder without terror, and therefore the most terrible of all, for that haunting murderer with his charm, his quick mannerisms, his air of indefatigable gentleness and suavity comes very close to us. We have seen his face before. We know those precocious mannerisms. Partly they belong to Charlie, but they also belong to Hynkel. He is Hynkel when, by some mysterious dispensation of fate, the power to command others is taken from him, and he can command only himself, and he is not unlike the suave Hitler who appeared in the princely drawing-rooms of Munich and Berlin in the days before he had created a ferocious party. So Monsieur Verdoux, without committing any murders that we can believe in, playing with murder as he plays with banknotes, concerned with the comedy of murder to the exclusion of the comedy of life, provides a sense of overwhelming menace. He hints. The hint is enough. We shiver because we know that in our own time murder is practised in the real world with the same suavity, the same gentleness and the most exquisite good manners, not by bank clerks but by diplomats. It is in this sense that the play was conceived as a tract for the times.

What is surprising is how successfully Chaplin jumped the hurdles, succeeded in performing miracles of improvisation on a stage and in a setting dangerously close to the edge of probability. We live in an improbable world, but this did not make his task any easier. Deliberately coating the pill with the vast resources of his wit, he saw to it that the coldness of the murderer came through, and some of that deliberate momentary coldness invaded the whole pattern of the film, with the result that there were some who claimed that it was cold beyond reason, and Monsieur Verdoux, however credible and however dexterous, was more ghoulish than Bela Lugosi had ever been. When Chaplin replied that this was exactly what he had intended, and that he regarded *Dracula* as a feeble discussion on horror, it was assumed that he was being clever or churlish. Instead, he was being desperately serious. 'To create pity, I have had to create terror,' he said. 'Here you see the most terrible image that has ever crossed the screen, and one of the most human.' Asked whether Monsieur Verdoux was the tramp in disguise, he answered: 'Of course they are the same. Isn't he delightful?'

In the same way, and with something of the same nonchalance, Goethe gave his best lines to Mephistopheles, and found him loathsome and delightful at the same time.

When *Monsieur Verdoux* first appeared, it was said against Chaplin that he had abandoned 'the lovable little man in the baggy pants'. He had, of course, done nothing of the sort. There was no change – only a reversal of phase. Charlie had never been a sentimental figure. He was the murderer, the pimp, the panderer, the seducer, the criminal, the artist and *l'homme moyen sensuel* from the beginning, just as we have been all these things ourselves. In *The Vagabond* and perhaps twenty other films he had clubbed his enemies and left them on the ground. We knew long ago that when he was aroused his fierce disdain for the proprieties would lead him to some inexcusable crime. The pinch-bottle coat, the underfed caterpillar of a moustache, the menacing predatory gleam, the mingled fear and contempt of the law, all these had been there; he had insisted on them; there was never a time when he excused himself for his failings; and it was our fault if we saw him a sentimental figure. 'Ah, if only he would make a film like *The Kid* again,' they complained. 'There was such a warm glow in him then.' Chaplin could reply that in that detestable film Charlie throttled a policeman and made a living by practising the trade of a glass-mender, a trade which was tolerable only because he arranged that Jackie Coogan should go round the streets of London hurling stones at window-panes. He had never earned an honest penny. He had lived under a number of bogus names. He had been to prison more times than he could remember. In *His Prehistoric Past* he had wielded a club, trampled upon a carpet of female adorers and knocked down a tribal chieftain. In *City Lights* he kicked a beggar, and in *The Pilgrim* he kicked a child. Why should he be expected to reform? Inevitably, since all the evidence led only to this end, he would become a murderer. If he lived long enough he might even become a clown. It would be a fitting end to a man who had been a shanghaied seaman, a petty thief, a burglar, a child-stealer, an escaped prisoner, a scene-shifter, a tout, a boxer, a musical barber and a great dictator. The odd, the engrossing thing is that Monsieur Verdoux did not even trouble to conceal the fact that he was Charlie in disguise, in the thinnest disguise, a disguise which could be stripped off him with the greatest of ease.

The old tricks were there – why were they not recognised? That smiling air of innocence when he committed a crime – we had seen it before in more than fifty films. The Monsieur Verdoux who thumbs the banknotes with appalling speed, is he not the same as the nondescript barber in *The Great Dictator* who shaves his customer to the music of a Hungarian Rhapsody? The Monsieur Verdoux who tenderly removes a caterpillar from his path is the same Charlie who shared his last sausage with a dog in *The Champion*. The Monsieur Verdoux who lives among the monstrous mediæval *bric-à-brac* in his shop is the same as the anonymous hero of *One A.M.* whose house is decorated with a stuffed emu and far too many cloisonné vases. In *Monsieur Verdoux* he enters the same prison which he entered once before in *City Lights*, and there is the same effortless shrug of the shoulders as the gates open. The harpies he murders, Lydia Floray and Thelma, whose smoke rose in goblets from the incinerator, have haunted his films time without number, and it is only reasonable that these women should be thrust once and for all from the screen. Monsieur Varney delicately cuts roses and offers them with an entranced smile to his victim; such offerings were almost Charlie's trademark. And when he was being thrown out of the factory in *Pay Day*, he offered a lily to the foreman. The exchange of flowers was a theme of the highest consequence in *City Lights*. It was said of Monsieur Verdoux that he was genteel, but Charlie was always genteel: witness his delighted disgust when Jackie Coogan wet the diapers. It is true that in *The Kid* he combined gentility with a suitable contempt for gentility, but if it is the mark of Pan that he should play music sweetly for the nymphs, it was also the mark of Pan that he would suddenly interrupt the music with a scream and send the nymphs packing. Terror and contempt, these too were present from the beginning. 'But he was really frightening in *Monsieur Verdoux*,' they exclaimed. 'If I see a comic movie, I want to see a comic movie – I don't want shivers going up my spine.' Which was strange, for the shivers went up our spines when he scribbled his terrible game of noughts and crosses in *The Face on the Bar-Room Floor*, and all the fire-bells went ringing in the last remoseless scene where he stared in a maze of grief out of the last twenty feet of *City Lights.* 'Yes, but *City Lights* was terribly amusing.' Was it? There never was a film more intimately concerned with death by drowning, shooting and hanging. Murderers hide behind curtains, the Thames opens its arms for the suicide, the very rope which is pulled to ring the bell in the boxing scenes must twist round Charlie's throat, and surely the drunken millionaire with the nickel-plated gun in his hand is a menace to be feared, so that we sit on the edge of the seats in a fearful anxiety and torture, waiting for the moment when the gun will pass into Charlie's harmless hands. But in *Monsieur Verdoux* Charlie takes the place of the drunken millionaire, and his hands are no longer harmless, and the gun is pointed at our own heads. 'I intended to create a pity for all humanity under certain drastic conditions.'

But in one sense of course the film was a complete failure. In the past he had been able to create pity for all humanity because he spoke no recognisable tongue. Now for the first time he spoke in cultivated English, with a faintly Bostonian accent mingled with the warmer accents of the South. It was such a voice as a Harvard graduate might use from his office in New Orleans. Though the name was French,[1] and so were the names of his victims, this was a subterfuge as outrageous as his impersonation of a honey-tongued bank clerk. He was pure American, and as though to put the seal on his Americanism he lifted one of his best lines from Calvin Coolidge's farewell message to the nation as he left the White House for the last time. Coolidge was asked to give that blessing which is demanded of Presidents when they have acquitted themselves of their onerous duties and retire from the scene. The newsreel cameramen and the reporters waited for the moment of benediction. Coolidge paused, raised his eyebrows and remarked casually: 'Well, goodbye.' As Monsieur Verdoux sits in his small cell,

[1] According to Chaplin the name Verdoux arose quite early in the preliminary discussions on the film. He was unaware that it could be translated as 'the sweet worm'. Adolphe Menjou played the part of Pierre Revel in Chaplin's production of *A Woman of Paris*, and it is possible that the name Verdoux comes from an unconscious mingling of the names Menjou and Revel.

a reporter comes to ask him for a final message, a final explanation. In his most ingratiating manner Monsieur Verdoux says: 'Goodbye, now.'

There are other borrowings from further afield. Somewhere behind Monsieur Verdoux there is the spectacle of Sweeney Todd, the demon barber of Fleet Street, and a little to one side of him stands the English murderer Joseph Smith who played *Nearer, my God, to thee,* on the harmonium while one of his wives was drowning in the next room. The sanctimony of Monsieur Verdoux is examined from all angles. 'Don't pull the cat's tail,' he says to his little son. 'You have such a cruel streak in you. I don't know where you got it from. Remember, violence breeds violence.' In conversation with a druggist he discovers a poison which leaves no trace. 'Think what an arch-criminal would do with it,' he comments gratuitously. At another time, reflecting gently on the permanence of wars, he says ruefully: 'Munitions? That's what I should have gone into.' On the eve of his most gruesome murder he leans from the balcony and gazes at the moon. 'This pale Endymion hour,' he murmurs. 'Our feet were soft in flowers.' Lydia Floray snarls: 'Get to bed'; but the beauty of the night still haunts him as he arranges the plates for breakfast, as he dances round the table, placing two sets of plates, until the absurdity of it occurs to him and he removes one set, for after all it will only remind him of the dear departed. He is appallingly vulgar as he hovers in those places which were once called 'the antichambers of death', but how rich is his vulgarity.

In the end he meets his match. One rainy night he finds Marilyn Nash huddled in a doorway, with a stray kitten huddled under her mackintosh. She is Monsieur Verdoux's *alter ego.* He, too, had once carried a dog in his capacious trousers or buttoned up in his cutaway. When he takes her to the dubious shelter of his apartment, she tells him she is Belgian, and has just come out of jail. Her Belgianness is as transparently false as his Frenchness; she is pure Cockney. He decides to murder her because murder has become a habit, but when she tells him that her husband died while she was in jail, he gives her money and weeps for her misery, and as she goes down the street his eyes follow her with a hangdog expression of grief – perhaps, he tells

himself, he should have murdered her to make her happy.
After all, the poison would leave no trace. Months later he
meets her riding in a Rolls Royce. She is now the wife of a
munitions manufacturer, the inevitable messenger of his own
death. He delays with her when the police are on his scent. She
asks him where he is going. 'I go to meet my destiny,' he says.
Yet he has already met his destiny. She is standing there in
front of him – she is his destiny, and at the same time she is
himself. The game of mirrors is played to the very end.

At this point the film might very reasonably have terminated.
The wheel has come full circle. Marilyn Nash, the gay and
impudent tramp, is only Charlie in disguise. Verdoux must
destroy Verdoux, since otherwise he is indestructible. The
imprisonment, the trial, the gates opening upon the courtyard of
the guillotine – but they are surprisingly similar to the gates
which opened on Charlie when he went to prison in *City Lights,*
and it is hardly possible to imagine that he will suffer grievously
– all this is in a sense an anticlimax. 'I go to meet my destiny,'
says the clown, but what other destiny has he but to clown
for ever? Put him under the guillotine, and his head will bounce
up, leap over the whole infernal machine and join the body
lying beside the basket. Grimaldi had cut his own head off and
laughed to see it grow again, and Charlie could do the same
without the slightest feeling that he was disturbing the order of
nature. We cannot believe in his murders; we cannot believe in
his own death; nor are we asked to.

The enemies of Chaplin have taken the film at once too
seriously and too frivolously. Years before he had said in an
interview with Alistair Cooke that there was 'a genuine danger
that the little man would become too fragrant, too much like
Everybody's Little Ray of Sunshine'. The danger had ceased
after *The Gold Rush,* but it haunted Chaplin, who was determined
that Charlie should grow with the times. Charlie had always
been the adventurer, stepping out alone into places where people
feared to tread. *Monsieur Verdoux* was many things, but it contained within it an implicit condemnation of a society which
condoned murder and made no serious effort to put an end to
cruelty. The Russians condemned it because they saw that it
assailed their authoritarian rule; the Americans condemned it

because their temper was vindictive. Both saw themselves parodied in the figure of Monsieur Verdoux, and neither recognised that in the film the forces of good were made to triumph. 'The man is devilish,' they said. 'He burns a woman in an incinerator, and then takes care not to trample on a caterpillar. What kind of devil is that?' It is a strange question, for most of us know that devil only too well, and from time to time we have observed him peering from the human heart.

When Chaplin was preparing *Modern Times*, he observed that there would be a few changes in Charlie. 'In the new film,' he said, 'he will not be quite so nice. I'm sharpening the edge of his character so that people who've liked him vaguely will have to make up their minds.' The sharpening was a slow process. It began with *The Circus*, many years before *Modern Times*, but in a sense it was not a sharpening so much as a further exploration and an attempt to bring Charlie into sharper focus. The old tricks remained, and so did the old ambiguities, the determination to have a foot on each side of the frontier. We laughed because we knew these tricks only too well – we have employed them ourselves since the beginning of our stay on earth.

Why, then, did the audiences for which he had created his comedies turn so bitterly against him? Perhaps, after all, the answer is a very simple one. The world of the clown is the world of extreme danger, a world where no one may relax and nothing happens according to the law, a no-man's-land where only the bravest may wander, determined against all the odds to preserve their freedom. Today, the clown's world has caught up with us. We live in that no-man's-land. Like the teetering hut on the edge of the abyss in *The Gold Rush* which would fall if a single ounce of snow were added to its weight, we know that the smallest things may destroy us. We hear the roar of the avalanche in our ears, and we do little enough to save ourselves. The one thing that might save us is the sense of human dignity, and this Charlie in all his disguises has possessed in abundance.

CHAPTER XX

PORTRAIT OF THE MORALIST

WE LIVE in ridiculous and desperate times; we are catching up with the Keystone comedies. We know that world only too well. The incompetent flat-footed cops, the mad bank presidents, the thugs in the alleyway, the pie-crusts which are disguised sticks of dynamite, the perpetual vision of peace in a world where every stone marks a hidden detonator and every road leads nowhere, all these we know because they are part of the world we now travel in. We travel blind, sustained by the hope that the blindness may miraculously fall from our eyes, and we do our best to remain deadpan in spite of the possibility that our cities and all the people in them and all the works of art may be instantaneously transformed in a rainbow-coloured cloud. There was something prophetic in Mack Sennett's world, that world which Charlie explored with the utmost abandon. There was a time not long ago when we laughed at the television face in the factory, of the mechanical feeders and the cog-wheels which forgot which way they were going. We do not laugh so much now. Today the thugs are waiting down the alleyway, and the cops overwhelm us always, and sooner than we think we may be living in flophouses or wandering down uninviting empty roads. The world is bleak and cold, with the wind coming through the worn rafters. In this dilemma, where do we stand?

We may, of course, take our consolations where we can. We pay our income-tax regularly and read the books on child psychology; it is up to God and society to protect us. It is pleasant to repose in the justice of our cause, but it is no longer sufficient. We live in desperate times. We have no real assurance of victory. We blunder, and do not know where we are going. The roads ahead are blacker than they have ever been. In this extremity the only certain weapon is defiance, the purely human and instinctive courage to go on, whatever the cost, however many bodies we stumble on. Like the hanged highwayman who kicks off his shoes in a final gesture of invincibility, we may find that the only final consolation lies in our determination to go on dancing to the end.

Charlie, who represents to such an extraordinary degree the whole human race caught in its habitual rat-trap, does kick off his shoes, and we are abundantly convinced of the validity of his gesture of invincibility. But the matter is not so simple. The joyful contempt he flings at the face of his enemies has many origins. It is partly pure *braggadocio*. There is warmth in it, and extreme cold. There is a sense of human dignity and a splendid nonchalance. He will whistle to himself, and take pleasure in the sudden panic-stricken look on the face of his conquerors when they see he is unconquerable. All his life Charlie has lived on the edge of things, as today we live on the edge of things, but he has behaved with decorum – the decorum is only too plainly under-scored – and when the last moment arrives he has no regrets, because he has a clear conscience. (He has stolen occasionally, but to steal food when one is hungry is, as St Ambrose observed long ago, one of those sins which are immediately pardoned in heaven.) Indeed, far more than Sir Galahad, he represents the heroic figure of the man who remains pure and undefiled, and he is all the more credible because he is reduced to a human scale. And since human heroism consists in the refusal, even the absolute rejection, of all those things which tend to degrade the human splendour, Charlie emerges as the knight-errant of the back streets, the knight of faith, the devout tightrope walker who, simply by maintaining his balance on the tightrope, holds the circus tent and everyone in it from falling into a bottomless abyss; and he can only do this out of his sense of impudent defiance – that complex defiance which, as we have seen, derives from so many different sources. He is a master of defiance, but sometimes when the highwayman kicks off his shoes he will imitate defiance by accident – there must be many times when what seemed to be defiance was no more than the nervous spasms of the trembling bones.

Kierkegaard has spoken at great length of the knight of the faith, the simple person who arrived at faith without difficulty, without ever having to cross the abysses, the man with no chink in his armour, the most enviable of the saints. It occurred to Kierkegaard that the knights of faith were subtly disguised. The great prelates who attained to holiness by the use of hairshirts and midnight flagellations, the philosophers who pushed thought to the very end of thought, the nuns who sacrificed themselves – yes, they possessed an admirable holiness, and it would be folly to dispute their love of God. But did God love them? It seemed to Kierkegaard that God loved most of all the tobacconist at the corner, the man who puffed at his pipe and had a little joke for his customers and took his family along the shore every Sunday afternoon. In such a man it might be possible to find a faith so final that it put the faith of the nuns and the theologians to shame. Something of the same thought must have passed through the mind of Flaubert when, seeing some peasants in the evening gathered at table, he said: '*Ils sont dans le vrai.*' The man who had spent his life in a titanic struggle with art, producing it little by little, chipping it from his breast-bone, came to see at the end of his days that art flowered naturally round the peasants'. table, so naturally that they were hardly aware of its presence and took its existence for granted.

In all this Charlie has his place, and there is nothing at all fanciful in seeing him as one of those rare archetypal figures like Don Juan, Pierrot and Faust, who arise unexpectedly and flower and take on the colours of their time, and inevitably there will be more Charlies later. Faust, passing through the hands of Marlowe, Goethe and a hundred others, demonstrated the human spirit's hunger for experience and power at periods when that hunger was keenest. Don Juan emerged from the hands of Father Gabriel Tellez, the dramatist Tirso de Molina, already a rounded figure, though he was to acquire a forest of cock's feathers in the year to come, and he was born anew, with a fierce aplomb and a studied indifference to harm, in the hands of the obscure Da Ponte. As for Pierrot, he had lived through a hundred lives before he was blessed with maturity from the hands of Deburau; and like Don Juan, who descended from the figure of Larva in the Jesuit tragedies and even beyond, he had a respectable ancestry. Don Juan demonstrated the human spirit's appetite for the conquest of women, but of Pierrot a more subtle claim must be made: he represented an awareness of pity, the knowledge that failure is important and often desired, and that out of failure arise the most triumphant conquests. Pierrot partakes of the glory of Don Juan, for all men in a sense fail to accomplish the one thing they most desire, which is to possess a woman, and Don Juan fails more tragically than most.

The dancing figure of Charlie represents a human and more practical quest. He has no desire for conquests. His desire is for freedom in a trammelled world. He is the virgin spirit of liberty who refuses to be oppressed, refuses to talk in mock profundities, refuses to concern himself with the origin of the universe or with anything except the practical things of the moment, *l'homme moyen sensuel* raised to the pitch of perfection, desiring above all that the world should provide him with sleep, rest, food and amusement, bewildered by machines, and still more bewildered by himself, by the fact that a man is a man. He is the least dangerous of the great archetypes, the most human, the most incorrigibly concerned with things as they are. His characteristics are a terrible enthusiasm and an odd mania for laughing at the world's incongruities, and in his own capricious way he is determined, like Cinderella, that the last should be first, but he goes further, for with the crook of his bamboo cane or a jab in the eye he ensures that the guilty are condemned. And since, as we have shown, he is nothing more than the great god Pan reduced to human size and wearing a human dress, there is no reason why we should be surprised to find him among the archetypes, and of all the archetypes he is the one whose emergence is fraught with most consequence, for he is the only one who is not evil.

Faust's sin, like the sin of Don Juan, was one of blazing spiritual pride. They knew no limits to their power. They were determined upon rebellion and presumption, on the breaching of divine law; and in the popular imagination they were always conceived in the glare of infernal fires. They were dark spirits, with the look of demonic majesty on their faces, cruel, merciless and terribly real, so that people recognised themselves in the flame-lit characters. They were cruel not in order to be kind or because they saw virtue in cruelty for cruelty's sake, but because they regarded other people as in their way; they must destroy others to achieve their victory, and every virgin and every honourable man was their legitimate prey. But Charlie is no hunter, desires no prey, is in quest of no El Dorados, and he remains a great personage because he transcends life and the limitations of ordinary life by his infinite resource in dealing with life as it is lived. In this sense he is a far more heroic figure than Faust who merely transacts a legal document with Mephistopheles or Don Juan who goes out of his way to erect barriers between himself and the women he inconveniently desires, for he lives in the real world, his enemies real enemies, his blunders real blunders from which he can only extricate himself by real and human acts. He is no Don Quixote wandering in a land of dreams. He desires the princess, and he knows that she is already married to her prince, and therefore he must go on his way. No windmills fall before him. He has a gypsy's love for simple things, the open road, flowers, the flesh of women, a good meal, and all the excitements of incongruity and irony. It is odd that it has been rarely recorded of him that he is essentially a moral figure, and that he came to birth in an age when morality was in decline and he could only have come to birth in such an age. What is even more astonishing is that the author of this prodigious archetype has been so bitterly attacked.

The failure of the public to recognise the validity and delicacy of *Monsieur Verdoux* springs from many causes: not the least of them was the blunting of our sensibilities by the war. Charlie was playing dangerously in the shadow of total annihilation, that shadow which we fear above all things; even in that shadow he dared to laugh, and not only because he was himself wearing the faintly sinister disguise of someone who pretends to be the agent of annihilation. Refusing to face such a shadow, we become a little like the resourceful Countess Aurélie who, living in her underground cellar, habitually read *Le Gaulois* of 22 March 1903, because this was the best issue the editors ever published, though she added that it was always a shock to see in the columns reserved for the lists of the dead the name of a close acquaintance who seemed to die every morning. When *Monsieur Verdoux* appeared we were still living in the past. 'Who wants to have imaginary people staring at us, especially strangers?' says one of the other characters in Giraudoux's wonderful play, and some-

thing very similar must have been said by the people who saw
Monsieur Verdoux and went away disgusted. If they had looked
a little closer they would have noticed that the imaginary
person was no stranger, but someone who lived far too close to
their hearts for comfort.

It had been like that from the very beginning: Charlie had
leaped out of space to find his home in the human heart. The
man who acted the part, and who was terror-stricken by the
creation of his imagination, was a prodigious actor who acted
with his whole body, limbs and torso, but it was Charlie rather
than Chaplin who gave back to the soul its earthly covering of
body. In time Chaplin will be forgotten, but Charlie will remain.
He will have a place in the cosmography of the imagination
which every generation maps afresh, but in every thousand
years only a few new legends are permitted to enter. He will live
in the world inhabited by Alexander the Great, Napoleon, and
the Borgias, with Robin Hood, King Arthur and the Wandering
Jew as his companions; Punch, Pierrot and Harlequin will be his
accomplices in mischief, and somewhere to the north of his
favour there will be Faustus and Don Juan, wearing their
legendary masks, striking their legendary attitudes, and like
them he will disappear out of history into masquerade. Don
Quixote lives there, and so does Ulysses. In this world, where
Nausicaa is for ever playing ball by the seashore and Falstaff is
for ever quaffing his flagons of rude ale, Charlie's place is
assured. It is even possible that his place is at the very centre of
the fabulous island, since of all the heroes he is most like ourselves once we have removed our false beards, ear-trumpets and
magnifying spectacles and show ourselves more naked than
we care to be. The formula for Charlie was potent. The elements
have been so mixed in him that the recreative activities of latter-
day actors will hardly be able to change him. For all the foreseeable
future he will walk down the brightly lit roads of the mind,
swinging his cane and dexterously picking up cigarette butts,
flaunting his absurdly human dignity in the face of the world's
importunity, a pirate nailing his flag to the mast, but instead of
crossed bones and a skull the flag shows a pair of battered boots
and a polished derby, those signs of our human dignity and
waywardness.

Charlie was not, of course, the only clown to show an appreciation of human dignity, and thereby launch himself into eternity. In our own age at least one other has appeared. Raimu, with his equatorial waistline, his buttony moustache and foolscap of knitted wool, had some of Falstaff's fervour and Falstaff's inability to recognise the harshness of the world, even though he complained about it. He takes his pleasure where he can. He, too, covers the soul with flesh, and he knows Charlie's trick of claiming a place in both worlds, the world of *bouillabaisse* and *provençal* women and the timeless world of contemplation. In *La Femme de Boulanger* Raimu is the proud possessor of a young and pneumatic wife. He is the friend of everyone in the village, and he even has a good word to say for an exasperating and long-necked priest, who is a model of the young curé who is determined to change the ways of the village. He is a baker, and therefore possesses a sacramental function in the village, but the baker's wife is a jade who runs away with a handsome farm-hand. The villagers attempt to comfort Raimu, and while comforting him they get drunk, and when in their drunkenness they bring him a pair of antlers, he refuses to accept their mockery. He refuses indeed to understand them. Why have they come? What are these antlers in comparison with what he has lost; and so he falls to bed, dreaming of his wife, patting and smoothing down the bedclothes where he expected her to be, and then jumping up in the middle of the night to hurl imprecations on a world so unjust that it removes from him his chief source of felicity. Even when he attempts to commit suicide, he is responsible only to himself, for no one else must suffer. The antlers, the drunken friends have nothing to do with his death. The act of suicide is no more than a bewildered recognition of the tumult in his own soul, a gesture of despair wrung from his heart rather than from their deeds. But in the middle of this nightmare he remembers the bread, and with a steadfast air of dignity he wanders from the bedroom to the bakery. There, at a slower pace and without the staccato rhythm which Charlie has made peculiarly his own, we are aware that we are in the presence of the same theme which runs providentially through *The Bank*, *The Kid*, *City Lights*, and half the intervening films. It is odd that in none of Chaplin's films except *A Woman of Paris* is there an unfaithful wife, for in the history of Charlie infidelity clearly has a place. An unfaithful wife is promised in *Limelight*, and this is perhaps as it should be, for only at the very end can Charlie be expected to reveal all his secrets.

Raimu and Chaplin share the eminence. Fernandel with his charming leer and his horse-face belongs to carnival, a face copied from the painted ten-foot dolls. The Marx Brothers possessed an anarchic fire until the seeds of Brooklyn respectability addled them. W. C. Fields was wholly given over to anarchic fire, but the fire alone is hardly sufficient. Donald Duck, the one great creation of the Disney studios, died of the weariness of repeating a single barking cackle, but he was majestic while he lasted, and in Elysium he follows on Charlie's heels. Close to the eminence are Ben Turpin, Slim Somerville, Harry Langdon and Buster Keaton, and Roscoe Arbuckle is not far behind. The great deadpan faces of the Keystone and Roach comedies were wonderful evocations of American legend, the stone faces springing out of the folklore of the tramps, the bums and the International Workers of the World. They came from the same cradle which produced the man so lean that he cast no shadow; six rattlesnakes struck at him once, and every one missed him. Charlie was not deadpan, though he would sometimes with great effort suggest that he could be. As for Chaplin, who can clown as well as Charlie, he is, as Mack Sennett has said repeatedly, 'simply the greatest actor who has ever lived', but this is probably the least important fact about him.

As he grows older, reflecting on the impermanence of fame and the permanence of legends, Chaplin has not lost his love of clowning. The great clown tends to be lost in the greater Charlie. It is probably a pity. There are times when Chaplin at his eternal game of mimicry could hoot Charlie off the stage; and there is as much magic about the man as in the character he invented. Charlie was an accident – we remember Mack Swain's moustache and Roscoe Arbuckle's trousers. What if they had not been there? There are a hundred comic characters which Chaplin could have played, if he had ever allowed himself to dwell for more than a few moments on the imps which crowd in his brain. I have seen him do things which I thought only Indian fakirs could do. His deep blue smoky eyes can change colour. In a moment his splendidly arched brow can become low and mean. His face and neck can swell out until he resembles to perfection the latest news photograph of Winston Churchill, or he can suck in his cheeks until he resembles some poor devil in a prison camp, and by some unwarranted process of magic he can speak the very words they would utter. He still enters a room so superbly quiet that you hardly notice he is there, and there is nothing about him in the least like Charlie. As in his youth he resembled Keats, so in age he bears (in the rare moments when his face is in repose) an astonishing resemblance to the elder Yeats, with a great mane of white hair, the face bronzed, the lips pursed, the hands at rest; and just as he enters quietly, so he can disappear as quietly – gone like a flash, leaving the air quivering behind him.

I have seen him many times, and it was always the same – the odd quietness, and the curious passion for disappearing, so that he gives at times the appearance of a man who desires to watch, and only to watch. He is not tall, but he gives the impression of tallness. He still talks with the faintest of Cockney accents, but the mellowness of southern American accents – where did he learn them? – is also there, a professor's voice, or a scholar's, the voice of a man who is accustomed to live alone, and is surprised to hear himself speaking. You are not conscious of his clothes; you are conscious only of that head, glowing in the sun, a head which grows stronger and more leonine as the years pass, so that you wonder how it was ever possible that a man who looks like a president of a vast company or a poet should be remembered as the little chalk-white tramp with the long boots and the waving cane, running madly in the face of authority, as a moth runs at a candle flame.

But when the mood takes him another Chaplin appears who is infinitely remote from the presiding genius of United Artists. Chaplin the clown has all of Beckmann's powers. He comes into the room unobserved and unannounced, very casually, with that curious power of self-effacement, and then suddenly, no one knows how it begins, he is the centre of the stage. He begins to gesture. He tells a story. It may be a story about a fishing trip to Santa Barbara or Catalina Island, but the story becomes something else – it becomes pure comedy. With gestures

Chaplin outlines the fish, the line, the ship, the watching seagulls, the way the line is thrown, the way the fish with greedy eyes runs scampering after the bait. You are no longer conscious of the presence of Chaplin, but of the roar of the sea, the desperate struggles of the fish, the creaking of the ship's timbers. The fight goes on. The fish butts the boat, the fisherman falls overboard, and now the fish has become as large as leviathan. The tremendous battle is waged in the room, and you are convulsed and helpless with laughter, and at the moment when you can bear the sight of the comic battle no longer, he introduces another fish which comes to the rescue of the first, and then the ship springs a leak, and then crowds of small fishing-boats come out of nowhere, and somewhere in the sea he is struggling in mortal combat with leviathan, and there is no end to it, for always at the moment when you think the story is coming to its conclusion Chaplin has introduced from nowhere some miraculous element, some new and outrageous adventure which must be followed to its conclusion, but there is no conclusion, and it is only when you are sick with laughing and crying that he will pause long enough to let you breathe again. Give him a lace handkerchief. He will become an old dowager, a senorita, a Russian noblewoman congratulating Chaliapin on his voice, the lace handkerchief becoming a fichu, a mantilla, the little square of silk in which the Russian noblewoman drowns her sobs. In the end, of course, with something of Charlie's nonchalance, he may wipe his nose very brusquely with the handkerchief, and so put an end to the performance, but when he was taking the part of the old dowager, she was there, and like Beckmann she brought with her the air she lived in, the whole furniture of her mind, her hobbling walk, the delicate way in which her fingertips touched the furniture in her room. With relish he will play the part of one of those girls who haunt Japanese bath-houses, or a city stockbroker, or any politician. They are all observed minutely, with love and irony. He could, if he wanted to, mimic the New York telephone book or the Selective Service Act, and at once they would become both ideally true and hilariously funny.

There are blind beggars who wander over North China with bells fixed to their knees and clapboards attached to their legs and a great collection of musical instruments slung over their chests or tied to their ankles; one blind beggar alone tells a story to the sound of a full orchestra. When Chaplin tells a story, you are conscious of the presence of a full orchestra. Somehow, by some miracle, he conveys the story in all its depths. There will be ten or twelve characters in the story. By a gesture, by a tone of voice, by some trick of shading, you come to know each of them as you know your friends. Then, when the story is over, it is quite likely that he will disappear from the room, vanishing as mysteriously as he entered it; it is only long afterwards that you remember he was wearing an outrageous red velvet coat and a pair of grey slacks.

There are mysteries in Chaplin which no one will ever dare to plumb. The perfection of the technique is bewildering; he is over sixty, but the casual sureness of gesture and mime remains, increasing in brilliance with every day that passes; and like the elder Yeats he seems to acquire power with age. There are moments when he wearies of Charlie. He will say, 'I am so sick of him. I'd like to wring his neck. I'll never make another film with him.' The next moment he is drawing out of the air the most impossible situations, the most ridiculous distortions, and through all these mazes he pictures Charlie at his wrecker's game, humbling the proud, falling in love with all the pretty women, almost delighting to be repulsed, at odds with the malevolence and idiocies of the world. Whole volumes concerning the life of Charlie have been left on the cutting-room floor; more volumes have been told by Chaplin with that quietly disingenuous air of someone revealing the sacred mysteries. I asked him once where Charlie was going during the fade-out, when he wanders down an empty lane, shrugging his shoulders and kicking at a stone. He said darkly: 'He is going nowhere. He is only the blind mole digging into his hole.' The blaze of neon lights from a deserted sandwich joint on Wilshire Boulevard fell on his face. For a moment he looked like Mephistopheles.

It was one answer; there were a thousand others. Like Proteus, Chaplin can assume a thousand shapes, hint at a thousand ironies, balance his thousand legs upon a thousand tightropes. Chaplin at his clowning has a wider range than

Charlie, but in some subtle fashion Charlie always included those possibilities which the clown has explored, and we know that when he is amusing himself quietly in some evil-smelling doss-house, where all the misery of the world is accumulating, Charlie will invent for himself those creatures who are continually being invented by Chaplin with prodigious abandon. Chaplin and Charlie have one thing in common: they are concerned with ultimates. The dowager is the ultimate of dowagers. The fish caught off Catalina Island is the ultimate of fishes. The Japanese bath-girl is the ultimate of Japanese bath-girls. And the mole digging into his hole is the ultimate of moles.

Because he deals with ultimates, Chaplin is inevitably the child of paradox. He will say, for example: 'Why shouldn't I mock poverty? The poor deserve to be mocked. What fools they are!' He will say this savagely, the face becoming a mask of horror-stricken accusation. 'Why don't they rebel against poverty? Why do they accept it? It is the ultimate stupidity to accept poverty when there are all the riches of the world – every man should have them.' The next moment, confronted with human misery, knowing that it is there, knowing that there is almost nothing he can do about it, he will say: 'The whole world is full of poor devils caught in the trap. How will they ever get out? I've tried to help them to forget the trap in my films, but the trap is still there.' He once told the Russian producer Eisenstein: 'You remember the scene in *Easy Street* where I scatter food from a box to poor children as if they were chickens? You see, I did this because I despise them. I don't like children.' Those were the words which Eisenstein remembered, and it is likely enough that Chaplin said them, but it would be absurd to accuse Chaplin of a savage intolerance on the basis of a remembered phrase. He has shown too many times a tenderness for children so real, so overwhelming that it is like a wound. It is possible to go insane by loving too much, by being tender too much. The tortured sensitivity of the artist is the price he pays for the abundance of his love, and when he scattered food to the poor children he was remembering, and subtly transforming, the way in which food had been served to him at an orphanage in London.

The presence of a comic genius in our civilisation presents

almost as many problems as the presence of Charlie. What rôle is to be played by the comic genius? The Roman Emperors took care that the great mimes should be close to the throne. Every manner of honour was showered upon them. They were known to be dangerous. They were like walking explosives. They had the power to turn the people against the Emperor, and they were known to be afraid of nothing. Two clowns were executed by the Emperor Tiberius for mimicking him, and so bringing his rule into jeopardy. The court jesters of the middle ages were sometimes roped to the throne by little golden chains, perhaps for fear they might escape and jest before the people. Dimly, it was recognised that they possessed powers denied to the Emperor. They were closer to the sources of life. They spoke when they spoke at all – for mostly they claimed a prodigious indifference, and were silent for long periods – only at moments of illumination, and so they were cousins to the sybils, who lived mysteriously in caves and uttered prophecies over braziers. The Emperor was thought to have absolute power over the empire, but he knew with one word, with one laugh pitched to the exact pitch, the clown could destroy the kingdom, as a singer will destroy a wineglass. It has never happened, of course, but it is conceivable that it might happen: in the totalitarian states comedians may never approach a live microphone. The dangers and triumphs of comedy are very real, and they are especially real in totalitarian times. The opposite of the dictator is the clown. Between them there can be no peace; hence Chaplin's dilemma when he attempted to play both rôles. Because he is the opposite of the dictator the clown is dedicated to playing a heroic rôle, perhaps the most heroic of all, for since his moral function is to remind us of our common humanity and take delight in it, he is the enemy of bureaucracy equally, of all the pigeonholes into which governments, acknowledging their incompetence to deal with human beings, attempt to squeeze us. Secretly the clown rules. More than the poet he is the unacknowledged legislator of our lives, and we may thank God that this is so. Out of the nettle danger he plucks a sense of our real humanity each for the other. There was a time when this was called morality.

The achievement of Chaplin was a singularly moral

achievement. He has invented an archetype whose purpose was a moral one, and he gave the game away when he came to utter the anguished and impassioned cry which concludes *The Great Dictator*:

> *The good earth is rich and can provide for everyone:*
> *The way of life can be free and beautiful,*
> *But we have lost the way.*
> *Greed has poisoned men's souls,*
> *Has barricaded the world with hate,*
> *Has goose-stepped us into misery and bloodshed.*
> *We have developed speed,*
> *But we have shut ourselves in.*
> *Machinery that gives abundance has left us in want.*
> *Our knowledge has made us cynical.*
> *Our cleverness, hard and unkind.*
> *We think too much and feel too little.*
> *More than machinery we need humanity.*
> *To those who can hear me, I say – Do not despair!*
> *The misery that has come upon us is but the passing of greed,*
> *The bitterness of men who fear the way of human progress.*
> *The hate of men will pass, and dictators die,*
> *And the power they took from the people will return to the*
>   *people.*
> *And so long as men die, liberty will never perish.*

So long as men die. . . . We might have known from the beginning that a clown's confession of faith would implicate mortality.

We are hungrier for mortality than we know, so hungry that we leave the flesh outside and go spinning after peace of mind. It is not peace of mind so much as peace of body which will put an end to our miseries; and we have not begun to learn to comfort others bodily. The clown does it by making us laugh, by pulling the curtain aside and showing us the world as it really is, the joyful abandon, underneath the frigid mask; and Charlie, hungry to the point of undiscriminating excess, feverishly in love with love, points the way to the substance of the moral life. He knows that men create themselves by their acts, not by their conventions; therefore he acts with the freshness of a child, and asks why one should act in any other way. He makes his conventions as he goes along, and always with daring, and always with courage. He cares not a fig for the dictators and bullies; he will throw them down as calmly as he will kick a lump of mud in the road. If we are frightened and would like to sleep because we are afraid, he will tell stories to keep us awake. He knows, as the elders of the Church once knew and then forgot, that divine grace is not conferred on all the schoolmen or even on all the prophets; the charwoman may be the possessor of a saint's nimbus; grace is not conferred only on certain individuals but on all alike. The moral of his story is that there is no moral except the dignity of man under heaven. As for Chaplin's own achievement, as distinguished from Charlie's (which belongs to another order), he knows mortality too well to care very much for recognition – to seek recognition as a person is foolishly to deny one's own doubleness. The world is as it is; men turn into clay; the canisters of film will also perish. But at least for a brief while he has held up a candle which dazzles with a joyful light. In the end his achievement is a part of the divine love in mankind which will one day succeed in abolishing the idea of particular persons altogether, those individual ghosts who haunt us all, packaged and labelled with our names, as though names were more than scratches haphazardly put together. Scotus Erigena believed that in the end we become mere points of light swimming in the divine consciousness, an unhappy fate, for the sunlit waves can do this sort of thing better. St Paul and earlier schoolmen believed in a nobler destiny: that on the Day of Judgment we shall arise in flesh and in joy. A pity we should have to wait so long.

Now that we live in the long shadow of the rainbow-coloured clouds, it is good to remember Charlie, who arises in flesh and in joy and impudence and sheer delight of the world around him, fiercely jubilant, as men often are when under fire, and with no cares to speak of, no guilt to wash clean. Like St Francis he tips his hat at the birds and trees, and will sing a song with the farm-girls. Smitten by the moon, he comes with the gifts of Pan, and in these treacherous days one can do worse than fall in step and beat a drum beside him.

www.ingramcontent.com/pod-product-compliance
Lightning Source LLC
Chambersburg PA
CBHW031559110426
42742CB00036B/252